SANCHO'S JOURNAL

To Both –
the River terrace in
Winter!

best,
David Montejano
feb 2014

Jack and Doris Smothers Series in
Texas History, Life, and Culture
Number Thirty-three

SANCHO'S

EXPLORING THE POLITICAL EDGE
WITH THE BROWN BERETS

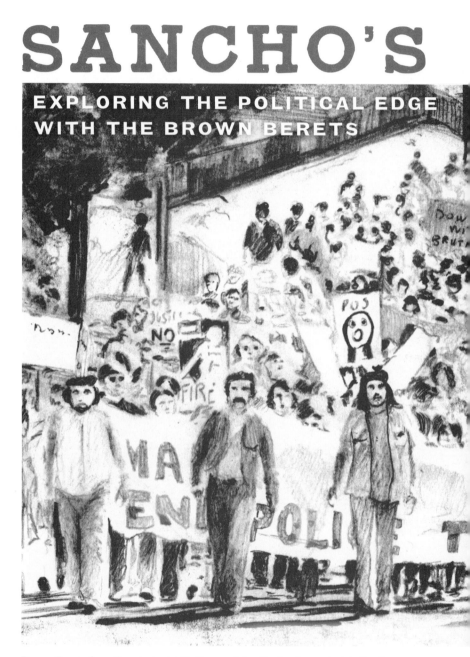

Brown Berets from San Antonio, Dallas, and Austin, lead a protest to the State
Capitol, Austin, October 11, 1974; based on photo by Alan Pogue

DAVID MONTEJANO

ILLUSTRATIONS BY MACEO MONTOYA

JOURNAL

UNIVERSITY OF TEXAS PRESS ✧ AUSTIN

Publication of this work was made possible in part by support from the J. E. Smothers, Sr., Memorial Foundation and the National Endowment for the Humanities.

Requests for permission to reproduce material from this work should be sent to:
Permissions
University of Texas Press
P.O. Box 7819
Austin, TX 78713-7819
www.utexas.edu/utpress/about/bpermission.html

♾ The paper used in this book meets the minimum requirements of ANSI/NISO Z39.48-1992 (R1997) (Permanence of Paper).

LIBRARY OF CONGRESS CATALOGING-IN-PUBLICATION DATA
Montejano, David, 1948–
    Sancho's journal : exploring the political edge with the Brown Berets / by David Montejano ; illustrations by Maceo Montoya. — 1st ed.
        p.   cm. — (Jack and Doris Smothers series in Texas history, life, and culture)
    Continues: Quixote's soldiers.
    Includes bibliographical references.
    ISBN 978-0-292-74239-0 (cloth : alk. paper) —
ISBN 978-0-292-74384-7 (pbk. : alk. paper)
    1. Mexican Americans—Texas—San Antonio—History—20th century.   2. Mexican Americans—Texas—San Antonio—Politics and government—20th century.   3. Mexican Americans—Texas—San Antonio—Biography.   4. Chicano movement—Texas—San Antonio.   5. San Antonio (Tex.)—Race relations—History—20th century.   6. San Antonio (Tex.)—Politics and government—20th century.   I. Montejano, David, 1948– Quixote's soldiers.   II. Title.
    F394.S2119M51737   2012
    305.8968'720764351—dc23
                                                2012016105

doi:10.7560/742390

Pa' los batos y rucas del Condado de Béxar—
¡que sigan soñando de mejores mundos!

c/s

Among other things, Don Quixote said that [Sancho Panza] should prepare to go with him gladly, because it might happen that one day he would have an adventure that would gain him, in the blink of an eye, an ínsula, *and he would make him its governor.*
MIGUEL DE CERVANTES, *DON QUIXOTE*, FIRST PART, CHAPTER VII

CONTENTS

PREFACE AND ACKNOWLEDGMENTS

THIS JOURNAL TELLS TWO STORIES. One is an account of my experience with a Brown Beret chapter, the Southside Berets of San Antonio, Texas, in the mid-seventies. The narrative is based on my journal notes written while "hanging out" with a dozen or so street men or "batos locos" (crazy guys) in 1974–1975, with various addenda tacked on over the years. I was interested in understanding how they acquired political consciousness and how such consciousness transformed behavior. Seven months of hanging out, coupled with intensive interviews, proved to be sufficient to develop a snapshot of the politicization process. I came to understand the manner in which these batos adapted their lifestyle and habits to accommodate their entry into the public arena of politics. A follow-up some thirty years later confirmed various features of that snapshot.

Interwoven into this account is a second story—my explanation of why it took more than thirty years to write this up. Basically this was a failed dissertation. Explaining that failure, and resolving it, is an integral part of the following narrative. My observations and note taking, in other words, did not stop once I left the barrio settings. The notes spill over to record the various academic settings and interactions that gave final shape to this dissertation project over time. They describe my search for an appropriate conceptual framework for my experience with the Berets. This journal, then, is an intellectual autobiography of sorts. It brings closure to a line of inquiry that began some three decades ago.

I have many people to thank for a project that has lingered for so many years. All those I acknowledged previously in my history of the Chicano movement, *Quixote's Soldiers: A Local History of the Chicano Movement, 1966–1981* (University of Texas Press, 2010), deserve another round of thanks for this companion ethnography. Drawing from that list, I again thank those who engaged me in discussion and supportive critique at some critical point—Diana Montejano, Mario Compean, Martín Sánchez Jankowski, David Montgomery, Emilio Zamora, Tobías Durán, Felipe Gonzales, Richard Fox, Carlos Vélez-Ibáñez, Ben Olguín, and Verónica García. For their reading of several manuscript chapters, I thank the members of my history writing group (spring 2010)—Alex García, Filiberto Chávez, Jordan Gonzales, Natalie Mendoza, and Joe Orbock. For their close scrutiny of the entire manuscript, I am most grateful to David Minkus and Andrés Jiménez.

Naturally I am especially indebted to the Southside Berets for allowing me to hang out with them. I am indebted as well to the leadership of the Valley, Austin, Waco, and Dallas chapters for their candid views. Because I have disguised their identities, I can only give them a collective "gracias." My decision to maintain their anonymity also meant that any illustrations had to be drawings rather than photographs. Half of the following illustrations have been abstracted from photographs, with the remainder reconstructed from my journal notes and memory. Artist Maceo Montoya, son of Chicano movement artist and activist Malaquías Montoya, drew the exquisite charcoal line drawings that accompany the narrative. I am deeply appreciative of his interpretive skills and patience. Maceo's work is a powerful suggestion of the continuity of Chicano movement culture and practice. Finally, I thank John Ledesma for last-minute edits of some images.

In closing, I gratefully acknowledge the various academic patrons whose financial support basically kept this project alive. Research grants from the University of New Mexico, the University of Texas at Austin, and the University of California, Berkeley, provided important life support for this project. Of special note were sabbatical residencies at the School of American Research in Santa Fe, New Mexico, and the Center for the Advanced Study of the Behavioral Sciences in Stanford, California. In conclusion, I extend *un abrazo firme* to the University of Texas Press staff, particularly editor Theresa May, for their support over many years.

I alone, of course, am responsible for the following interpretation.

Berkeley, California
June 19, 2011

SANCHO'S JOURNAL

ON SLOW WRITING

1 SOME THIRTY YEARS AGO, when I was searching for a dissertation topic, I carried out an ethnographic study of a Brown Beret chapter that formed during the Chicano movement of the late sixties and early seventies. For seven months in 1974–1975, I hung out with a group of thirteen young men as they learned about the Berets and the Chicano movement. I was interested in understanding how they acquired political consciousness and how such consciousness transformed behavior. If I could somehow capture the essence of becoming political, I reasoned at the time, then perhaps that essence could be reproduced and disseminated. And what better material could I have to search for that political essence than the working- and lower-class street youths who were marching and protesting and calling themselves Brown Berets?

As an engaged activist, I felt that I understood most components of the broad-based civil rights movement that I was part of—farmworkers, working-class barrio residents, college students, young professionals—except for these "batos locos" (crazy guys) who identified themselves as Brown Berets. Sometimes also called "pachucos," these young males were generally considered to be delinquents or gang members. Their evident politicization looked like a promising subject for my dissertation.

Thus, when the time came to choose a dissertation topic, I decided to focus on the Chicano movement and, in particular, on the street youths who had organized themselves into Brown Beret chapters. To this end, I carried out an ethnographic study but then struggled to write it up. The experience was so charged, and the theoretical contexts so inadequate to capture and portray this experience, that I shelved the project. The study never became a dissertation. I was unable to finish it.

Thirty-something years later I returned to the material. The passage of time had provided a sense of distance and anonymity, elements that now permitted the space for a frank description and assessment. The earlier constraints no longer held: this project was not a dissertation or a study written to gain tenure, so I was basically free to shape the book as I pleased. Although there have been recent sightings of Brown Berets, the Chicano movement of which they were part no longer exists, thus eliminating the complications of movement politics and associated police surveillance problems. Just as importantly, the development of a significant literature in ethnic history and sociology in the last two decades has established the background necessary for this kind of specialized ethnography. My previous work, in particular, has described the context for the following narrative. This book, in other words, is not for beginners.

On another intellectual front, recent developments in interpretive social science have provided an opening for my material. Thirty years ago the inability to write up an ethnography as an objective study, aimed at testing certain sociological tenets about politicization, would have been seen as a sign of a failed project. Today, in the aftermath of a postmodernist critique of ethnography, this very difficulty and inability seems to constitute a sign of honesty and understanding of the ethnographic experience. The postmodernist critique provides an opening for my material—that is, for writing an ethnographic interpretation laced with autobiographical and literary references. Indeed, an undercurrent of the following narrative deals with the experience of writing, or not writing, the book. Describing this experience will help the reader understand the ambiguities and tensions of ethnographic representation that partly froze my writing. In short, the writing blocks have become part of the narrative.

In dealing with these blocks, I have leaned on those anthropologists and investigative journalists who have passed through similar experiences. I found both solace and inspiration, for example, in the predicament that social critic James Agee faced in writing *Let Us Now Praise Famous Men* (1941). Originally commissioned to write a documentary on southern tenant farmers for *Fortune Magazine*, Agee discovered that he lacked the detachment, condescension, and self-confidence necessary to produce a typical "Life and Circumstances" article. He was troubled by the question "Why we make this book, and set it at large, and by what right, and for what purpose, and to what good end, or none." He lacked the quality that anthropologist Clifford Geertz called "ethical ambiguity."

Within the discipline of anthropology, such self-consciousness and uneasiness about the sharp inequality in the encounter between observer and observed created a crisis of mission beginning in the seventies. In a telling statement, anthropologist Vincent Crapanzano noted that however much the ethnographer "wishes to separate his ethnography from the ethnographic confrontation, the writing of ethnography is a continuation of the confrontation." "Indeed," he added, "at one level the writing of ethnography is an attempt to put a full-stop to the ethnographic confrontation." To this insightful statement, I would add that *not writing* the ethnography—or in my case writing it in ambivalent fits and starts over thirty years—is another way of putting a full stop to the ethnographic confrontation.

It is best to discuss the writing blocks now and be rid of them.

The Harder They Come

In retrospect, I can see that I had set myself up for disappointment. Looking for the key to political consciousness was a naïve undertaking, but it was symptomatic of the heady political idealism sweeping the country in the late sixties and early seventies. The convergence of an antiwar movement, a civil rights movement, and a farmworkers' campaign on college campuses filled many of us with visions of an egalitarian and just society. We drew inspiration as well from the Cuban and Algerian revolutions and other Third World liberation struggles. Domestically and internationally, the old social order of privilege and status was being challenged. How could we advance this challenge? Ideology to me seemed to hold the key. If we could harness the power of ideas, then all types of social change were possible.

The catalysts for the Chicano movement were the farmworker strikes in California and Texas in 1965–1966. The Mexican American youth had been primed for mobilization by the black civil rights movement, then a decade old. The farmworker strikes incited Mexican American college students to organize various efforts for ethnic-racial equality, and these quickly evolved into a cultural nationalist political movement. The movement spread beyond college campuses to the impoverished segregated neighborhoods as activists mobilized barrio youths in various campaigns against "gringo oppression." For their motivating lessons, movement participants drew on Mexican and Mexican American history and culture.

The Mexican Revolution emerged as a major source of inspiration. Others emphasized an indigenous past and renamed the American Southwest "Aztlán," after the ancient northern homeland of the Aztecs. The despised lower-class identity of being Chicano and Chicana was embraced and invested with new meaning as poetry and literature, political theater, art, and music gave expression to a cultural-political renaissance.

Some young activists, influenced by the Cuban Revolution and the revolutionary image of Che Guevara, began wearing berets long before any official organization existed. The name "Brown Beret" was supposedly coined by the Los Angeles Police Department (LAPD) in the late sixties in reference to members of the Young Chicanos for Community Action (YCCA), many of whom sported berets. In a satirical swipe, the YCCA adopted the tag and the LAPD slogan "to serve, observe, and protect" as the organization's official name and motto (modified by some chapters to read "to serve, educate, and protect"). Its members dressed and organized themselves in paramilitary fashion to suggest a militant posture. The Berets first acquired notoriety and national publicity with the Los Angeles high school blowouts of 1968.

The idea of the Berets as a community police force quickly spread across the country wherever substantial numbers of Mexican American youths lived, reflecting considerable frustration over segregated living conditions and life chances. By the early seventies Beret chapters were involved in various local projects and manifested different levels of development. In general they all provided security at community events and protests and monitored police conduct in the barrios. The more developed chapters sponsored breakfast programs as well as after-school youth programs and published newspapers. The most advanced also ran community centers and health clinics.

This activism among barrio youth generally unfolded against a backdrop of gang conflict and neighborhood divisions. Wherever these Beret groups emerged, almost invariably one of their first goals was to end the warfare prevalent in their barrios. Chicano nationalism signified the transcendence of neighborhood identities to an overarching ethnic-racial identity. Accepting the ideas of "la raza unida" (the united people) and "carnalismo" (brotherhood)—what I mean by politicization—broke through the provincial identities of neighborhood cliques and exposed individuals to a larger world and larger sphere of action. The batos and "rucas" (girls) learned that power could be used for securing justice and righting the wrongs of the community. Understanding the change in behavior and perspective from a "street lifestyle" to the lifestyle of a Chicano or Chicana militant was what interested me.

The case of the Chicago Berets illustrates the potential and problems associated with their emergence. According to "Duque," the prime minister of the Westside (Chicago) Berets, in 1972 the Berets occupied an old settlement center (the Hull House) in the Pilsen neighborhood and converted it into a barrio center. Thus was born Casa Aztlán and eventually the Benito Juárez Free Health Clinic. Duque, with his impressive knowledge about the health politics of Cook County, made clear that the Chicago Berets were very involved in maintaining and defending the free clinic at Casa Aztlán. The Beret newspaper *Mi Sangre* carried accounts of what the clinic meant personally to individual Berets. One Chicana, Dolores Espinosa, wrote that not many years before she had been a "lady lord" who used to "go wild in our neighborhood streets. NOTHING CONSTRUCTIVE." Then she came across the Brown Berets. "ALL of a sudden, my life experimented a 360 degree change and my life course found a goal. Somehow, I saw the light for the first time." Espinosa was working as a volunteer at the Benito Juárez Free Health Clinic. Another Chicago Beret explained that they were militant but nonviolent and that their "militancy came from wanting to open up the eyes of the people to see how the establishment kept us down" (December 1971).

But the mobilization had not been without problems. Not all eyes were being opened. The established gangs saw the emergence of Berets as a new gang, and this created conflict. Duque noted that the cliques and gangs picked out enemies and that some had identified the Berets as enemies. The same point was made by a Dallas Beret, who said when he lived in Chicago as head of the Latin Counts he would talk about how he was going to nail (*pañar*) one of those guys with the "funny caps." The experience of the Chicago Berets was typical of the Beret chapters in the southwestern cities. Often the Berets as a group acquired all the personal enemies of new recruits. Personal ideological change did not necessarily mean a change in perception by an individual's friends and enemies.

Although the Chicano movement drew inspiration from various sources, international as well as national, and used culturally distinctive symbols, it was clearly informed by the black civil rights movement, especially in its "black power" phase. While Che Guevara may have inspired the wearing of the brown beret, the Black Panthers were an evident influ-

ence on the Berets' posture as a paramilitary organization. Although the
ideologies of the Berets and Panthers were different, the similarities in
their organizing approach were apparent.

The Black Panther strategy called for the organization of the lumpen
proletariat or, as Elaine Brown put it, "the gang members and the gang-
sters, the pimps and the prostitutes, the drug users and dealers, the common thieves and murderers." In this they departed from Karl Marx, who
had described the lumpen as the wretched of the earth who had no rele-
vancy in a socialist revolution. Based on their reading of Frantz Fanon's
anticolonial writings, the Panthers believed that members of the black
lumpen, unlike Marx's working class, had absolutely no stake in industrial America and thus were the most motivated sector to lead a revolution. The urban riots had already demonstrated their rage and their readi-
ness. The Black Panther Party intended to create politicized soldiers from
that mass of energy.

In the early seventies the Brown Berets had not yet developed an elaborate ideology beyond cultural nationalism and community service. But like
the Panthers, they drew upon the young male and female lumpen of the
barrios, known as "pachucos" and "pachucas" or "batos locos" (crazy guys)
and "rucas locas" (crazy gals), for their membership. Many young adults
and teenagers were attracted to the Berets by their uniforms, various mar-
tial performances at rallies and protests, and their aggressive flaunting of
Anglo (white) authority. The militancy they espoused was seemingly natural, formed in a barrio world of gang conflict and street life.

I was curious to explore the individual and group dynamics of the
Brown Berets and the manner in which political consciousness was acquired. The politicization of these youths and adults fascinated me. I believed that their political "awakening" signified a change in identity and
purpose in life. I wanted to understand such a conversion experience. Using my family and movement connections, I secured an invitation to observe and participate in such a group in San Antonio, Texas. I saw this
as an unparalleled opportunity to observe the experience of politicization
firsthand.

The invitation was to accompany the Brown Beret leadership on a visit
to Cuba. In late October 1973 the Cuban government had extended an invitation to the Brown Berets and their friends to visit the island. They had
accepted. Ten to fifteen chapter leaders were expected to go, and I had
been invited to accompany them. Given the cultural nationalist orientation of the group, I considered this to be a potential critical development.

Observing the interaction of the Beret leaders with one another and their reaction to Cuban socialism promised to be politically engaging.

The entire situation reminded me of the Jamaican movie *The Harder They Come*, featuring singer Jimmy Cliff, which played for a record-setting eighty weeks at a Harvard Square theater in the early 1970s. After seeing it for the first time, I understood why it had become such a classic. It reflected the sentiment of resistance then sweeping university campuses. The soundtrack, which included hits such as "Many Rivers to Cross" and "Sitting Here in Limbo," was also a favorite for those writing dissertations, as I remember.

This Jamaican movie follows the life of a country boy (Jimmy Cliff), a recent arrival to Kingston, as he tries to make a name for himself in an alien and oppressive world run by corrupt police, politicians, and businessmen. When Cliff is unable to make it as a singer, he plunges into the drug world and again finds himself challenging established monopolists. He ends up running from both cops and drug dealers. His only chance of escape is a fishing trawler on the way to Cuba. In a dramatic conclusion, Cliff swims out to meet the trawler but does not make it. He washes up onshore and dies shortly thereafter in a gun battle. Although he dies as a bandit, the implication is clear: his consciousness would have been radically different had he been able to board the trawler bound for Cuba.

In some part, my involvement with the Berets was inspired by an interest in testing such a conclusion. But the Berets never visited the island. The trip was postponed indefinitely. Trip organizer George Velásquez said that the Berets were demanding to take their *cuetes* (handguns) on the trip but gave no other reason for the cancellation. The trip was never rescheduled. What impact might it have had? Later I learned that a high-level Soviet delegation, led by Leonid Brezhnev, had paid a state visit during the time when we would have been on the island. Security concerns had undoubtedly been the reason for the cancellation.

In spite of this, I was still interested in the Berets as a possible dissertation topic. In the summer of 1974 I began to hang out on a daily basis with thirteen members of a Brown Beret chapter in San Antonio's Southside. The founding chapter from the Westside, the group I had hoped to spend time with, had disbanded a few months before my arrival. The Southside Berets had regrouped with four veteran members and nine new recruits. They offered the opportunity of observing a Beret chapter in the making. Through them I became acquainted with Berets across Texas. I met the leaders of six other chapters—from North Dallas, West Dallas,

Waco, Austin, Hondo, and McAllen—and carried out what sociologists call "participant-observation" as well as structured interviews. I also interviewed the Beret veterans of the original Westside chapter. In short, I acquired a good sense of the diversity of the Texas Brown Beret chapters, whose ideology ranged from sophisticated class analysis to rudimentary ethnic nationalism. All chapters, however, saw themselves as a community police force or as soldiers in defense of the people. They considered themselves the vanguard or leading edge of the Chicano movement.

Publicizing such an image was the main reason the Southside Berets had invited me to hang out with them. They expected me to write a portrayal of heroic *soldados* (soldiers) defending the community and expected that their names and true identities would be part of that portrayal.

The "political edge" I was interested in was different. It was plain at the outset that I wanted to understand how and why these batos locos from the much-disparaged underclass had become political. I wanted to see if they had experienced a political conversion—something akin to a transformative religious conversion—that signified a sharp change in personal behavior. Initially I was drawn to Eric Hobsbawm's notion of "primitive rebels" or "social bandits" as prepolitical phenomena lacking only a philosophy through which to couch their rebellion. The story of Jimmy Cliff again loomed large. My preliminary dissertation notes made it embarrassingly clear that I was interested in understanding "the transition from the 'false consciousness' of gang delinquency to the developing 'true consciousness' of the Brown Berets." Basically I was looking for a magical key to politicization of lower-class Chicano men. This was the political edge I was interested in. Why did these guys join a political organization, and what did it signify to them?

My crude formulation ran smack into social reality. I was unprepared for the inadequacy of key sociological concepts when observing actual living people. Within a month of being "out in the field," I began to sense how naïve my formulation had been. What became clear almost from the beginning was that being political was really no big deal: these guys were just like everyone else in the way they learned to be political—through learning, sharing information, and interacting with like-minded individuals. In this respect, the dense organizational network we call the Chicano movement provided a critical environment for the emergence of the Brown Berets. Within this network, they learned to discuss politics, participated in local actions, and acquired a civic reputation. The young men began to learn how the larger society beyond their barrio was constructed.

At the typewriter, about 1977

They acquired a political literacy. Without the support of the movement network, the Berets floundered and finally disappeared.

The key to understanding the politicization of street youths was realizing that no rigid or necessary contradiction existed between "being political" and "being loco." A bato could accommodate the behavior expected of the first while still practicing or maintaining the lifestyle of the second. Although a few Berets seem to have experienced a transformative conversion, for the great majority becoming political did not signify a major change of personality or of personal habits. Nor did it necessarily imply a disengagement from an underground economy, where everyday hustling might include petty theft and petty drug dealing. They did not have to speak "in tongues," however, to experience a break with the past.

Thus, aside from difficulties with the conceptual language and framework of the sociological literature, a good part of the problem of not being able to write the dissertation had to do with the fact that my original story line about the nature of politicization had vanished. The story would not be about dramatic events or about messianic conversions. Nor would it be the romantic portrayal that the batos wanted. In short, this story had no climax, no discovery of a secret key to mobilizing and transforming the lower classes—except the negative discovery that discipline is essential and that obtaining information and planning are vital steps in carrying out political action. Nonetheless, there remained an interesting story about my experience in attempting to understand this group and its social world.

The problem lay in writing it up.

On Being Embedded

The paralysis I sensed also came from a feeling that I was airing dirty laundry. The Chicano movement can be credited with bringing down the remnants of segregation in the Southwest, a major achievement. But the struggle was not romantic or pretty. This is particularly true if the lens is focused on the intimate details of underclass men as they came to understand politics. I wanted to write a candid appraisal that noted both the good and the bad. Soon I realized that the bad would have been sufficient to embarrass a still-active group and perhaps even the Chicano movement. This brought the self-doubts about my project into sharp relief.

At the base of my discomfort was a sense that I was betraying the political and personal trust I had been given. The Beret leaders expected a heroic telling of their exploits; why else would they invite me to hang out? Naturally I had been straightforward about my desire to write a book about them. This still created awkwardness, as the new recruits tried to understand what a non-Beret was doing with them. After several weeks, I had no real way to justify my hanging around in terms that made sense to them. Apparently it was an issue for the leadership as well. This ambiguity was dissipated, at least for the group members, when they unexpectedly made me an advisor and fitted a brown beret on me. Suddenly I found myself faced with an acute dilemma: how could I be an advisor to a group whose political development I wanted to study? How could I avoid what social scientists call an "interaction effect"—that is, how could I make sure that my presence didn't influence the outcome that I had come to observe?

I came to understand the dilemma from the Beret point of view: it was an organizational move to gain resources and skills and to exert some control over my writing. It was also a move to ensure my loyalty to the group. Only a Beret-affiliated writer could have license to accompany them on their various excursions. Many types of controls over my activities as a fellow member were possible—controls based on the Beret oath, on the rank hierarchy, and, importantly, on personal friendship. The Berets were keeping me close to them. To use a word popularized by the recent Iraq

War, when journalists were assigned to military units, I was "embedded" in a Brown Beret chapter.

I dealt with the dilemma posed by my advisory role by devising working rules that would maintain a balance between participation and observation. One was not to give any orders. Another was never to set the pace for a discussion, to speak only after everyone had spoken—in other words, when my input would have little impact on the final outcome—and then only if I really felt that it was important to comment on the subject or to ask for a clarification. A third rule was not to give any instructions or advice unless requested. Because I adhered to my working guidelines, most of the guys soon accepted that I was there to write a book. They stopped asking me to make speeches. Generally I managed to remain an observer and "participated" only when asked to do so.

Once accepted, I was treated just like anyone else in the group. I was an equal, subject to being reprimanded like any other Beret for having missed a meeting or for not wearing the beret. I imagine that most viewed me as a somewhat straight guy. I didn't curse as much as the others, didn't cat-call women, didn't even litter. The guys joked that I would not make it in the woods because there were no books to read. Nonetheless, I developed some genuine friendships. I came to know their families. We visited each other's homes whenever we wished, and my house became a stopover for out-of-town Berets passing through. We became "camaradas" (friends).

The great advantage of participant observation or ethnography is that most information comes from natural or unstaged situations and conversations. This is also its great disadvantage, because natural situations provide an overwhelming amount of information, most of it irrelevant for the research interest at hand. Understandably, the Berets kept pointing out what was important. Occasionally they would say to me: "Now put that in your book." The Beret leaders mentioned activities that I should include, and several individual Berets shared stories of past exploits with my book in mind. Yet there was always an uncertainty about which details of Beret activity and stories I was going to describe. The seeming open-endedness of ethnography, especially in this movement setting, gave my exploration the sheen of an undercover investigation. One Beret jokingly said that I was going to write, "¿Qué hacen los Berets? Juegan con pistolas" (What do the Berets do? They play with guns).

Sorting out the important and relevant observations from a mass of unstaged and staged moments may be the most difficult and trying task of the ethnographer. Clearly this is one reason why ethnography remains the most problematic of all scientific methodologies. As anthropologist Clifford Geertz put it, the great irony of ethnography is that its authenticity rests on a peculiar species of good faith between ethnographer and informant that verges on bad faith. For some form of reciprocal pretense between anthropologist and host must exist, reflecting their situational agreement to welcome one another into their respective cultures regardless of the few realistic grounds for such participation. Thus, reasoned Geertz, a certain "moral tension" or "ethical ambiguity" between anthropologist and informants "lies at the heart of successful anthropological research."

That tension and ambiguity clearly permeates my field notes. Offering my grant writing services for Beret projects did little to temper it. Nor did it fully satisfy the curiosity of the leaders, who occasionally wondered who I really was and why I was really hanging out with them.

Another source for my paralysis, a corollary to my embedded position within the Berets, had to do with the fundamental race-ethnic division of the segregated society I was part of. Would my work expose barrio youth and the Chicano movement to ridicule from an "Anglo" reading audience? As a translator or interpreter in the segregated setting of Texas and the Southwest, I was aware that I was only a few steps removed from the status of "native informant." For what purpose was I writing a book that would expose the intimate behavior of lower-class Latino men? Was I a voyeur? An interpreter? An informant? In what sense was I different from a Western-trained "native" anthropologist reporting on restive youth back home in the hinterlands?

Such questions stopped my writing on this project for many years. I now realize, as I reread the materials I collected some time ago, that my hesitation was not merely a reflection of an internal personal conflict. It reflected my understanding, inchoate at the time, of the special importance that appearances or representations take on in a segregated setting. In such a setting, stock stereotypes and images generally seemed to float along, unchecked by particularistic or complicated explanations. Thus the entire Mexican American community could be shamed by the public—or publicized—misbehavior of an individual or small group. In fact, as I discuss later, a few months into my field research, a senseless killing among two friends provoked a very public and acrimonious discussion about the meaning of Mexican masculinity.

The possibility of being shamed may help explain the acute sensitivity of many Hispanics to public discussion of problems in the barrios. A mixture of embarrassment and defiance moves many to keep things hidden, for it has been clear that Anglos have very different conceptions of Mexican culture. Mexican Americans have been conscious of the tenuous claim they have over the representation of their culture in the public media. The basic reflex has been to close ranks or at least not to break past them. In such a politicized setting, how does one communicate across the cultural-ethnic divide?

Unfortunately the divide was evident at the universities as well.

On the Books of Sociology

It is September, 1975, my first month as an Acting Assistant Professor of Sociology at the University of California, Berkeley. The position is contingent on my finishing the dissertation. I have just given a lecture to the faculty about the Black Panthers, the Young Lords, and the Brown Berets, explaining that their politicization was unexpected, given the general views of lower-class lifestyles.

After the lecture, Professor Leo Lowenthal of the famous Frankfurt School, the European Marxist I had wanted to meet, stopped me in the hallway. He turned and asked, in German-accented English, "Are they illegal immigrants?" I was struck by the question. Why was this the first question? I quickly realized that Professor Lowenthal knew little about Mexican Americans and their historical presence in the Southwest. His question illuminated a canyon-like breach, a wide fault line of knowledge and perspective, that separated us. My hesitation spoke clearly.

"Is my question irrelevant?" he realizes. He aborts the discussion quickly. "You better hurry and finish if you want to stay here," he says, referring to my dissertation. He turns away. I watch as seventy years of him limp down the hallway. I want to believe that the threat is well intentioned. Yes, I better hurry, I think irreverently.

Yet the encounter left me feeling numb. It was a familiar numbing feeling. As a young professor-in-the-making I had found that I could not speak about my interest in barrio politics or social life without confronting naïve or insulting generalizations. I had to deal with the texts of other professors who were clearly not as well intentioned as Lowenthal. Professor Walter Miller of Harvard, for example, had condensed the lives of lower-class youth into a few "focal concerns" of "toughness," "thrills," "getting into" and "staying out of" trouble, an ability to "outsmart" while avoiding being "outsmarted" or "taken," and so on. Professor Edward Banfield, also of Harvard, had described the lower-class individual as living from moment to moment, unable to imagine a future. In his words:

> Impulse governs his behavior, either because he cannot discipline himself to sacrifice a present for a future satisfaction or because he has no sense of the future. . . . In his relations with others he is suspicious and hostile, aggressive yet dependent. He is unable to maintain a stable relationship with a mate; commonly he does not marry. He feels no attachment to community, neighbors or friends, resents all authority. . . . He is a nonparticipant: he belongs to no voluntary organizations, has no political interests, and does not vote unless paid to do so.

In a fitting conclusion to this type of analysis, Banfield suggested that lower-class infants be auctioned off to middle-class families in order to break the vicious culture of poverty.

Sociology as I knew it spoke generally of containment and control, revealing a profound sense of suspicion and fear about an underclass, which was almost always a "colored" underclass. Nor was this grim assessment confined to a nasty American right wing. On the left were European intellectuals who maintained the disreputable view that Marx had of the "lumpen," that their history could only be one of political tragedy. Eric Hobsbawm and George Rudé had shown that the urban and rural masses could rise on a crest of near-suicidal insurrectionary zeal but fall as quickly because of their narrow view of the enemy and their short list of goals. No less an author than Antonio Gramsci, the great theorist of political culture, noted that "hatred is a poor organizer, and the lessons of hunger rarely expand a man's horizons." Gramsci saw such hatred as merely the "first glimmer" of class consciousness, "the basic, negative, polemical attitude."

A few texts suggested that angry lower classes have political agency—Frantz Fanon's *The Wretched of the Earth* was a doctrinal text for university activists—but generally, regardless of which way one looked, literature of all political persuasions saw lower-class culture, and particularly male culture, as violent-prone, pleasure-seeking, and authoritarian: to be eradicated, according to one side; to be dismissed, according to the other. Enter, then, the Panthers, Lords, and Berets, marching into the face of such

"You'd better hurry and finish."

"right" and "left" views. Segments of the U.S. racial underclass already organized in adult cliques and gangs had become politicized in varying degrees. Now here was something worth looking at and comprehending.

That had been the substance of my dissertation presentation. As I saw Professor Lowenthal slowly walk away, I sensed a profound and frustrating distance. At its base, the distance reflected a divide of race and class, but it also pointed to a lack of shared knowledge and even of a common vocabulary. I had no text—no sociology, no history—that I could give to him or to my other colleagues so that they could begin to comprehend the basic context and language of my ethnography. How could I bridge the chasm or even begin looking for a way to cross? I muttered, "Yeah, I'll hurry."

I didn't hurry, obviously. Or to put it another way, thirty or so years ago I decided to work on developing the missing historical and sociological context. At that time it was no exaggeration to say that Mexicans generally made only cameo appearances in history textbooks as bandits, criminals, or immigrants. The absence of a serious treatment had allowed a popular amnesia about the Southwest and its long Mexican presence to set in. Some commentators even questioned whether Mexicans had experienced racial discrimination and were deserving of civil rights protections. The focus on immigration, which dominated the sociological and political imagination in regard to Mexican Americans, further distorted the complex history and the politics of the Southwest. Lowenthal's view of Mexican Americans, I later realized, had been informed by attorney general William Saxbe's much publicized comment that he intended to deport a million illegal aliens and "then find those who have burrowed more deeply into our society." Clearly, before I could talk about lower-class Mexican American men and distinct subsets of barrio society, I had to talk about the entire community and its *American* history. I had to point out the contradiction in "remembering the Alamo" and portraying Mexicans simply as immigrants. I had to establish the long Mexican presence.

Laying the Groundwork

Thus my first book, *Anglos and Mexicans in the Making of Texas, 1836–1986,* was a sweeping outline of the changing relations between the two peoples over the century and a half after the "fall of the Alamo." Essentially the "narrative explanation" described the evolution of a conflictual relationship born in war and annexation and nurtured for most of the twentieth century by segregationist policies to one that by the end of the century was based on the politics of accommodation and negotiation. Reclaiming and explaining the long history of Anglo-Mexican relations was a critical first step.

Twenty-something years later I applied another layer of context to the canvas. My second book, *Quixote's Soldiers: A Local History of the Chicano Movement, 1966–1981,* zeroed in on the frenetic fifteen-year period when a social movement "from below" challenged and began to brush away the last vestiges of the segregated social-political order in San Antonio and South Texas. Unlike the telescopic scale of *Anglos and Mexicans,* where market forces and class structures had taken center stage, the ground-level focus in *Quixote's Soldiers* dealt with organizational formation, leadership, and specific political projects and campaigns. Of particular relevance to the present work, I noted that a remarkable but generally overlooked achievement of the Chicano movement had been the calming of barrio gang warfare for a decade.

Having laid out the historical and sociological contexts in detail, I have returned to the ethnography that in a sense inspired them. I can now describe what I learned from the everyday experience of hanging out with the Berets. With these journal notes and reflections, I bring closure to a line of inquiry that I began some thirty years ago.

This book, then, can be considered the last installment of a trilogy about a particular Mexican American experience. Thematically, the trilogy has been an inquiry into the nature of economic development, social change, social movements, and race-ethnic relations. In historical terms, the first book ranged over 150 years, the second focused on 15 years, and this, the last, basically chronicles 7 months. So these works might be characterized in terms of different temporal scales—a *longue durée*, an intermediate or *meso durée*, and now a "micro history" or account of everyday life. Sociologically, the trilogy can be read as traversing different scales of analysis, from historical to societal to individual. Making those connections—linking "private troubles" with a greater structural reality—is what C. Wright Mills called an exercise of the "sociological imagination." Readers should keep that greater reality in mind as they follow the microhistory of private troubles that I am about to narrate.

This concluding installment of the trilogy introduces the anthropological method of ethnography to my previous historical and sociological analyses. In contrast to the sociological imagination that calls for thinking beyond immediate circumstances and daily routines, we can speak of an "ethnographic imagination" that requires immersion in these circumstances and routines in order to understand the "inner reality" of agency or social action. Such an ethnographic imagination seeks to understand how people negotiate structural reality in light of their aspirations and perspectives. I aim to apply such an imagination to my account of how and why a group of lower-class men organized and presented themselves as the leading edge of a political movement.

As my recollection of my hallway chat with Professor Lowenthal suggests, my observations and note taking did not cease once I left the so-called field. My journal notes also cover the experience of interpreting and writing this book in various intellectual environments. I describe the evolution of my thinking according to the "loci of enunciation," to use Walter Mignolo's felicitous phrase. As the title of this book (and of the previous one) makes obvious, my search for an interpretive framework or metaphor led me away from sociology to literature. Describing the places where I haltingly "enunciated" this work will help explain this particular literary turn. By happy coincidence, as I note in a later chapter, such a turn allowed for a form of reconciliation—figuratively speaking, of course— with Professor Lowenthal. I finally answer Lowenthal's question about the Berets with language that I believe he would have understood and appreciated.

The Social World of Los Batos

If my interest in the politicization of batos locos had left me with some-what anticlimactic and prosaic conclusions about the importance of disci-pline, this was more than offset by the unexpected cultural shock I expe-rienced in hanging out with the batos. My experience was an immersion in the lower-class male world of the pachucos or batos locos, now become Brown Berets. This world was so distinct that once-familiar physical sur-roundings appeared strange and different. As a San Antonio native, I had traveled down the streets and through the impoverished neighborhoods of the Southside for years. Now I was learning about one of the resident "social worlds." This was a stark world of guns and knives, drugs and al-cohol, tough talk and tough looks, but it was also a world of brotherhood, honor, compassion, and a deep desire for justice. The mixture of these el-ements imparted a surrealistic and bittersweet quality to my experience, with many moments of frustration, anger, excitement, and feelings of soli-darity. Luisa, the Westside Beret who had introduced me to the group, told me that I didn't know what I was getting into.

The particular chapter I was hanging out with, I later learned, was seen as the most "loco" of the seven Beret chapters in the state. The new recruits to this chapter-in-formation, a diverse group of unemployed or semiemployed batos, were still being introduced to Beret discipline and practice. To make matters worse, by the mid-seventies the Chicano move-ment had splintered and slowed considerably. Increasingly there was less need for Beret security, less interaction with an organizational network, and less reinforcement from a supportive community. Thus, for the period I was with them, the Southside chapter did not have regular or frequent opportunities to put on a "public face." Some members never really pulled away from the routine of street life. The result was a group whose actions were at times lauded as heroic and at times subjected to ridicule.

The following narrative of my sojourn with the Southside Berets sheds some light on what happened when los batos ventured into the public arena. These notes also make clear the importance of an organizational network, the ideological diversity among the Beret chapters, the difficul-ties of organizing, and the necessity for discipline. What should stand out from the talk and interaction were the efforts of lower-class men to maintain a movement and to engage in politics. Given the stock characterizations of this lower-class male subculture, this seemed nothing short of miraculous.

The following journal account also makes clear the paralyzing tensions unleashed by my participant-observation. The notes reveal the vetting and negotiation that took place between the Berets and myself. They reveal the Berets' doubts and suspicions about my intentions as well as my own self-doubts about what I was doing.

A final word about the following account: as previously mentioned, one problem with participant-observation stems from the vast, unfiltered information collected by the ethnographer. Immersion in the field means experiencing a flood of observations, as the observer learns and absorbs many things simultaneously. In this sense, relating the process of discovery through field notes and interviews can produce an overwhelming and boring read. Much discovery, in fact, comes in jerky roller-coaster fashion rather than as the calibrated results of a smooth linear ride. Thus, for the sake of presentation, some selection, editing, and even reordering of the observations must take place. I have made such clustering (where it has taken place) transparent.

While my narrative follows a general chronology, my observations are organized into thematic chapters that attempt to preserve the experience of discovery. To emphasize the "field experience," I set off excerpts from my actual field notes as extracts.

REGENERACIÓN

IN APRIL 1974, after three years of activism against police brutality and barrio warfare, the Westside Brown Berets (the original San Antonio chapter) decided to go "underground"—that is, it disbanded. Internal tension among members, along with loss of support from Chicano movement organizations, had finally collapsed the confederation of barrio youth from different neighborhoods. A few months later, in August, the Southside Berets regrouped and reconstituted the San Antonio Brown Berets. The half year I spent with that chapter is the foundation for these journal notes.

In the second half of 1974 the Brown Berets made a resurgent appearance in San Antonio. They participated in several political protests organized by an immigrant rights organization, began to work with glue-sniffing youth, and prevented the hasty eviction of a family from public housing, to mention their most notable activities. Through "visits" or interventions, the Southside Berets soon made the local network of social service agencies and civil rights organizations aware that they had resurfaced. In a seven-month period, the Berets appeared three times in television or print media. One of those incidents—the prevention of an eviction—earned the Berets exclusive focus for several days, including an excoriation by muckraker columnist Paul Thompson of the *San Antonio Express-News.*

From outward appearances, the Berets were determined, militant, and, depending on perspective, either intimidating or reassuring. It was not apparent that this was an organization in the process of formation, basically a group of batos locos from the Southside with a desire to do something "por la causa" (for the cause). Other than expressing a basic ethnic nationalism forged by a legacy of pervasive segregation, the young recruits knew little about politics or organizations. They had only the vaguest ideas about the Berets and had been recruited through familial and friendship networks.

In this chapter I introduce the Brown Berets and describe the manner in which they reconstituted themselves and began to learn about politics. During the first six weeks of the Berets' rebirth, an intense and exhilarating period, the recruits were introduced into the network of organizations that made up the Chicano movement. They began to learn not only about the Chicano movement but also about the rituals expected of Beret members—the special handshake, the maximal wearing of the beret, and proselytizing or spreading the word about "carnalismo" (brotherhood). Wearing the beret, in particular, was an important marker that reinforced the sense of a unique status or membership.

For the following discussion, I have selected two events from this initial organizing period—an immigration conference and a recruitment trip—that provided opportunities for the recruits to practice and hone their rituals. These "performance opportunities," as I call them, would prove to be important in reinforcing commitment to the group and its ideals. In this initial period, the Berets also dealt with my strange, anomalous status as a participant-observer within the group.

The Southside Berets: An Introduction

The Southside Berets, with one or two exceptions, resided in Columbia Heights, one of the poorest sections of San Antonio. Developed during the forties and fifties when zoning requirements were lax or nonexistent, this sprawling Mexican American neighborhood was characterized by substandard wood frame houses, dirt streets, and poor drainage. It had an image, in the words of social worker Ernesto Gómez, as a place "where addicts and hoodlums live, where immoral and unethical people live, and where illegitimate babies are born daily." This perception was in large part due to the barrio's Circle Gang, "known throughout the city for their raids into other barrios, resulting in stabbings, shootings, and killings." The gang boys, according to the sociologists and social workers involved with the Wesley Center Youth Project, came from "action-oriented maladapted families." These families consisted of an unstable female-headed household with either a weak adult male figure or a "male figure in and out of the house." The Berets were drawn from this social material.

BEGINNINGS [AUG. 15, 7:30 P.M.–2 A.M.; AUG. 19, 7:30–11:30 P.M.] I arrive at the Wesley Community Center, an old settlement house in the deep Southside, in the early evening. The Center is located in an impoverished barrio of run-down houses and unpaved streets. The Westside Berets, the group I had intended to work with, have stopped meeting. Toro, the Southside leader, knowing my interest in writing about the Berets, has invited me to the first meeting of the new chapter. The Wesley Community Center is closed, and the meeting is taking place outside in the parking lot. Thirteen batos have shown up.

Present were Toro, Chivo, Loso, and Tino, all veteran Berets; the cousins Java and Primo; Java's brother Abe; Abe's friend López; two teenagers named Benny; and three guys Chivo brought from Castroville, a small town twenty miles west of San Antonio, so that they could organize there.

Toro (meaning "bull") was the *jefe* or leader of the group. He was short but muscular, fair-skinned (*güero*), wore glasses, and had a missing front tooth, giving him a classic toothless grin. At thirty, he was among the oldest in the group. He was employed at the Wesley Community Center as a part-time welfare worker. He studied auto mechanics for two and a half years at Gary Job Corps. He clearly could make more money as a mechanic than as a field-worker, but he said he liked to "work with the people." Toro boasted about his fight experience, noting that before he joined the Berets he was a gang leader of Los Osos (The Bears). Once the batos from the other gangs saw that he was coming out on TV and the radio and in the newspapers, they began to respect his ideas about carnalismo, and his image changed. Toro used to be a neighborhood organizer for the Mexican American Neighborhood Organizations (MANO) and a member of Chicano III, an ex-*pinto* (ex-con) organization involved in social action and service delivery. Toro appeared to be quite an astute tactician, demonstrating an awareness of which people were in power at various organizations, who to hit for leverage (*palanca*), and how things get done (*movidas*)—in short, the politics of bureaucracy. He was obviously the catalyst behind the regeneration of the Berets.

Chivo (meaning "goat"), Toro's older brother, was thirty-two years old, dark-skinned, with handsome features and a scar on his cheek. He appeared to be the wise man, experienced in barrio street ways, quieter and more settled and self-assured than his brother. Chivo said that he got his nickname from parents who would scare their kids by telling them that El Chivo would get them if they misbehaved. Like Toro, he had been part of MANO until government funding was exhausted, and he had been a member of Chicano III until he was kicked out. Now he was painting houses. Toro mentioned that Chivo had knifed about forty batos and killed one. Chivo had to carry a *cuete* (handgun) in order to protect himself. He had a plastic stomach as result of a *plomazo* (shooting) four years ago.

> Chivo drives an old '64 discolored red Chevy truck with a bumper sticker that says "VAMOS RECIO." This means literally "We're speeding." In a political sense, it means "We're moving fast" or "We're in a hurry." The sticker was a gift from someone who belonged to an organization of the same name. Chivo says that Recio used to be a great truck that could outrun any patrol car. He recalled two times when he eluded the Border Patrol while giving a ride to some "mojados" [illegals]. Looking at the truck, I can't help but wonder how much of what I'm hearing is exaggeration.

Loso, a tall veteran Beret about twenty-six years old with an olive complexion, came across as sharp, articulate, and confident about his opinions; he was an organizer and strategist. Toro said that Loso's only drawback was that he had many personal problems. Loso used to be minister of finance but was removed because he spent the fourteen dollars they had in the treasury. He wasn't kicked out of the organization, because he demonstrated dire family need.

Tino, in his mid-twenties, was another veteran member who had come back. Presently he was on leave from the army. Intellectual-looking, bespectacled, and soft-spoken, he had been with the Berets for two years the first time around. He was dropped because he was selling *carga* (heroin) and was also strung out. At that time he had the rank of major and was the minister of information and security. He wanted to rejoin the Berets as a private but had to undergo some severe and skeptical questioning, especially from the new recruits. Toro expressed some pride in the recruits, saying that he knew that they were Beret potential because of the way they challenged Tino. Tino had been organizing glue and paint sniffers from his Flanders barrio.

Toro, Chivo, Loso, and Tino had been with the original Berets of the Westside. Now that the Westside had stopped meeting, they were striking out on their own. For this first meeting of the reconstituted San Antonio Berets, they had recruited nine potential members.

> The initiation of the new recruits is unritualized, but there is much talk about dying for the Berets and the people. This appears to be the underlying criterion for Beret membership. A recruit has to be invited and sponsored by a Beret. Chivo says that it's not necessary that the recruit know all the movement stuff, only that he adhere to the idea of carnalismo, and that he be ready to die for the cause and for other Berets. "Would you be ready to shoot a gringo tomorrow if ordered?" Chivo asks rhetorically.

Toro asked each new recruit why he wanted to join or, more precisely, what "his problem" was. Javalina, who had been invited by Toro, spoke first. Java was a stocky and broad-faced twenty-seven-year-old. With his glasses and shoulder-length brown hair, he had a disheveled intellectual look. Java worked as a mechanic at Kelly Air Force Base. He saw his membership as an attempt to avenge his uncle's lynching in San Antonio back in 1923. Other than his uncle's cause, and some mention of union organizing at Kelly, Java did not express any political ideas or interests.

Next up was Java's cousin Primo, age twenty-five, of average height and a skinny build; he had dark features and curly black hair. Primo, a driver for a soft drink bottling company, was an impressive recruit, knew quite a bit of history, and had pieced together an ideology from reading movement newspapers like *Chicano Times*. A Vietnam veteran, he was very frustrated because they wouldn't let him into public swimming pools because of his tattoos, which were "done in Vietnam while serving this country." Since then he apparently has generalized his frustrations to "gringos."

Primo and Java had both sought out the Berets and had talked of joining for a long time. Java had also recruited his brother Abe, a hulky, hairy twenty-year-old who in turn had invited his best friend López, also twenty years old, to the meeting. Bespectacled López thought of the Berets in terms of fighting paint and glue sniffing. Both Abe and López were high school dropouts.

The other recruits seem to have drifted into the Beret web by accident of geography or proximity. Mosca, about twenty-three years old, was a neighbor of Chivo and the reason why he and his two brothers were at the meeting. Mosca was short, stocky, and dark-skinned. In contrast, his brother Terco, about nineteen, was small-framed, thin, and olive-complexioned. Chuy, the oldest brother at twenty-six, was a strikingly short man who immediately became tagged with the moniker "Green Giant." The three brothers hailed from nearby Castroville. They wanted to join because they believed that they had been discriminated against, but their claim about discrimination turned out to be a family argument that had landed the brothers and their father in jail. They were still bitter about that.

> Toro emphasizes that the Berets "no se meten en problemas personales o familiares" [do not get involved in personal or family problems]. Toro further tells all new recruits that if a Beret gets drunk or crazy with his beret on or gets arrested for some *pedo* [stupid thing], the Berets will leave him in jail. Moreover, if a bato gets drunk or crazy very often, if he insults (*chotea*) the Berets through some activity not related to the Berets, or if he doesn't come to the meetings, they can expel him from the Berets after a hearing before everyone.

The two remaining recruits were teenagers who quickly earned the monikers "Fat Benny" and "Skinny Benny." Fat Benny, nineteen, was big and stocky, with light-brown hair, a fair complexion, and a good-natured disposition. He had just returned to the eleventh grade after being out of school for two years working as a carpenter's helper. He was really into paint sniffing a year ago and had been selling *mota* (marijuana). Java, who was one of his regular customers, started to talk to him about the Berets. Fat Benny seemed quite interested and serious in learning about the political movement that the Berets represented.

Skinny Benny, age sixteen, had Indian-looking features highlighted by waist-length hair. He had just dropped out of the tenth grade. He was the youngest recruit and the "rawest" of the group. He seemed primarily interested in rucas and getting stoned. He had two bad cuts stitched up on his right arm, due to a recent attempted burglary of a Goodwill store during which the window came crashing down on him. He was lucky that he didn't get cut more severely and that the cops didn't catch him. He was completely drunk when this happened. He said he got home all bloody but smiling.

With the admission of nine guys, the group now had a wide range in age, from sixteen to thirty-two, with one cluster of guys in their mid- to late twenties and another cluster of guys of high school age or a little older. Kinship was an important element in the group, as evident with the brothers Toro and Chivo; brothers Mosca, Terco, and Giant; brothers Java and Abe; and cousin Primo. Of the thirteen active Berets, only five (Fat Benny, Skinny Benny, López, Loso, and Tino) did not have a close relative in the group. Neighborhood ties were also important: all the new recruits were neighbors (or relatives of neighbors) of the Beret leaders.

Seven of the thirteen were unemployed. Five were unemployed unskilled laborers, including one unemployed "elevator operator." One was an unemployed truck driver, and another an unemployed house painter. Of those who were employed, one was a "shoe shine man," one was a "body and fender man," and another was a private in the army. The most secure and best compensated jobs were held by Toro (an occupational therapist's aide), Loso (a nurse's aide), and Java (an aircraft painter). Most of the batos were high school dropouts, so their prospects for stable or well-paying work were minimal. Some might describe them as members of an "underclass."

Why did these batos join the Berets, subject themselves to conduct rules, and begin attending rallies and meetings? Most were not searching for a group to join. Camaraderie was clearly an important lure, as evidenced by a recruitment process based on familial, friendship, and neighborhood networks. Otherwise the members seemed to have drifted into the group. Nonetheless, they shared a basic understanding, even if vaguely expressed, that the Berets were doing good things for la raza (the people). Reinforcement of this sentiment came from an admiring public. Toro was correct: being a Brown Beret conferred immediate recognition and status within movement circles. For a bato who had never belonged to anything or participated in any public event, such recognition was exhilarating and gave the sense of being part of something grand.

Later, while slightly drunk, Toto loudly proclaims that the Berets are the only organization with chapters in every state, organized and united. The other organizations are "just fucking around, not knowing what they're doing. Los Berets saben lo que están haciendo y como es el ultimate one can go in the movimiento, no nomás aceptamos cualquiera [The Berets know what they are doing. And since this is the ultimate one could go in the movement, we don't just accept anyone]. This is the highest honor one can get."

Name	Age	Rank	Occupation
Core Group			
Toro*	29	prime minister	occupational therapist's aide
Chivo*	32	lieutenant	unemployed house painter
Loso*	26	major	nurse's aide
Tino*	24	sgt.-major	army private
Java	28	sgt.-major	aircraft painter
Monte	26	major	graduate student
Primo	25	private-major	unemployed truck driver
Mosca	24	private-major	unemployed elevator operator
Fat Benny	19	private	unemployed unskilled laborer
Skinny Benny	16	private	unemployed unskilled laborer
Terco	19	private	unemployed unskilled laborer
Abe	20	private	unemployed unskilled laborer
López	20	private	body and fender man
Giant	26	private	shoe shine man
Later Core Members			
Marty	30	major	machinist
Rosado	27	sgt.	unemployed semiskilled laborer
George/Jorge	21	(refused rank)	college freshman
Concha	25	no rank	homemaker
Peripheral Members			
Catriz*	28	major	unemployed railroad laborer
Manuel	29	no rank	unemployed unknown
Pedro	53	no rank	semiemployed house painter
Mexicles	24	no rank	unskilled laborer
Mique*	30	no rank	unknown
Alberto*	26	no rank	unknown

*Veteran members

Roster of Southside Brown Berets, 1974

Learning and Performing

Within a week of their initiation, the status and excitement of being a Beret were demonstrated at an immigration conference. The batos would provide security at a "Sin Fronteras" (No Borders) Conference organized by Trabajadores Unidos–Centro de Acción Social Autónoma (TU-CASA), a progressive immigrant rights organization. Toro explained that the Berets supported TU-CASA because the "mojados [wets] are our brothers" and because TU-CASA was against the "migra" (immigration police). Chivo stressed to the new recruits that they must not show up "moteado o to-mado" (stoned or drunk), because those attending the conference, especially the undocumented, were putting their lives in the United States on the line. The immigration police might show up to disrupt the conference. The security of the people was up to the Berets.

The conference was an opportunity for the Berets to perform their security role. This event would also provide an occasion for intermingling with other movement activists, especially with Berets from other chapters. This interaction would be an important source of information and political education and the main way the new recruits acquired political literacy. Finally, the conference, the first political event for the new recruits, would bring the Berets immediate recognition and admiration—in a word, status.

THE SIN FRONTERAS/NO BORDERS CONFERENCE
[AUG. 16, 7 P.M.–3:30 A.M.; AUG. 17, 11:30 A.M.–8:30 P.M.;
AUG. 18, 3 P.M.–12:30 A.M.]
We meet at the Centro Cultural Ruben Salazar, where a three-day Sin Fronteras Immigration Conference is being held. The Centro is named after a journalist who was killed by police in an antiwar protest rally [August 29, 1970] in Los Angeles. The Centro Cultural is basically a house with an attached outdoor pavilion surrounded by mesquite trees. Located on the far western outskirts of town, it sits just a few hundred feet from a major runway of Kelly Air Force Base. All weekend long the sounds of jet aircraft landing and taking off would be mixed with Marxist polemics, nationalist discussions, and condemnations of U.S. immigration policy.

About fifty people were in attendance at this No Borders Conference sponsored by TU-CASA, which was part of a national network of immi-

grant rights organizations, with headquarters in Los Angeles. The San Antonio chápter was a membership organization of about three hundred immigrant families fighting for the rights of immigrants and of the working
class in general. This was its first state conference of immigrants and followed an earlier March conference in Los Angeles. Bert Corona, secretary-
general of CASA, had flown in from Los Angeles to headline the roster of
speakers.

> Fourteen Berets, including one from Dallas and six from Austin and
> Hondo (a small town west of San Antonio), are present. The Beret as-
> signment consists of providing security for the undocumented immi-
> grants and interested Chicanos attending the Conference. Toro acts the
> boss part. Toro assigns perimeter duty to various Berets and keeps one
> of the walkie-talkies. I can tell Toro is walking back and forth by fol-
> lowing the loud chatter of walkie-talkies.
>
> Chivo is more and more coming across as the educator and trainer
> of the group. He tells the recruits that pants should be cuffed around
> boots. He gets down on Java and Primo for the stems on their berets,
> saying they look like chefs. Chivo takes out his knife and cuts off the
> stems. Java and Primo are wearing berets for first time.

A few Berets were busy directing parking, but most were content to
stand on the periphery of the open-air gathering. They showed little interest in participating in political discussion. Nonetheless, simply being at
the conference immersed them in an intense political environment, and
learning seemed to happen through osmosis. The interaction with the veteran Berets from the other towns, in particular, had a definite educational
impact.

The leaders of the other Beret chapters impressed me with their political sophistication. Perales, age twenty-five, the prime minister from Dallas, could have been the poster model of a heroic revolutionary. With flowing black hair and a thick beard, good looks, and a smartly cocked beret,
he seemed like a cross between Jesus Christ and Che Guevara. Perales
was a part-time college student and a full-time drug abuse worker. An excited and eloquent talker, he claimed to have written about fifteen songs
and poems about the *movimiento*. He was an impressive if self-centered
guy. Equally impressive was Clavo from Hondo. Clavo, a Vietnam vet,
had attended the Colegio Jacinto Treviño, an alternative Chicano college.
He knew about the work brigades to Cuba and had plans to visit that win-

ter. He talked about conflict between Mexican immigrants and Chicanos; mentioned communism and alternative systems; and said that Chicano and black soldiers were killing the Vietnamese people who were fighting the same battle they were. He didn't know this when he was in Vietnam; he learned afterward.

Toro agreed with Clavo that we had to change systems, but he didn't say to what. Java and Primo expressed a dislike of communism but also showed a reflexive anger when Chivo and Toro talked about how Chicanos had been treated; that's why they thought the Berets were okay. Given the varying opinions about communism, the ideological glue that seemed to bind everyone together was cultural nationalism.

There was no sense of contradiction with this anti-Communist sentiment when some Berets began to praise Che Guevara moments later as their revolutionary hero.

> While at TU-CASA, Java came over and asked me if the poster of the guy wearing a beret was César Chávez of the Eagle; I told him no, that it was Che Guevara. The other guys laughed at Java's mistake. This provided Primo and Toro an opportunity to show how much they knew about Che, which was considerable. Primo knew that he suffered from asthma and had some foot ailment, Toro said that he has read everything about Che, and both engaged in a discussion about where he was killed, what position he had in the Cuban revolution, and so on. Fat Benny also made a comment about Che. A TU-CASA person offered the poster to the Berets, and Primo assumed the responsibility of taking care of it. I'm not sure what Java thought of all this, since he seems such a staunch anti-Communist, but he now knows quite a bit about Che.

Because of the presence of other Beret chapters, organizational questions that the Southside leadership preferred to defer or hadn't thought about kept arising. The presence of three Chicana Berets from Austin raised the gender question.

> The Chicana Berets said they feel frustrated in the male Beret organization but do not yet feel left out. The guys put down their ideas, like taco fund-raising in Austin; they feel they haven't been given a chance to prove themselves; they can shoot guns as well as guys can. They can defend themselves and the community, just like the guys. The rucas did

provide security for a good part of afternoon and morning; the batos lent them a handgun.

Toro and Chivo had already voiced their objections: the rucas caused too much *pedo* (trouble); they were busy with fashion concerns; they were not ready (except for a few); the guys fought over them; they were the reason the Westside dropped out.

> Later Clavo from Hondo and Perales of Dallas come down on Chivo ["me hicieron garras"] because of the seven chapters in the state only San Antonio has no women. It gives the chapter a backward image. Java agrees that it would be good to have rucas for demonstrations and public meetings, for a positive image. Chivo mentions that the rule about rucas is that nobody messes with them. This comment elicits many *bújales* [oh no!] from the guys. The subject is left hanging in the air.

But the Berets certainly appreciated the attention and support of women at the conference. Java was happy and proud that the rucas wanted to take "chingos de [lots of] pictures" with the Berets. One activist told Java that she was tired of talking; she wanted action. That was why she liked the Berets. Java agreed and said that the Berets were not violent if things could be worked out another way, but they would not back down; they would use violence if they had to. The admiration of women for Berets was regularly mentioned as recognition of the Berets' special mission to be "chingones" (male heroes) in defending the people. Toro remarked, "Por esa razón los Berets siempre tienen chingos de rucas atrás de ellos" (That's why the Berets always have lots of women after them).

Among the non-Beret activists who interacted with the Berets was noted poet and ex-con Raúl Salinas. Salinas spent a lot of time talking to the Berets, which made an evident impression on the recruits. In short, the intense political environment of the conference provided a basic learning experience for the new Beret chapter. They met other Berets and other activists, discussed political ideology and history, and began to learn about the rituals and rhetoric of the Chicano movement.

> The high point of Beret presence at the Conference comes when Chivo gives a brief speech about the history and mission of the Berets to the gathering. I complimented him on his speech, that he had done well.

Chivo was pleased and accepted the compliment, saying that it was difficult for him to speak without cursing or hurling insults. He remembered he spoke at a campaign rally for Sheriff Jimmy Flores where he said, "No me caí pa' nada Jimmy Flores, pero es raza y tenemos que trabajar juntos, y si gana y no nos ayuda, vamos a meterle en su culo" [I don't like Jimmy Flores for anything, but he's raza (people) and we have to work together; and if he wins and he doesn't help us we'll go stuff it up his ass]. And the people applauded like crazy. Chivo saw a picture of himself speaking and said that it looked "bien de aquellas" [really great]—"flanked on both sides by two Berets with full uniform, with their trousers bloused, their berets, and their sunglasses."

In spite of all the talk about the *migra* crashing the conference, the only incident occurred at the Friday night dance when a drunk Chicano Marine, in full dress uniform, walked through the middle of a group of Berets and said, "Those are funny uniforms."

Java replied, "Hey, carnal, somos los Brown Berets" (Hey, brother, we are the Brown Berets). When one of new recruits started cursing and "echando madres" (throwing insults), the drunk Marine responded in kind, and then most of the Berets present joined in. Nothing physical, just words. When Chivo found out, he got angry at the way they had acted—"como van a aprender de la causa de los Berets si les echan madres!" [how are they going to learn about the Beret cause if you curse them!]. The guys just laughed until Chivo threatened to take away their berets—"The Berets have to educate the people, not curse them."

Recruitment and Reinforcement

A week after the conference, the importance of the beret as a visible cue was again highlighted when the Berets ventured into uncharted territory. It would be the first recruitment effort of the reconstituted San Antonio Berets. Java and Toro organized a recruiting trip to Devine, a small town thirty miles southwest of San Antonio. Toro said that some batos there were interested in forming a Beret chapter.

Java impressed me with how quickly he adopted some of the rhetoric, though he still lacked the polish and knowledge of older Berets. Java was focusing on the ritualistic features of Berets, including basic sayings of carnalismo. The day after becoming a Beret, Java was instructing others on the Chicano handshake and talking to his family about carnalismo and the Berets because they thought that it was nonsense. As a result of his enthusiasm, Java has been made the new minister of discipline, with the rank of major. He was given the charge of calling members to meetings and activities and finding out why some didn't show up. He was also responsible for picking up berets from inactive members. "Anyone who misses three meetings is out; leaves of absence are possible if someone has a personal problem," according to Java. He had become a most energetic, almost compulsive advocate of carnalismo. Both Toro and I agreed that Java's rap had changed dramatically within a week. Now Java wanted to recruit others in San Antonio and surrounding towns.

FULL MOON OVER DEVINE [AUG. 23, 6:30 P.M.–I A.M.]
About ten batos have shown up for the recruitment trip to Devine. Toro warns everyone to behave themselves in the small towns; there the people pay a lot of attention to the way an individual behaves; those Berets who misbehave will have to answer to the rest of the Berets. We take off in "Recio," as we jokingly call Chivo's truck, and in another pickup down Interstate 35. Barely outside San Antonio, Java stops to pick up a Mexicano hitchhiker. He turns out be a Quechua Indian hitchhiking back to Bolivia after traveling around the world. As he tells us of his travels throughout China, I sit stunned. What are the chances that we would pick up a Quechua hitchhiker returning from a world tour? Is he a shaman? I wonder. As we head south to Devine, toward Bolivia, I think that this may be an interesting evening.

We arrived in Devine about 7:30 P.M. It was a small segregated farm town of 3,000 people. Mexicanos made up 60 percent of the population. As in many small towns, the city center, consisting of a square with a courthouse in the middle, was dead by early evening. We saw no one downtown. There was no one at the ice station, close by the square, that was to be the rendezvous point. The ten Berets were milling outside the ice station wondering what to do next while Toro and Chivo talked about the disappointments we would have to face working with the people. Soon, however, we began to attract attention. A car full of batos had circled the block to look at us and had returned with other cars. Soon ten cars full of guys from the town converged on the ice house, and Toro was talking with the apparent clique leaders about what we were doing in town. None of these guys had heard anything about a scheduled meeting, but that didn't matter anymore—contact had been made. Meanwhile the town police car had circled the block several times.

> Having been led to their hangout on a country road outside town, the ten Berets begin mingling with the twenty or so batos, mostly of high school age, who have been drinking, smoking, and sniffing glue. The light from the full moon gives the scene a strange appeal. It's an impressive sight as the Berets introduce themselves and begin educating the batos in the ritual of the Chicano handshake and in calling each other "carnales" (brothers)—rituals that most of these Berets have just learned in the past few days. The Devine batos seem overwhelmed by the unexpected rush of *política*; they respond by asking eager questions—"What age do you have to be? I'm in school; is that okay? Mi ruca no quiere; que debo de hacer?" [My girlfriend doesn't want me to join; what should I do?].

Java shouted for all to gather around the back of Toro's pickup and for anyone who wanted to speak to get up on the truck.

> Both Java and Toro jumped onto the bed of the pickup. Toro introduced the *soldados* (soldiers) and began talking about the significance of the beret: "The color of the beret is brown because we, the Chicano people, are brown. The brown circle of the *parche* [emblem] represents the world of all the bronze people; the red background of the *parche* represents the blood which Chicanos have lost in Vietnam and in gang fights in the streets; the eagle because we support the farmworkers' strike of César Chávez; and the hands shaking because we believe in carnalismo [brotherhood]."

Toro explained that carnalismo meant that "a Chicano should not raise his hand against another Chicano. On the contrary, we should help ourselves, so united we can fight the gringo." He added that as soldiers of the people they would be trained in karate and to shoot guns and carbines; there were chapters all over Texas, and now they wanted to start a chapter in Devine. Java rapped about doing this because you want to—"We're not compensated—nadie nos paga." The Berets "speak from the heart to help the people." Java also pointed out that "somos mexicanos y no importa de cual lado" (we are Mexicans and it doesn't matter from which side) and

Full moon over Devine

that "we help the *mojado* also." These were themes that he had just picked up at the No Borders Conference.

> Someone shouts "hay viene el tío loco de uno de los batos, que no le gusta que se junten los batos pa' tomar o fumar y que a la mejor trae su shotgun" [here comes the crazy uncle of one of the guys, who doesn't like the guys to get together to drink or smoke, and maybe he has his shotgun]. We split.

We got back to San Antonio after midnight and had a short meeting to review our impressions of the Devine batos. Toro said that he was proud of the group, the way it conducted itself. Java was now Toro's "hero," or so joked Toro. Java had salvaged the Devine trip after no one showed at the designated place; he had spoken eloquently to the guys who didn't know anything about the Berets. Java now appeared to be the chauvinistic convert. He announced that he intended to do some casework at the Wesley Center with Toro. This was another way, he said, in which the Berets could help the people.

The Devine trip clearly impressed upon the new recruits that the Berets were okay. Although this was only their second activity as Berets, Fat Benny, Skinny Benny, and Terco had aggressively introduced the Devine batos to the "Chicano handshake." Fat Benny, the "old" high school junior, mentioned that one of the batos had confused them with the Green Berets but that he had corrected the guy. Primo also did well speaking to the guys about helping the people, "que no debemos de levantar la mano contra otro Chicano" (that we shouldn't raise our hand against another Chicano). Primo was dead set against the paint sniffing the Devine batos were doing. Chivo noted that the Devine guys had split into two groups when someone said that no drugs were allowed in the Berets. Java ended the discussion by saying that we shouldn't make them Berets because they were too young; right now it was enough to talk.

My Ground Rules for Hanging Out

After two weeks of hanging out on a near-daily basis with the group, I felt that I was off to a good start. I was somewhat disappointed about the no-show of the Westside veterans, but this new Southside chapter provided an opportunity to observe the political development of raw recruits.

MY INDUCTION AND DILEMMA [AUG. 25, 6–11 P.M.]

We meet outside Chivo's house, one of a row of barrack-like structures along an unpaved alley, hidden between Quintana Road and the Pacific Railroad. One could drive by for years, as I had done, and never see these shacks; obscure dirt roads running off Quintana reveal a whole set of look-alike *cantones* [houses]. Being so close to the rail yards, these probably were once the living quarters of the railroad laborers. Chivo mentions that he often sees the *mojados* [illegals], just arrived from *méxicles* [Mexico], come off the boxcars. Tonight we see the rail workers assembling and disassembling chains of boxcars, the locomotive pushing the boxcars until they slam into a string of boxcars. Blam! The sound of boxcars slamming each other punctuates the night air.

I was not prepared for all the beer and *mota* (marijuana) consumed at our gatherings. I have been writing my field notes late at night, somewhat drunk and half-awake. My notes say simply, "I have to cut down on the beer drinking." Overall I felt accepted by the group. Chivo had given his okay on what I was doing—"what benefits a Beret benefits everyone." Later I found out that Toro had asked everyone what they thought of me, how they liked the way I talked to them. Apparently they liked me.

Two weeks after starting out, I am inducted into the Berets. Although I had told Toro and Chivo that I wanted to write a book about the Berets, it took a while before the *soldados* really understood that. The new recruits were puzzled by my ambiguous status, and they constantly asked when I was going to buy a beret. Tonight Toro asks me if I had made up my mind on the Berets. I reply that I had no problem with the goals of the Berets; I just wanted to write about them. Toro then tells me directly, "To write ese libro, tienes que ser minister of information" [to write that book, you have to be the minister of information]. This was not said as an ultimatum but simply as a matter of fact. Toro then commissioned me as a minister of information with the rank of major.

This was an unexpected move, and it took place in front of the group. I had no problems with assisting the group. Previously I had committed myself to writing a grant proposal for their youth outreach work. I saw my assistance as a trade-off: I would provide information and advice as well as write letters and press releases, and they would let me hang out with them, knowing that I was writing a book. Basically I would be an advisor-secretary of the Beret chapter. My advisor role was clear: Toro said he wanted to develop his mind and wanted me to help him. Chivo said that I was going to go far with the Berets if I wasn't killed first.

But there was an obvious problem, of course. As minister of information, I was expected to "educate" the members. Yet that was why I was hanging out with them! I wanted to observe the development of their political consciousness. How could I balance my role as observer with that of participant-officer? That seemed to be inherently impossible. My dilemma surfaced that very evening after the meeting.

> The eleven of us basically take over the dirt alley in front of Chivo's house, as we continue drinking and talking. Everyone is a little drunk. Chivo introduces us to his dog Nixon and his cat Spiro. Chivo begins joking about Nixon, Spiro, and later about President Ford trying to eat a tamal without unwrapping the corn shuck, and this at a banquet in front of the Alamo. We're laughing and howling.

The mention of Gerald Ford brought up a discussion of his amnesty proposal regarding the "draft dodgers" who had gone to Canada instead of fighting in Vietnam. Java spoke out against amnesty and said he was proud of the number of Chicanos who had received medals while fighting. He said too many Chicanos had died over there "pa' dejar los gringos que se rajaran" (to allow the gringos to "turn tail"). Toro was in full agreement and said the Berets should go on record against Ford's amnesty plan and that I should prepare a statement to that effect. I asked if that meant we were in favor of the Vietnam War. Toro said no. I then mentioned what Clavo, the Beret leader from Hondo, had said about how the United States acted as the dog police ("perros") of the world and that they were sending Chicanos to be the dog police of Vietnam. "Were we now on the side of the dog police?" I asked. The subject was left unsettled, an easy thing to do considering our drunken state.

> I could not refrain from speaking out on the issue of amnesty, not so much because I was in favor of it, but because we were all drunk. Did I exert too much influence here? What would a conscientious advisor have done? I think I will wait to see what they remember tomorrow, when we can have a sober discussion on the question. This is my first act as an advisor.

Gathering in the alleyway

This situation forced me to clarify (to myself) my working rules as an ethnographer. One was not to present myself as some expert or representative of the group. Already Chivo had asked me to address the No Borders Conference as such a representative; I had refused, saying that the honor should be his as a Beret veteran. Another rule was to refrain from initiating or participating in a discussion until I had a clear sense of where everyone else stood. A related third rule was that I would never give any orders; I would regard my officer rank as an honorific status. A fourth rule was that I would provide assistance and information when asked. In spite of such ground rules, reconciling observation and participation still proved to be tricky.

The discussion drifted off to other matters. Skinny Benny mentioned a bato who had been selling hot *cuetes* taken from Sears; he had to sell them quick. Chivo and Toro were sorry to hear that the bato had already sold them. This began a group discussion about make, calibers, and so forth, illustrating a sophisticated familiarity with handguns. Toro then showed off his handgun and shoved it in his pants. Java joked that Toro was waving the *cuete* around to prove that he was the *jefe* (boss).

> Chivo then recalls a time when all the Berets were *pedos* [drunk] and Beret founder Juan Guajardo started to daydream about taking over the Alamo, and another guy said just give me a machine gun on top of Joske's [next to the Alamo], and another guy said just give me a Browning automatic rifle, and that's the way the talk went, with the guys asking for carbines, grenades, and tanks—"chingos de tanks"—and when it was his turn to ask for something, he said, "I want to hand in my beret." Chivo said that all the batos broke out laughing and they couldn't stop laughing. This recycled memory still draws laughter, this time from a second generation of Berets.
>
> Spiro the cat sat nearby, listening to the entire proceedings with disinterest. Nixon the dog had wandered off to pee against some tree.

Wearing the Beret, Going Public

After two weeks of hanging out, I felt that I had witnessed a necessary first step in acquiring political consciousness, with the great emphasis placed on rituals—the special handshake, the meaning of the *parche*, and the wearing of the beret. In contrast to the veterans, who could at times become relaxed about symbols and rituals, the new recruits were keenly aware of maintaining them. Java had emerged as the fierce enforcer and fanatical adherent of the smallest rituals, and those most concerned about ritual practice were the teenagers—Abe, the two Bennies, Terco, and López.

The most important ritual called for the maximal wearing of the beret. The beret symbolized carnalismo. As Toro put it, "The beret means more than the crucifix for me, because when I was a Christian I was going around shooting [*polmiando*] my people, and when I became a Beret I stopped doing that." According to Chivo, however, protecting the beret was one of the few things that a Beret could fight for: "A Beret can fight, but only for three reasons—for his *waifa* [wife], for his *jefita* [mother], and for his beret."

Buying the beret, then, was an important part of the rites of passage of becoming a Brown Beret. Only one military store in the entire state sold them, at $3 apiece, and that store was in San Antonio. Berets from other towns had to make a special trip. Thus four Berets from West Dallas had driven 300 miles to San Antonio to buy fifty berets for a new Ledbetter chapter.

The accouterments of the beret were one set of crossed rifles, centered and placed two fingers above the head band, and the *parche* or emblem of the organization, which had to be sewn slightly to the left of the crossed rifles, four fingers above the head band. Any rank insignia had to be placed immediately above the crossed rifles. This—a fully dressed beret—constituted the basic uniform. The brown military jacket was deemed optional if a member didn't have the money. The cost outlay, which varied because the storeowner was well aware that he had a monopoly, could be considerable for an unemployed bato:

Brown beret	$3.00
Crossed rifles	.75
Rank insignia	.75
	$4.50 minimum
Military jacket	8.50 optional
	$13.00

This did not include the *parche* of carnalismo, which could no longer be obtained from the manufacturer with whom the Berets had contracted previously. That meant that new Beret members often found themselves competing with each other for the fully dressed beret of a veteran member who had been kicked out or had withdrawn from the organization.

The beret was an explicit marker of membership. It defined who belonged to the group. In my case, it minimized my conspicuous and constant presence as a participant-observer.

WEARING THE BERET [AUG. 30, 7–10 P.M.]
Chivo spends about 45 minutes trying to fit a beret on me. In saying something about the beret, I refer to it as a "cachucha" [cap], and Chivo quickly and firmly corrects me—"It's not a cap; it's a beret." . . .
Toro mentions the book I want to write, and he passes around a magazine article (from *La Luz*) I had given him in our first contact. The batos seemed interested, but no question is asked of me. I said my book would be like the article. I wanted to say more, about the need to get life histories, but I decide to defer for the time being.

While wearing the beret reduced my obvious presence, it did not erase questions about who I really was, what organization I really belonged to, and what I really was writing about. These questions would surface throughout my field experience.

Wearing the beret, besides being a visible display of membership, was also important as a public declaration of commitment to "la causa." This type of self-imposed visibility, especially when the beret symbol appeared ambiguous or dangerous to some, demonstrated and reinforced commitment to a militant posture if not ideology. Its use brought praise or admiration as well as negative reactions from many in the community. Even those who did not know what the beret represented generally showed a minimal reaction such as stares, smiles, frowns, winks, disapproving nods, and so forth. A significant feature of wearing the beret lay in this everyday vulnerability to public reaction. I would not have understood this fully had I not donned the beret.

Sometimes the beret attracted guys who were interested in the group. It was not uncommon for strangers to approach the Berets and ask about joining them.

> A few days ago, while walking with Toro and Java downtown, we were approached by a bato loco. This guy wanted to join the Berets or the Raza Unida Party; he was confused about the distinction. The guy said a number of ex-*pintos* [ex-cons] wanted to join. Toro was going to follow up.

At other times the beret attracted hostility, particularly from old gang members. A Beret could never be sure of what to expect. The Westside Berets had told me many stories of being accosted in cantinas. Java mentioned being confronted in a tavern by an ex-Beret because he did not have the patch of carnalismo on his beret; the guy thought that Java was mimicking the Berets. The ex-Beret was ready to protect the integrity of the distinctive symbol, but he left Java alone when he recognized Toro standing outside. Fat Benny and Skinny Benny described an incident while walking past the housing projects. Both had their berets on. Some guys accosted them for money; they didn't have any and began to explain the notion of carnalismo. A guy later asked them to back him up in a fight, but the two Bennies refused, again explaining the idea of carnalismo. Wearing the beret made a member open to all sorts of reactions.

In sum, both positive and negative reactions to the beret reinforced the mission of the group—to fight discrimination and work for a raza unida. For the recruit, the buying and wearing of the beret heralded a break from previous life history. It was a public announcement of commitment to the cause. Whether this signaled a change in personal behavior was another matter, as I discuss in a later chapter.

POR LA CAUSA

AS NOTED BEFORE, the Southside Berets constituted a "second generation" chapter, consisting of four veteran Berets—Toro, Chivo, Loso, and Tino—and nine recruits. Three more recruits joined later: Rosado, sponsored by Java; George, sponsored by Toro; and for a brief period Concha, also sponsored by Toro. I describe them in a later chapter. At its height, the chapter had sixteen members.

Most of the recruits had never been part of any organized efforts, and thus they had to learn that the circle of "camaradas" (friends) was not just another social clique but in fact an organization with public goals. They also had to learn that they were part of a larger network of organizations with similar goals, or what is called an "organizational field." This network constituted the most important audience or public for Beret performances. Awareness of their organizational status was extremely important, and most Beret veterans were quick to use it to differentiate their present situation from their past biographies as gang members, *tecatos* (addicts), or delinquents. But the recruits had to learn what it meant to belong to an organization.

The previous chapter describes the emphases placed on ritual practice as constituting a basic learning step in acquiring political agency. Occurring simultaneously was a second step of learning that the Berets were an organization as opposed to a clique or social club and part of a broad organizational field with shared goals and beliefs. Interaction with this movement's organizational field—and in particular with the statewide network of Beret chapters—was key in shaping the perspective and actions of this emergent Beret group.

In this chapter I describe the recruits' evolving understanding of their membership in a movement organization. I have selected early journal entries that highlight important aspects of this learning experience. One basic item dealt with behavior in public. Wearing the beret not only signified membership but also made the member "public." Thus following behavioral rules—that is, the nagging question of discipline—was important. A second aspect involved interacting with a broad movement organizational field. Such interaction provided information, resources, and "performance opportunities." Related to this was a third aspect: defining a specialized niche and identity within the movement field. This had the potential of becoming a specific expression of Beret political agency.

Following Rules

Although the Berets consciously distanced themselves from a gang identity, their past nonetheless haunted them. This had been a public relations problem for the original Westside chapter, even though it had consistently portrayed itself as a civic group. The problem did not disappear with the reconstituted Southside Berets. The older batos—Toro, Chivo, Loso, and Tino—were ex-gang members and had a trove of tales from their gang days. One of Toro's favorite stories, when explaining the meaning of Beret membership to non-Berets, concerned his gang past and how the Berets had transformed him.

[SEPT. 18, 7 P.M.–1 A.M.]
Losoya, Toro, and Java talk with two "Mexican American girls" who happened to be at Wesley and wanted to know more about the Berets; they had some negative preconceptions about pachucos and the Berets.

Toro comes on strong and articulate about his personal life history and what the Berets are about. About four years ago, Toro says, he was the leader of Los Osos, a very active street gang, and he got into an unfortunate incident where two brothers were beating him up and he took out his *cuete* and killed one of the guys. The case was thrown out of court due to a lack of evidence. One or two months later about eight guys jumped Toro and Chivo and left them for dead all *filiorados* (knifed up). Several months later when both Toro and Chivo had recuperated, they shot the other brother.

Toro said all this as a way of underscoring his personal change as a Beret who believed "in unity, la familia, and carnalismo, in not lifting a hand against another Chicano unless in self-defense." The Berets "are here to help people," concluded Toro, "but we're not angels." This was a life story that I would hear a few times during my time with the Berets. It was the story of transformation that I wanted to understand and document.

The Southside Berets always struggled with the gang tag and behavior of some of its members. Because they were aware that their "loco" label still followed them, displaying public etiquette was basic to supporting their dual claim of personal change and organizational legitimacy. In his pre-Beret days, a bato's behavior might have been restricted by the clique or peer group, but generally these restrictions had not called for following conventional public etiquette. Now with the Berets everyday street behavior such as verbal curses, body curses (such as shooting the finger), wolfing at women, relieving oneself in public, touching one's genitals, getting drunk, using drugs, fighting, and any other behavior that embarrassed the group was frowned upon and could become the subject of group discussion and reprimand.

Conventional behavior, of course, was functionally important for the organization's effectiveness. An organization could hardly afford to alienate the very people whom it wished to organize, educate, and protect and who might be the source of the few resources the organization could rely on. Even among the members, getting drunk or "loco" was dysfunctional for the organization's survival, as illustrated by the disintegration of the citywide Beret organization. Thus the batos who joined the Berets had to adhere to rules regarding comportment.

The rules regarding Beret behavior were explicitly written down in a list, but for the first two months of the regenerated Southside Berets all strictures about correct behavior, especially regarding the practice of carnalismo, were simply verbalized. Not until mid-October did the batos engage in a focused discussion of the chapter rules.

RULES FOR THE BERETS
[OCT. 16, 5 P.M.–3 A.M.; OCT. 17, 7 P.M.–1 A.M.]
Java produces a copy of the Rules for the Brown Berets, a document from the days of the Westside chapter. Toro wants us to review and amend the rules. Java reads the rules one by one. There is not much discussion. Rule number four regarding contact is relaxed quite a bit, with soldiers and officers needing to contact one another a few times a week

In order for an organization such as ours to survive, we must have a love for our people, dedication, and discipline. If you really love your people, you yourself will straighten out. The following rules apply to each and everyone of us. These rules were not made to be broken.

Rules for the Brown Berets

The following rules are for the San Antonio chapter of the Brown Beret Organization. Any member of the organization found guilty of breaking any of these rules, is subject to disciplinary action and will either be put on probation or permanently terminated from the organization.

1. Every member will attend all called meetings, rallys, pickets, or demonstration.
2. any member absent from 3 consecutive meetings without a good excuse or failure to call in his excuse prior to the meeting will be **punished and then** ousted from the organization.
3. Every Brown Beret will be in uniform at all Brown Beret functions.
4. All soldados will contact their officer ~~once a day~~ **twice a week** and all officers will contact the Prime Minister ~~twice a day~~ **three times a week**.
5. Under no circumstances will a Brown beret indulge in the possession, sale, use or distribution of ~~narcotics~~ **hard drugs (excluding mota).**
6. While in uniform, no Brown Beret will be seen in public while heavily intoxicated.
7. It is an absolute must that all Brown Berets preach "carnalismo." **This rule will be enforced!!**
8. No Brown Beret will speak against another carnal unless he is present.
9. Under no circumstances will a Brown Beret raise his fist against another Chicano, unless in self-defense.
10. All Brown Berets will show respect for each other and to the people at all times.
11. **The case of** any Brown Beret arrested for an offense not having to do with the causa, will ~~swim alone~~ **be reviewed by 3 officers who will decide if any assistance should be given.**
12. Every brown Beret will always look and act his best.
13. All orders will be obeyed.

EL CARNALISMO UNE   –NO SEPARA

QUE VIVA LA CAUSA Y LA REVOLUCION

HASTA LA VICTORIA

Brown Beret Rules as Modified for the Southside (edits are shown through strike-overs, inserts through boldface)

rather than daily. Rule number five regarding no use of narcotics draws
the most comments. "What?" ask several of those present. This leads to
a clarification that "mota" is not a narcotic or hard drug. Rule number
seven about preaching "carnalismo" or brotherhood will be strictly enforced, says Toro.

The first four rules dealt with internal communication; the amendments
suggested a decreased level of activity from the Westside days. The next
six dealt with behavior. Being drunk or wasted or disrespectable in public was explicitly prohibited by rules five and six. Rule seven stated that
preaching carnalismo was an "absolute must," and rules eight, nine, and
ten basically specified what this meant in terms of practice. These four
rules seemed to suggest the difficulty of maintaining group solidarity.

Enforcement of these rules, of course, was an entirely different matter.
Although all the new recruits professed their acceptance of the rules, only
Java, as the minister of discipline, appeared to take them seriously. Java
had been placed in charge of enforcing attendance at meetings and activities. He was also in charge of picking up berets and other uniform items
from inactive members. With control over the assignment of repossessed
berets, Java attempted to reward and discipline members. The expense or
scarcity of berets, *parches*, and military jackets had created a "token economy" of prized articles.

The question of discipline would be a recurrent issue within the
chapter.

Working with Other Organizations

A second point about "becoming political" concerned the importance of
the movement's organizational field. In the absence of any structured
political education lessons, political understanding for the new recruits
came about through interaction with the network of Chicano movement
organizations.

A major source of information and reinforcement naturally came from
the statewide network of Beret chapters. In 1974–1975 the network consisted of eight recognized chapters—Austin, Hondo, Houston, McAllen,
North Dallas, West Dallas (Ledbetter), San Antonio, and Waco. The existence of these chapters had impressed the new recruits with the idea of
a great, unified organization. They had heard about the Hondo chapter
and its newspaper, about Austin and its police brutality campaign, about

the Dallas Ledbetters who ran a community center with a boxing ring—
in other words, heard about chapters that had projects that they might be
able to follow. They were impressed that a Beret could travel throughout
the state and the Southwest and visit other Berets who would provide a
place to stay and food to eat. This point was brought home when a Dallas
Beret, a truck driver returning from California, passed through San Antonio on his way back to Dallas in mid-September. He had been on the road
for a month and a half and had stayed with Berets the entire time.

"Che," as everyone called him, was twenty-three years old and had
been a Beret for three years. He was a seventh-grade dropout, but his
knowledge and eloquence made him graduate student material. His nickname had originated from his tongue-in-cheek claim that Che Guevara
was a relative. But with his big nose, unkempt black hair, and very dark
skin, he looked nothing like Che. Jokingly we called him "el hijo de Che"
(Che's son).

CHE'S NATIONAL REPORT [SEPT. 12, MIDNIGHT–2 A.M.]
Che from Dallas has just driven into town. He's been in Califas about
a month and a half. He provides us with a national report on the status of the Berets. He tells us that the Berets in Califas "están muy que-
mados" [are very burned] and have gone underground. They can't wear
the berets in public; "nomás los tienen en sus cantones" [they just have
them in their homes]. Che says that David Sánchez sold out, "nadie sabe
lo que paso con toda la fería que pañaron con la Caravana de la Recon-
quista" [no one knows what happened with all the money they collected
during the Caravan of Reconquest].

Speaking of the Caravana, Toro recalled that they didn't like the attitude
of Sánchez and his officers when they arrived in San Antonio, that they almost came to blows when Sánchez paid an unwelcome visit to the house
of one of the Beret women. The Berets in El Chuco (El Paso), Che continued, still believed in Sánchez, that he was right about infiltration, and that
for a while a Federal Bureau of Investigation (FBI) informant had headed
the Los Angeles chapter.

Frequent interaction with Berets from other chapters was a source of
information as well as an occasion for political education.

Che then proceeds to test some of the San Antonio Berets (Primo,
Skinny Benny, and Terco) by asking them "¿Quién es Lucio Cabañas?"
[Who is Lucio Cabañas?]. Primo and Skinny Benny didn't know, and

Terco knew very little. Che turns to Toro and says, "These guys are Berets and don't know about Cabañas. What kind of Berets do you have here?"

Toro said he was embarrassed. He explained that Cabañas was a campesino revolutionary fighting in the Mexican mountains.

The whole subject was raised when someone mentioned Aztlán and Primo said, "What?" Toro then started on a mini-lesson about how the Southwest was the home of the Aztecs, which they called Aztlán. Now the batos knew what Aztlán meant, and who Lucio Cabañas was. For the recent recruits, this had been another lesson in politics and history, administered at one in the morning.

While other Beret chapters were an important source of information, the local movement network provided the immediate context for Beret learning and action. The most active members of this network in San Antonio consisted of the Raza Unida Party, the Mexican American Unity Council (MAUC), Barrio Betterment, the Mexican American Legal Defense and Education Fund (MALDEF), the Southwest Voter Registration Education Project (SVREP), the League of United Latin American Citizens (LULAC), and Trabajadores Unidos–Centro de Acción Social Autónoma (TU-CASA). Through their meetings, conferences, and protests these organizations disseminated information and reinforced the importance of Beret membership by providing opportunities for Beret public appearances. The events sponsored by these organizations created moments that furthered the recruits' understanding of their membership.

TU-CASA, in particular, had developed close ties with the Berets. Established in early 1973, TU-CASA was an immigrant rights organization and part of a national network of other CASAs, with headquarters in Los Angeles. Its leadership had close ties with progressive political organizations in Mexico. Although immigrant rights were its main focus, TU-CASA was also involved in community issues. In its brief existence TU-CASA had organized protest marches against high utility rates. These marches had drawn support from the San Antonio and Austin chapters of the Brown Berets, from a few unions (the United Steelworkers, the clothing workers' union, the meat cutters' union, and the United Farm Workers), the Raza Unida Party, and various church groups. TU-CASA was plugged into a wide local, national, and international network.

The TU-CASA leadership continued to work with the Berets once

the Southside chapter regrouped. Restaurant owner and well-known activist Rosario was in regular contact. The batos had provided security at
TU-CASA's No Borders Conference in August, which was the first political event for the new recruits. At a subsequent meeting (September 22),
the TU-CASA leaders invited the Berets to join them in a protest before
the Mexican Consulate to commemorate the massacre at Tlatelolco. The
date was set for October 2, the anniversary of the Tlatelolco killings in
Mexico City. Rosario gave a rundown on the protest and the significance
of the timing. Much of this had been said before at TU-CASA meetings
when the Berets had been present, but now it was being said "personally" only to Berets. The Berets said they would not hand out leaflets or
picket but would provide security, which is what they did for political
organizations.

PROTEST AT THE MEXICAN CONSULATE [OCT. 2, 9 A.M.–9 P.M.]
In the early morning of the anniversary of the Tlatelolco massacre in
1968 we went to protest in front of the Mexican Consulate in downtown
San Antonio. The protest is meant to commemorate the massacre and
to draw attention to the ongoing political repression in Mexico. Ten Berets [Toro, Java, Primo, the two Bennies, López, Chivo, Terco, Abe, and
Loso] have shown up. This is the first demonstration for most of these
batos.

The batos form a perimeter around the twenty or so protesters who
are picketing the Consulate. A squad of five policemen stands close by,
monitoring the protest. The only hint of trouble comes when a rookie
patrolman—we call him a "rookie"—approaches the Berets and says we
are breaking the law by not moving. This creates some tension; no one
likes the rookie's tone of voice, and thus no one is in a mood to comply. We are to follow Toro's lead if *pedo* [conflict] erupts; he mentions a
possible sitdown. Later a sergeant comes by and tells us just "not to ob-
struct," but until that point there was some tension. Another tense moment came when an old gringo cursed a girl who was handing out leaflets; the Berets immediately responded *con madres* [with curses], with
the gringo rejoining by calling us "Communists."

Afterward we passed by Beret headquarters and heard positive reaction to the TV footage that showed some close-ups of Berets doing security
duty at the protest. Skinny Benny, Primo, and Mosca felt good about coming out on TV. The camera focused on Skinny Benny; several comments
were made about the cameramen liking Benny's long hair. Everyone felt

Protesting at the Mexican Consulate

proud, and Chivo drank vodka straight in honor of these batos. Toro said, "The Berets have hit town again!"

Within the first six weeks of the regeneration of the Berets, TU-CASA had provided them two important occasions for learning and performing. There would be more. TU-CASA was courting the Berets.

Thus interacting with an organizational network went hand in hand with the formation of political consciousness. Java, Mosca, and Primo, all in their mid-twenties, seemed to be learning quite a bit about this network of organizations and its importance. The teenagers were for the most part unfamiliar with or unconcerned about the network of barrio organizations. Beret veterans Toro, Chivo, Loso, and Tino were already aware of this network, yet even they, as the new leadership of the reconstituted Berets, were in a learning mode.

In the barrio world of these batos locos, the Berets represented one of the few avenues of introduction to the movement organizational field. An introduction into political life involved training and learning techniques of formal organizational life that were irrelevant or nonexistent in barrio society. Thus the new recruits were learning to speak before rallies, to ask questions at meetings, to act as marshals at marches, and basically to act in a chivalrous manner in public. These experiences constituted basic political training.

Primo, for example, said that he didn't realize until he was speaking in front of a TU-CASA crowd that this was serious shit he was involved in: "que no somos una bola de payasos" (that we're not a bunch of clowns). It was a realization that he was not just in a *clica* (clique), a social grouping of camaradas, but in an organization. Mosca likewise had never hung around with a group of guys before, much less a group that considered itself an organization. Variously employed and unemployed, a loner who interacted mainly with his kinship group, basically illiterate, Mosca had spent most of his life handling day-to-day matters. Politics were abstract, very distant, irrelevant things. Although he was twenty-six years old and a native Tejano, he didn't know that the Democratic and Republican parties existed. Mosca had no idea of how government functioned other than that gringos controlled everything. Likewise his brother Terco had formed a racial conflict perspective from his negative experiences with "a gringo policeman" but otherwise knew nothing about politics. The other teenagers were similarly uninformed. Being with the Berets introduced them to a world of organizations and to a source of knowledge about history and politics. In a sense, they were becoming politically literate and politically vocal simultaneously.

Working with Barrio Youth

A related third point that surfaced early in the rebirth of the Berets resurrection had to do with staking out a specific organizational mission. As self-identified *soldados de la raza* (soldiers of the people), the Berets' role at minimum consisted of providing security at conferences and protests. But the Beret leaders also wanted to put forth their own ideas on how to protect the community. In the first months of their resurrection, the Southside Berets searched for issues that they could stamp as their own. The leadership immediately resumed one project of the Westside Berets: working with glue-sniffing and paint-sniffing youths.

FILMS FOR GLUE SNIFFERS
[SEPT. 17–18, 21–22, 25–26; MANY, MANY HOURS]
Chivo says the drug abuse problem is widespread and results from the *chavalos'* (youths') attitudes at being *chingón* (manly); they have brothers who are putting in 10–15 years in the pen and are considered heroes and they think very easily "pues que yo le voy a poner 20 y ser todavía más chingón" (well, I'm going to put in 20 and be even more manly). Chivo says if we can just get that attitude of wanting to be *chingón* and use it for la raza that would be great; that's what we must do. The idea is to talk to them, keep them busy, show them films, and so on.

The Berets were capitalizing on the desire to be macho, which had resulted in much internecine gang fighting. They were attaching this desire to the concepts of Chicano brotherhood and manhood. (Chivo wanted me to write a grant proposal on this.)

As part of an outreach effort, we began showing films in the parking lot of the Wesley Center. Beret veterans Loso and Tino had connections with the street youth from the Wesley, Flanders, and Villa Coronado barrios.

The next evening, we went over to the Wesley Center to show films to glue- and paint-sniffing batos, all adolescents. Loso had selected a film to screen. About ten guys from the Flanders area are picked up, and another ten from the Wesley barrio show up. We sit outside in the parking lot next to the building waiting around. The program is not well organized. The Center is closed, so Java and I look for a bedsheet to pin on the wall as a screen. There were no drinks and the popcorn was nearly all eaten by the time the show started. The film is about glue-sniffers and to the point—except that it puts down the Berets, shows them taking reds, smoking dope, and getting drunk! This is a damaging, unexpected, and ironic twist that Toro tries to minimize in the talk after the films. Chivo criticizes the film as middle class.

Upon Chivo's instruction, Primo led a rap on the *mono* (movie).

> Primo lays out what struck him most. His rap reflects his life experi-
> ence about taking drugs and being labeled deviant. He tells *los chavali-
> tos* [the youth] "every time I apply for a job, I gotta tell them that I was
> dishonorably discharged del navy and that I've taken drugs." But Primo
> adds a wrinkle to his rap that I hadn't heard before—that "this is our
> land, that we were here first, before the gringos." Fat Benny backs him
> up with many "yeahs."

The film series had provided an opportunity for the new recruits to display their understanding of movement concepts.

This campaign with youth later flared up into a full-blown crisis in late
September. The response of the Berets revealed old behavioral tendencies
and an incomplete comprehension of the movement's organizational field.

Loso had been meeting regularly with a Southside high school group
that had first started as "a drug abuse thing." Then some batos were suspended for long hair. So other batos formed a committee to propose a dress
code change, and they in turn were suspended. Loso said "que se les fue
a la cabeza y comenzaron a hacer lo que les deban la gana" (they got big
heads and started doing whatever they wanted). Now the batos were looking for some guidance. More discussion with them brought out other complaints that amplified the issues beyond the question of dress code—allow
smoking, allow Spanish, get rid of the racist coach, and of course allow
long hair.

At the Beret strategizing session, Toro pushed for some dramatic action,
while Loso counseled patience and called for seeking parental support.

THE SOUTHSIDE HIGH CRISIS
[SEPT. 21, 4 P.M.–8:30 P.M.; SEPT. 22, 12 NOON–7 P.M.]
Toro wants to know what the Berets should do. Loso and Chivo say that
we should let the high schoolers lead the school action with Berets just
helping organize them. Chivo says we must follow proper channels before resorting to Beret action; Loso says we must have community and
parental support also. Toro responds that the Berets do not have to follow proper channels, "Is that the image of Berets we want to give?" Toro
is tired of doing little stuff, thinks time is ripe for something big, says
that he is ready to go to the penitentiary. Toro says now is the time for
action. No, says Loso, we must broaden the issues to extend beyond

dress code—"los batos were suspended porque no la jugaron fría; se
creían muy chingones [because they didn't play it cool; they saw themselves as big men] because they raised the dress code issue." Toro is per-
suaded to change his tactics but keeps insisting on "action" to show the
principal we're behind the suspended batos.

Toro was in an excited state, eager to get into the fray. He raised the spec-
ter of a riot and talked about taking over the principal's office. Some Berets
were as eager as Toro to get into the fray; there was much talk about getting arrested. Loso urged everyone to calm down and said that we should
get parents behind these issues. Toro replied that he wanted to go by the
principal's house "just to let him know we're around." The leadership decided to secure some parental support.

The first two weeks of October were spent trying to mobilize community support for the suspended youths from Southside high. They organized a meeting at the Villa Coronado Center, a youth center in an out-
lying barrio south of the city. Villa Coronado was an unincorporated
settlement of shanties and outhouses, a true equivalent to the Latin American *colonia* or *favela*. It made the Columbia Heights neighborhood of the
Berets look like a middle-class suburb.

IN VILLA CORONADO [OCT. 16, 5–8 P.M.; OCT. 17, 7–11 P.M.]
The Berets distributed leaflets in Villa Coronado announcing a meeting
at El Carmen Church to discuss the Southside High problems. This was
the first proselytizing experience for most, and everyone was struck by
the apathy of the people. Skinny Benny concluded, in a matter-of-fact
tone, "que no les importa madre que les esta pasando en el Southside
High School" [that they don't give a mother about what is happening at
Southside High School]. The meeting the next day turns out to be disap-
pointing; it is well attended by youth, but the parents are noticeably absent. Even more frustrating, the meeting results in no plan of action.

Afterward, in a gathering of Berets and high school students, someone offered the now familiar solution of burning the school down. No one took
this proposal seriously. This was a symbolic statement, representing frustration and anger.

During the Southside High troubles, Toro, Loso, and I approached several organizations (Barrio Betterment, MALDEF, TU-CASA) to enlist support for the stalemated situation at Southside High. At some point, we

went to Hondo, a farming community forty miles west of San Antonio, where a prominent sign tells all passersby: "This is God's country, so don't drive through it like hell." Only the bilingual can sense any contradiction as we drive through in a truck that proudly proclaims "Vamos Recio."

[OCT. 21]
We went to Hondo to drum up support from the Hondo Berets for the Southside High issue. Chivo has a high opinion of Berets from Hondo, says they're very dedicated. The Hondo chapter has a newspaper, and they organized a high school walkout last year. While we were driving around crowded in the back of "Recio," some rucas in Hondo flirted with us and the guys responded by giving the brown power salute.

An observation from my field notes in mid-October: as we circled organizations to see who would help, I realized that this was Toro's first experience as a leader of a group with "public" goals, that is, as leader of an organization that was attempting to effect some change.

This was different from being a leader of a gang, which has no group objectives or program other than protecting its territorial boundaries and membership integrity. Still Toro seemed to feel that Berets could do it by themselves and that there was no need to gather support from other organizations; this was evident in his insistent, impatient call for action. Loso, on the other hand, acknowledged that he had no extensive experience organizing people and counseled that we should start attending meetings of other organizations.

The last serious effort on the part of the Berets regarding the Southside High issue took place in mid-November. It demonstrated the difficulty they had in relating to other movement organizations. The Berets showed up at a Barrio Betterment board meeting to demand action. Toro, Primo, Skinny Benny, Rosado, and George were at the meeting. Rosado thought there was going to be *pedo*, so he took a .22 Magnum with him to the meeting.

HITTING THE BBC [NOVEMBER 16, EVENING]
Toro and Loso talked about how they hit the board of the Barrio Betterment Committee really hard ["les caímos pesado"] last night, that they scared everyone. Loso says that "those pinche [stupid] rules about vot-

ing and making motions y todo ese pinche jale [and all that stupid stuff]
are worthless," that a guy should be able to stand up, say what he feels,
"se 'cabo todo el pedo" [and that's it]. The result is that the BBC will talk
to Channel 12 about a thirty minute spot on the Southside problems and
that if BBC doesn't get it the Berets are going to take over Channel 12.
Toro said that those who don't want to be inside with the Berets should
be outside marching.

Loso and Toro were upset at Robert Anguiano, director of the BBC, because they thought he was holding the Berets back. Toro noted that he
knew where Anguiano lived and that Anguiano knew that Toro could go
by "pa' desmadrar su casa" (to mess up his house). Bobby Anguiano of
BBC later told me that they were bothered by the proposed tactics but denied being scared. He said that he was working on getting a meeting for
the Berets with Channel 12.

The Southside High issue lingered for a few months and was never resolved. According to Loso, one of the suspended guys, who was depressed
and had nothing to do, died from an overdose. Toro laid the blame directly
on the school. The Berets were learning about the difficulty of community
organizing.

Feeling Efficacious

In the first months of their resurgence, the new recruits were learning
that they were an organization and not a clique or gang and that they were
part of a larger network of movement organizations. Wearing the beret
signaled that they were members of an organization, but understanding
what that meant was tied up with learning the Beret credo about brotherhood and following certain rules of comportment. While in uniform, each
individual was to adhere to conventional public etiquette as well as practice and preach about brotherhood among Chicanos. Awareness of membership also came through their interaction with other Beret chapters and
movement organizations. Wearing the beret, behaving respectfully, participating in conferences and protests, and engaging in community projects were all signs of political consciousness; these were essential for the
group's claim to be a political organization and not a gang. Defining and
carrying out a special mission of working with marginal youths reinforced
such awareness.

The Southside Berets continually ran into problems, however, because their preferred tactics usually implied a confrontational style. This was clearly a carryover from gang culture, where conflict resolution occurred through intimidation or physical blows. The Berets frequently flexed such muscle with other Chicano organizations, which generated mixed results and always created negative feelings. Although most of the Beret recruits had never been in an organization and knew little about the community's organizational field, they nonetheless felt efficacious, to use that favorite political science term. They seemed quite confident that they could influence the actions or positions of others. They were acquiring political agency, but it was not clear what this might mean.

SOMOS CAMARADAS

FROM THE OUTSET it was evident that the Southside Berets were an unusual, if not unique, political formation. Even as the members were learning about the political movement they had joined, they were forming an encompassing social group that exhibited many of the features of a gang. The chapter was a male clique laced with kinship and pseudo-kinship ties. It had a charismatic leadership, expected exclusive membership, and sported an aggressive posture. Add the distinctive argot that the batos spoke and one would be hard pressed not to call this group "a pachuco gang with uniforms," as some barrio residents described them. Rosado, one of Java's recruits, remarked that his relatives had warned him that the Berets were "a gang that gets drunk and into trouble":

> Rosado's aunt and cousin have told him that the Berets are "pistoleros," among other things. Rosado acknowledged that that they were armed but that didn't mean that they were going to shoot guys "nomás asina" [for no reason] like they used to in the gang days, and that if they knew the Berets they wouldn't say those things.

Although not a preexisting clique or gang, the Southside Berets nonetheless quickly acquired many of the features of a long-standing organized group. The older guys, and particularly Toro through his leadership style, set the climate for the entire group. The mode of aggressive interaction, the tolerance of petty crime, and the comfortable acceptance of weapons were all an inheritance from the social world of gang cliques.

Another inheritance, perhaps a counterbalance of sorts, was the solidarity and sense of familial belonging that the group provided. The intense, intimate relationships among the Berets were apparent. Even the mothers of Primo and Java knew all the Berets. The intimacy was demonstrated by the ease with which a member could drop by unannounced at each other's houses and by the freedom to talk about personal matters.

Members could count on each other for help when needed. An observer accustomed to routine and structure most likely would have viewed the lives of these batos as generally unplanned and spontaneous, but there was a pattern oriented around survival. A bato who was unemployed and felt discouraged about looking for work had plenty of time to spend with friends who would provide beer and cigarettes, would accompany him if he had someplace to go, or would help out in part-time work or a one-shot money deal. I witnessed many instances of carnalismo among the Berets. One instance took place after Primo announced that he was leaving for Idaho to look for work. He had lost his job with the bottling company because they thought he was a thief. We drank a bottle of tequila at his *despedida* (farewell).

FOR TWO SODAS & ONE PACK OF COOKIES [OCT. I, EVENING]
I went to see the guys after not having been with them for four days. Toro, Java, Chivo, Terco, Mosca, the two Bennies, and Primo were at Chivo's house. Seeing Primo was a surprise since he was supposed to be in Idaho; he didn't make it beyond Comfort, Texas (approximately 50 miles from San Antonio), where his car burned out. He came back and had Toro help him tow the car back to San Antonio. "All for two sodas and one pack of cookies," Toro kids. Primo is not sure now when he might leave for Idaho.

Brotherhood was not just ideology but practice as well.

In this chapter I describe the male solidarity of the Berets and the manner in which this was manifested.

On Male Camaraderie

With only three exceptions, all core members of the reconstituted Southside chapter were unemployed or casually employed. Thus there was con-

siderable hanging out on a daily basis at Chivo's house and later at the garage that the Berets converted into a headquarters. Beret gatherings were
taking place all the time.

NEW HQ [SEPT. 17, 6–11 P.M.]
Mid-September, one month after the regeneration of the San Antonio Berets. The newly reconstituted Berets has a core group of thirteen members, and a headquarters has been set up in a garage. The headquarters
is a dilapidated mosquito-infested wood frame garage behind the house
rented by Skinny Benny's brother. It is not much, but it is a beginning.
The headquarters belongs to everyone, in case someone gets run out of
his house. The two Bennies, Toro, and Java are living or sleeping at the
headquarters at the moment, but others drop by daily and spend good
chunks of the day there. It is not uncommon to find eight to ten guys
hanging out in the evenings. Informal beer and barbeque parties are
a regular event. Tonight Chivo shows up with a *taquache* [possum] he
caught to barbeque.

Drinking liquor or beer and smoking marijuana were commonplace activities at these gatherings. Aside from an occasional contribution during a
"pitch in" from these unemployed, the beer and food for the daily gatherings were provided by the three regularly employed members (Toro, Loso,
and Java). This was a considerable expense, because the group could easily consume two or three cases of beer at one get-together.

The batos would often play a verbal "put down" game among themselves as if they were looking for a fight. I had come to enjoy the game and
had forgotten how threatening it might appear to others. My friend Cecilio
García-Camarillo, a writer and publisher of the Chicano journal *Caracol*,
had accompanied me a few times to Beret gatherings and reminded me of
this. Cecilio noted that the guys talked unity but still held on to the "gang
style" of relating and behaving. He had just seen Toro make a motion to
reach for the gun at his waist after Java had put him down badly. I told
him that I had seen Toro make that move too many times before. I considered the game to be a performance about toughness. The "tough guy" look
and behavior was the one natural resource that the batos brought with
them as they entered the public arena of organizations.

My having become accustomed to such performative behavior was a
sign of my assimilation into the group. I was treated much like everyone
else: a camarada among camaradas.

[SEPT. 19, 7 P.M.–10:15 P.M.]

We joke around, capping on each other. Toro and Chivo cap on Java, saying "que es una espinia grande con dos patitas" [that he looks like a giant pimple with two little legs]. Toro wants to go camping for a couple of days to show us survival techniques and to have target practice, sometime in February or March after the deer season. Where?—probably at the Mosca family ranch. "We're supposed to eat what we catch— por eso no queremos ir muy lejos del pueblo [that's why we don't want to go too far from town]," cracks Toro. Laughter. In this connection, someone jokes about all the weapons that the Berets had: "toda la bola nomás tiene una arma" [the whole bunch has only one weapon]. Laughter. At that time I was cleaning my fingernails with my pocketknife, when they said, "Y aquí está" [And here it is]. More laughter.

Chivo laughingly satirized why each of us wouldn't make it for two days: Abe and Fat Benny for lack of food; Java, Skinny Benny, and Tino for lack of *mota*; and me for lack of books to read.

Java interrupts the reverie to ask why we have to go camping; we should learn to survive in the city. Because, Chivo responds, if there is a revolution, are you going to stay in town or are you going to the woods? "I can see Java now going to a policeman and identifying himself as a Beret and asking for directions." Much laughter. Java quietly says, "Pues, estos batos están hablando de revolución; pero no somos comunistas" [Well, these guys are talking about revolution; but we're not Communists]. Java mentions the possible loss of security clearance if his employers at Kelly AFB found out. "But why? No somos comunistas," Java repeats. The talk continues.

Java had again raised an important question about ideology that was brushed aside by the joking banter. This was not an ideological issue, because Toro and Chivo hated Communists as much as they hated "gringos."

Whatever tension the group sensed came not from its political character but from being a tight and encompassing male clique. The tension centered around time spent with the guys and time spent with their families.

On Women and Wives

The all-male character of the Southside Beret chapter encouraged the public perception that the batos were simply a gang. Java was eager to recruit

women into the group to dispel that image, but initially Toro was reso-
lutely against admitting women into the Berets. The batos weren't ready,
he said. They would compete and fight over the women. His opposition to
female membership stemmed from a desire to maintain the male camaraderie of the group.

This position was critiqued by the leadership of various Beret chapters,
as noted. Another type of critique came from the wives or significant others of the Berets. Even though the leadership wanted to avoid the tension
that the presence of women might introduce into the group, the Berets
still had to deal with "woman trouble." The trouble revolved, not surprisingly, over conflict between spending time with the guys and spending
time with one's family. This became especially pronounced beginning in
mid-September, one month after the regeneration of the Berets, when they
acquired their garage headquarters.

Chivo had already made clear to the camaradas that his commitment ("onda chicana") to the cause came before his wife. It was an explicit "love it or leave it" philosophy shared by Toro and the other guys.
Loso had talked about his placing the Berets and la raza (the people) first
before his family; his ruca had to understand that. This issue of Beret
membership versus family obligations was not solely a matter of "Berets primero." Many times the matter was couched straightforwardly in
terms of "macho versus ruca" and "male liberty." The attitudes toward
"waifas," at least those that Chivo, Toro, and Primo expressed, were typical of many males: women should serve men and their male friends.
The instability of their marital relationships was thus perhaps not unusual. Toro had been married four times, Chivo three times, and Java
twice.

Only Loso and the three Castroville brothers (Mosca, Terco, and Giant) were married at the time, but Toro and Chivo maintained various relationships. Toro had expressed a desire to settle down several times. He
said he was tired of going from house to house, of sleeping in his car; he
wanted to settle down with a ruca and have kids. Chivo laughed and said
that he wanted the same thing but every time he went home he was just
there "like a lion in a cage, pacing up and down, thinking what am I doing
caged up when I can be outside with the guys."

Women could not be part of the clique. After Toro had brought his
"wife" to a few parking lot meetings—she would wait in the car—Primo
remarked to Toro, as a mild rebuke, that "todavía trais tu vida personal
contigo" (you're still carrying your personal life around with you). That
the *jefe* could be criticized for violating male time was revealing.

[SEPT. 19, 7 P.M.–10:15 P.M.]

The "waifas," of course, frequently voiced their displeasure. On one occasion, Toro's wife finally got tired of waiting in the car while he was trying to settle issues that were coming up unexpectedly at a meeting. Toro does not like being pushed, especially in front of guys; so he ignored every attempt she made to hurry him. She honked the horn, waited, then turned on the lights of the car, waited some more, then turned on the ignition, waited a bit more, and then finally just drove off. It was a quiet but eloquent backdrop to the meeting.

Another time Chivo came to one parking lot meeting with his ex-wife. He drove in and parked but didn't get out. After several long minutes, he drove off without saying a word. The leadership was not exempted from personal conflicts.

For the married rank and file, the Berets offered an excuse to get out of the house. According to Java, Mosca, Terco, and Giant were all using the Berets as a convenient excuse and neglecting their families. Java had once discovered an anonymous note in his ledger of Beret names and phone numbers. The note, later traced to Mosca's wife, asked why, if there was so much carnalismo among the Berets, did they waste it drinking so much beer instead of giving it to a camarada who needed it? A more dramatic objection was voiced by Terco's wife during the Southside High crisis.

GOING TO ESPADA

[SEPT. 25, 3 P.M.; SEPT. 26, 8 P.M.–MIDNIGHT]

We are supposed to meet with the Southside High youth in a clearing by the historic Espada Aqueduct. The aqueduct was built in the 1700s to support the nearby mission. I wonder how many protest meetings have taken place there since then.

I go by Terco's house on Southcross Blvd to take some Berets to the meeting. Primo, the two Bennies, and Terco are playing craps and drinking. They have either forgotten about the meeting or thought it was later, but in any case they expected to be picked up by somebody; they don't have a car. We crowd into my car and have already pulled out onto the busy street when Terco's wife runs out and stands in front of car *echando madres* [cursing] at Terco, screaming that she was not going to move until Terco got down. Terco gets down, pushes her to ground, and gets back into car, but she gets back up cursing and jumps in front of car again. Those of us in the car are stunned at the unfolding drama. We are in the middle of a busy boulevard, with cars and buses passing around us. We tell Terco to deal with his personal stuff, that anyway quite a few Berets are going. Terco reluctantly gets down, and we finally leave. Terco, of slight build, was about to get a lashing from his wife.

Such family tensions sometimes engulfed the Berets. The female companions of the Berets were not passive or weak individuals. Within the year, the wives of the brothers Mosca and Terco would leave them.

Controlling Anger

A fundamental role played by the group was its containment of violence by individual members. Although much barrio violence has been blamed on gangs, in some sense the unattached bato loco—the "free radical," to use a molecular metaphor—has been more unpredictable and dangerous. Except for periods of gang conflict, youth cliques have generally acted to control the behavior of their members. That dynamic was certainly evident in the Southside Berets.

Anger management was a feature (for me) of Beret internal dynamics that I had not expected to observe. On one occasion, the meeting dealt with some loud emotional male drama, with the Berets acting as a male therapy group. Sixteen-year-old Skinny Benny wanted to shoot his girlfriend María because she refused to do what he wanted. He didn't like her claiming she was not his property. Benny in fact had a loaded gun, but his brother Mike had taken it away.

> [OCT. 1, 8 P.M.–12 A.M.]
> Toro handles the situation by tying in the Berets to Benny's threat.
> Toro notes that the *perros* [police] and the reporters would merely
> play up his membership in the Berets, that the cameras and news me-
> dia would stop and highlight the eagle, the brown beret; they would
> give a bad impression of the entire organization to the people, asking
> what kind of carnalismo is this when a Beret murders a 15-year-old girl.
> Chivo, on the other hand, thinks that Skinny Benny is dishing out *pura
> racla* [exaggerated bullshit], so he keeps encouraging him "to go ahead."
> I also think that Skinny Benny is venting anger. So his decision not to
> shoot his girlfriend is a somewhat anticlimactic "OK, I wouldn't do it"
> murmur.

In response to Skinny Benny, the Berets had essentially acted as a male therapy group. Such encounters reinforced Toro's strong opposition to admitting women into the Berets. These guys were not prepared to handle female Berets, not only because guys would compete for them, but also, as Toro emphasized, because the women were liberated and ready to go out with anyone they liked.

Being drunk was usually a precondition for angry explosions by one of the batos. Both Toro and Chivo, for example, tended to lose their polished, suave demeanor and become increasingly aggressive as they got drunk. One notable occasion came when Chivo fired his gun at headquarters. Chivo had gotten angry at Java because of Java's constant *racla* (nagging).

SHOOTING A HOUSE [SEPT. 22, 12–7 P.M.]
At the meeting I learn that last night took some strange turns. Chivo, while drunk with the other batos, had pointed the gun at Java and then fired off a round into the ceiling. Loso, who brought up the issue, voiced strong disapproval of the move. The others are reluctant to criticize Chivo, but they all agree that it looked *gacho* [very bad]. Chivo, stubborn, says "¿Porqué me aregañan? ¿Porque mate el garaje?" [Why scold me? Because I killed the garage?]. Chivo defends his action by noting that he was aiming above Java's head, that he was testing Java out, and that he never carries a gun but that he was taking care of the *cuete* for Toro. The end result is that members unanimously vote in a new rule that any Beret who points a gun at another Beret, even if playing, will lose his beret.

The vote is dramatic because it is in effect a censure of the action of a leader. Chivo stubbornly says that the rule will not change his behavior, but he is clearly hurt by the vote and interprets it as a scolding. The tension is relieved by Loso joking that everyone better show up at Southside High Wednesday now that he has given them a new rule to control Chivo.

This dramatic unanimous vote surprised Toro. He later told me that this would never have happened with the old group, which always spent the meetings talking about "personal shit. The old group would never have passed a rule governing use of guns. The new group was willing to criticize its leadership." As a result, Toro thought highly of the new group. As for Chivo, Toro believed that his brother would be a good leader except for his anger. Toro said that at times even he got scared because he couldn't

control Chivo. He related an incident when he had to take a pistol away
from Chivo, who was ready to kill a bato.

Presented in this light, the Berets were attempting to bring some pre-
dictability and order to their social world. The intensive talks with Skinny
Benny about his treatment of girlfriends, the rule against Chivo's gunplay,
and the constant reminders about the importance of the beret and carnalismo were all examples of social controls placed on individual behavior.
Although the batos drew up the rules, however, they had difficulty in following them. Perhaps the most difficult rule to obey involved staying off
hard drugs.

Controlling *Tecata*

I had been with the group several weeks when I realized that the Beret
chapter or, more precisely, a subgroup of the chapter had a whole other
side that I knew little about.

> [SEPT. 18, 7 P.M.–I A.M.]
> Apparently Primo, Skinny Benny, and who knows who else "borrowed"
> a truck, drove it to Castroville somewhere, stripped it, and set it on fire.
> The fire looked *de aquellas* [swell], said Skinny Benny, who got excited
> talking about it. Primo sold the radiator, battery, and alternator for $23.
> Hearing this gets Chivo upset because Primo could have gotten much
> more than that.

Hearing about this episode with a "borrowed" truck also took me aback.
Illegality was still tied up with the private life of some Berets.

Initially I didn't understand Primo's involvement. I considered him to
be one of the most astute and politically aware recruits. But he always
seemed to be thinking of schemes to get money, which should have tipped
off my inquisitive sense. When Primo told the group that he had lost his
job with the bottling company because they thought he was a thief, that
should have been another tip-off, in spite of his denials. I was still thinking in naïve, ideal-type terms: that being political signified a disciplined
lifestyle or at least steps in that direction. Then Java told me that he was
"down" on his cousin because Primo was strung out on heroin; Primo had
lied to him about being clean. Java was worried that Primo wanted to use
the Berets for his own personal needs. Toro had apparently known about
Primo since the TU-CASA Conference. Primo had become sick and pale,

and Toro, who suspected why, had told everyone to talk to the bato and not to let him leave. Now things began to make sense. No wonder Primo was always "finding" bikes.

FINDING MORE BICYCLES [NOV. 14, DEC. 20]
After the meeting, I give Primo and Skinny Benny a ride home. Primo mentions the ten-speeds that were "given" to Skinny Benny and himself because they're so "chulos" [good-looking]. Primo said that they were almost caught, that a lady came out and shouted to them what were they doing with the bikes, and that Primo answered, "We're just trying them," and that they took off. As he relates the story of his latest gift, I wonder why he senses no contradiction in his behavior. I do not understand what part of Primo is political.

Primo was not the only *tecato* in the Berets. Tino, who had just left for the service, had previously been "busted" by the Berets (when the Westside was still active) because he had been selling *carga* (heroin) and was also strung out. Now I learned that all the guys knew that he was still strung out. The two Bennies and Tino had snorted heroin together. Later, according to Java, "Tino attempted to inject the Bennies, tried to convince them to try it, and Skinny Benny's mother found the needles and everything, at which point the Berets almost lost their headquarters."

Primo added another account about the night Tino took him, the Bennies, and Abe to Southcross Park to shoot up.

[OCT. 21]
Tino prepared the stuff in front of them and Primo and Tino got turned on together. The other guys had previously said that they weren't going to shoot up, but Primo says what actually happened was that "Tino se tiró toda la carga" [Tino shot up all the heroin]. The immediate consequence was that Tino and Skinny Benny tried to steal the lawnmower that belonged to Benny's family. And again they almost lost their headquarters.

Tino was not kicked out despite his heroin use because the guys liked him; the rank and file kept him in even though the officers wanted him out. His departure for the service made the question moot.

Primo told me he would get out of the Berets before he gave up *carga*. He was staying off "for now," which he rationalized by saying, "Well, I can take up the stuff anytime I want to." The last time I heard Primo give the Beret rap to glue-sniffing youth, he seemed to acknowledge a sense of contradiction:

[OCT. 13, EVENING]
Primo goes through the standard rap about being *soldados*; he makes an interesting comment that "many believe that we're a gang, and I get upset when I hear that because the people who say that don't know us, we're not a gang, we're not angels and we do *jales* [jobs] by ourselves, *solos*, well, because sometimes we have to."

Rude Realizations

By the end of my second month of hanging out, there seemed to be little I didn't know about these guys. My main hypothesis about a "political conversion experience" seemed increasingly naïve if not absurd. I told myself that two months was an insufficient period for observation, but still I felt that my idea was gradually being shredded to pieces. I was learning that "being political" and "being loco" were not necessarily contradictory. Why did I think they would be? Some recruits had participated in a political protest and later had "borrowed" a truck for its tires and parts. "Finding" bikes was commonplace. Although there were recurring exhortations about the need for discipline, and although the group did act to control individual violent behavior, these batos locos were still tied to their previous lifestyle and habits. They exhibited most of the features of what urban anthropologist Diego Vigil has called an "irregular lifestyle," characterized by "drug use, drug dealing, intermittent, if any, legal employment, dependence on parents, siblings, and girlfriends for a place to live, and inattention to parental duties toward their offspring."

For the unemployed batos, the underground economy of drug dealing and peddling "found" goods provided necessary income. Money-making ventures, particularly selling marijuana, were difficult to resist in this barrio world of scarce opportunities. At times the "found" goods were put to political use.

[SEPT. 17, 6 P.M.–11 P.M.]
Chivo talks about an arrangement with Rosario concerning a handgun; the *cuete* is hot because it messed up a guy in the eye and Rosario would like to send it to Mexico. I know Rosario and about his reputed connec-

On the way to a meeting

tions with peasant guerrilla movements. I am surprised to learn of a connection to the Berets. Chivo says it's for the struggle over there. This arrangement is convenient for everyone, and the Berets will be 25 dollars richer.

Seven of us pile into Chivo's truck "Recio"—five are sitting in the truck bed—and drive over to Rosario's restaurant to deliver the one *cuete*. I stay in the truck while the rest of the batos go in. There was no need for me to witness the transaction. When they return, Chivo provides another layer of deniability by saying that the *cuete* doesn't work. I know he is saying this for my benefit.

The funds were to be used the following night to treat the glue-sniffing *chavalos* (youths) of the barrio to sodas, popcorn, and a film at the Wesley Center. Chivo noted, as an aside, that Rosario wanted more *cuetes* and that this could be a way of adding to the Beret treasury. Primo, who was upset at his ex-wife, talked about ripping off her food stamps and cashing them for the Beret treasury.

I was learning that behavior that I used to consider diametrically opposed—heroin use and theft on the one hand and material support for Mexican revolutionaries on the other—could be found in the same class of guys. Both deviant and revolutionary impulses were present in the same group. The result was an inherent ambiguity in motives and behavior. These batos, I was beginning to realize, were occasional small-time participants in the binational smuggling trade that saw American manufactures (guns) go south and Mexican agricultural products (marijuana, heroin) come north. I had stumbled upon a small corner of this underworld trade. The Westside Berets had warned me that I didn't know what I was getting into.

That was my first realization. My second had to do with the dissertation. "How was I going to write this up?" I began to wonder. An acrimonious public controversy that broke out in my third month with the Berets added to my growing unease and self-doubts about my research. The controversy had to do with the meaning of "machismo" (Mexican masculinity), which made this public debate especially relevant. As I followed the controversy, I could not help but think of Skinny Benny and of Toro and Chivo before they became Berets.

Debating the Meaning of Machismo

In early October, a story in the *San Antonio News* about a senseless killing on the city's west side provoked a remarkably open discussion about machismo and its place in Mexican American culture. The sensationalist reporting, which attributed the killing to "the Alamo City's love affair with machismo," sparked angry letters to the editor, denunciations in Mexican American radio editorials, a survey of Mexican American male attitudes, and an editorial statement by the newspaper defending itself against charges of racism. For three weeks, the meaning of machismo was debated in public.

On Tuesday, October 8, 1974, a killing took place between two teenage friends. Domingo Guerra, Jr., was whipped in a petty argument by his friend, who then offered him a ride home. Domingo, eager for retribution, bolted into the house, returned outside with a pistol, and pumped two bullets into his friend. Mike Hess, the police reporter on graveyard shift, framed the incident as an illustration of the depravity of machismo. The prominent front-page article was titled "MACHISMO: Manhood's Proof No Joking Matter" and accompanied by a photo of Guerra with the caption "MACHO: male, masculine, strong." With a touch of literary license, inspired perhaps by working on graveyard shifts, Hess described the incident as follows:

> Domingo told his story to police freely and quickly, his dark eyes sparkling as his tongue wagged his guilt. His self-image soared. His macho was blown to a golden bubble by his own breath. His spirit rose with it. He exploded in action and words.
>
> Domingo couldn't explain fast enough for police. He couldn't relive his macho success with enough fury.

Behind Guerra's back, a police officer says, "It's a cheap killing. I hate cheap killings." And the clerk at the courthouse describes Guerra as "just a punk." But Hess, apparently with some knowledge of popular anthropology, placed the blame for the tragedy on the culture of machismo. As he put it, "Macho is a gutter culture. It wanders ruthlessly looking for a fight. Tight, tie-dyed jeans, a muscle shirt, a glint of defiance in unfeeling eyes—that's its outward look." Inwardly the macho has an alter ego: "It is the cowardice of evil, a weakness to accept what it is. Men are not wild animals, destined to forever prove their masculinity."

The Hess article set off a firestorm of protest. Two days after it appeared as front-page news, the popular Spanish radio station KUKA aired (six times) an unusual and sharply critical editorial, which began:

> The Mexican American community is tired of the attacks and misinterpretations of the Chicano or Mexican American culture. At a time when all efforts should be directed to a better understanding among all of us, there are still persons who block these efforts.

Referring to the Hess article, the editorial stated that

> the reporter made a completely distorted analysis about the reasons for the killing and wrote his own personal version of machismo. . . . The inclusion of the word machismo, with its wrong definition, was a mistake.

Machismo is not vengeance, lack of compassion, or murder as some people would try to picture it. Machismo is, for the Mexican American, manhood, strength, character, and decision.

The editorial expounded on specific instances of machismo:

Machismo is, for the Mexican American, the ability to fight discrimination; the decision to do what his conscience dictates to him; and manhood to defend himself with all the strength and spirit that he believes is right within the framework of the law. When a man like César Chávez fights for a brighter future for the farm workers . . . that's machismo.

But, noted the editorial, "when a man kills another man, be it Mexican, or Chinese or Jewish, that's murder not machismo." The editorial concluded by inviting reporters and editors of the media "to do some research before writing about something they know too little about."

San Antonio's most prominent Spanish radio station, KCOR, issued its own critical editorial a few days later. Like Radio KUKA, it also offered a very different view of machismo: "Para nosotros machismo es el valor innato del hombre, para defender su hogar, su dignidad, la familia, la patria" (For us, machismo is the innate valor of a man to defend his home, his dignity, the family, the country). The macho was not "el delincuente que pelea, macho no es quien abuse del debil, o quien humilla al caído" (the delinquent who fights, a macho is not one who abuses the weak or humiliates the fallen). Moreover, noted the KCOR editorial, the macho was the one who worked hard to provide for the family, raised a voice against injustice, honored his father, mother, and woman, and said with pride, "This is my home." In short, "macho es dignidad" (macho is dignity).

Logan Stewart, a well-known maverick talk show host, made sure that these salvos were heard on the English-speaking side of town. On his regular talk show on KTSA in mid-October, Stewart told his largely Anglo audience that "perhaps the most glaring misuse of 'machismo'" in the Hess article was "the inference that 'machismo' was an inherent characteristic of criminals. Ladies and gentlemen: it is not." Referring to a "machismo" survey of local Chicano males, Stewart noted that most felt that machismo entailed the courage to meet the responsibilities of family, community, and country. One thing is certain, Stewart said: "Any man who has 'machismo' never needs to prove it. Any man who does not have it cannot achieve it through bravado, over-reaction, or violence." The violent behavior of "a teen-aged rebel," intoned Stewart, was not machismo. He then closed dramatically: "I'll tell you who has the courage of 'machismo': Ramsey Muñiz in his struggle upward within the laws of men to improve the lives of his people: that is the courage of machismo!"

After nearly three weeks of such negative reaction to the Hess article, the *San Antonio News* responded in a lengthy editorial defending its portrayal of machismo. The editors flatly rejected the idea that its critique of machismo was "an attack on Mexican American culture or Mexican-Americans." But they did not waver from their equation of machismo with the "cult of masculine superiority." They said that this view of machismo had "always been accepted"; it was this view that they rejected.

> If machismo means that man is something less than a man if he doesn't get his wife pregnant every year—then we oppose machismo.
>
> If it means that a man of means is not quite all he should be unless he has a mistress—then we oppose machismo.
>
> If machismo means that a man has to kill another man over a fancied or minor insult—then we oppose machismo.

The editors then noted: "It is ridiculous to see any link between this [machismo] and genuine Mexican or Mexican-American culture." They concluded by pledging their "support of all things that make the people of San Antonio and Texas—whatever their ancestral background—aware of the contribution of Mexican-American culture."

Thus ended a three-week public discussion, a break in the normal polite discourse of the city, over the meaning of the word "machismo." No converts appear to have been made. In spite of the Mexican American protest in the media, the *San Antonio News* stood by its "always been accepted" caricature of machismo as senseless violence (fecundity, adultery, and so forth). The community response indicated that machismo, like many other traditional concepts attributed to Mexican culture, possessed remarkable complexity and flexibility. To some it signified being hard-working and industrious; to others it meant being independent-minded; and to still others it meant defending, even aggressively, one's honor and integrity. Mexican American women certainly had their own critical views of machismo, and women in the Chicano movement had been actively challenging old practices and thinking. But in the face of perceived Anglo insults, the Mexican American community closed its ranks.

This public discussion of Mexican male honor pointedly revealed how far apart Anglos and Mexicans were in their understanding of Mexican culture and barrio life. It was a polarized debate. The editors of the *San Antonio News* refused to back down from their conception of machismo, and the Mexican American community responded in a united and vigorous fashion.

The standoff obscured a tragic reality: barrio youths were capable of doing "stupid things," as the Berets called them. They were not shocked by Guerra's murderous retribution. The element of senseless violence or *locura* (craziness) was an integral part of the lives of lower-class males. The brutal world suggested by the controversial Hess article was in fact a reality. But the *locura* of unpredictable angry outbursts and aggressive behavior was not a Mexican cultural trait. It was more a mind-set shaped by poverty and marginality. What else did the barrio kid have going for him other than his honor and his camaradas? An affront to either had to be dealt with—and what if the dishonor came at the hands of a camarada? In the eyes of a sixteen-year-old impoverished youth, male honor may have been his most important possession, and defending it overshadowed any thoughts of reprisal and punishment.

La Locura

There was a reason why the street guys were often called loco or crazy. At times the stress and frustration of "trying to make it" for oneself and one's family resulted in "stupid *jales* [actions]." Anger could be skin deep and readily set off. Alcohol and drugs were daily sedatives. Combined with an indifferent or defiant attitude, being drunk or high frequently resulted in senseless behavior, including physical conflict. The possibility of fisticuffs or worse was part of the social landscape that batos locos had to navigate regularly. The male world of bars and nightlife in particular was fraught with tension and uncertainty. Hanging out with the Berets introduced me to this rough-edged world of lower-class males.

The Berets made a sharp distinction between those who were sane ("buenos y sanos") and those who were drunk or strung out. Most Berets understood the mistaken rumor (*chisme*), the stupid act (*pendejada*), and so on, as a result of being drunk or high on drugs. This was not necessarily a pardonable excuse, only an understandable explanation. The craziness came from being drunk or being drugged or being angry at one's situation, but it didn't matter what the precipitating circumstance was. What mattered was to be aware that it was easy for a guy "to lose control." It was this uncertainty that the batos referred to as "fate" or "destiny." Thus being prepared was a survival tactic, whether in taverns, on the street, or at a political rally. If possible, they carried weapons; there were too many crazy guys, too many unpredictable guys.

Locura has been described by anthropologist Diego Vigil as a mindset about "acting in a daring, courageous, and especially crazy fashion in the face of adversity." According to Vigil, preadolescent barrio youths who spent most of their time in the streets under the influence of older peers learned many coping street habits and customs, including how to manage their sense of personal fear. The mind-set of *locura* was part of fear management. Gang or *clica* members who were filled with anxieties, frustrations, and aggressions tended "to find a ready outlet in loco acts and locura behavior generally."

In such an unpredictable environment, group identity and loyalty became paramount. It was vital to be able to count on a camarada's loyalty and courage. Camaradas and carnales were supposed to back each other up in any fight. *Culeros* (cowards) were the ones who didn't stand behind the group in a group conflict, and *relajes* (stoolies) were the ones who squealed to the outside or to the opposition. The *relajes* and the *culeros* were at the bottom of the barrio world. "Everyone hates them, and everyone kicks them in the balls," said Luisa. It was not a good omen for Beret solidarity, then, when Chivo let it be known that he had no confidence in Java in a bar: "que el bato se culea en un plieto" (that the bato becomes chicken in a fight).

Three Months In

By month three of the ethnography, I felt I knew the batos well. Naturally the "backstage" reality of the men who made up the Berets was less romantic than their public image. This I had expected. The difficulty I was experiencing was reconciling my argument about acquiring political consciousness and agency with the reality of lower-class male life. "Becoming political" did not mean that they gave up street habits or beliefs. The men exhibited genuine solidarity with one another, but this generally came at the expense of women. They were *machista* in their thinking about women, and this caused problems with their resistant wives or girlfriends. The group did exert some control over individual acts of *locura*. They acted as a male therapy group, made rules against gunplay, threatened to take away berets, and constantly reminded everyone of the importance of practicing brotherhood. They drew up rules of conduct, even though they had difficulty in following them. In fact, some batos never gave up their street lifestyle during the seven months I hung out with them.

The prospect of misinterpretation or distortion added to the difficulties I was having. The charged public debate over machismo, which dominated the domestic media for some three weeks, was a constant reminder that my description of barrio life and youth would be traversing some delicate terrain. This was no longer a question of describing an emerging Brown Beret chapter of batos locos but a matter of representing Mexican American culture and society. Mexican Americans might understand the internal distinctions and nuances of barrio society, but what of the general reading public?

Three months into the project, I was not about to abandon it. While San Antonio debated the meaning of machismo, I had renewed and expanded my contact with some impressive Beret leaders from other towns at a statewide meeting in Dallas. The San Antonio Berets had returned from that meeting with a renewed sense of purpose. Although doubts about the project were piling up, hopeful signs kept me going.

A DALLAS VAMOS

IN THE WEEKS FOLLOWING the No Borders Conference, there had been much discussion about a forthcoming statewide Beret meeting in Dallas. Everyone was excited. Now the newly reconstituted San Antonio Berets were about to meet their comrades at an executive committee meeting composed of representatives from all the Beret chapters in the state. I was excited. I had met some politically sophisticated Berets from other towns at the conference and looked forward to meeting them again.

Java said that everyone had given blood so they could each have $5 for the trip, but some had spent it Thursday night at the movies, and Fat Benny had used his money to buy another beret. Java was uptight about "los batos que no están camellando" (the guys who are not working) and didn't have the $5 for the trip. He showed me a $108 bill for beer expenses for Berets for the last two weeks. When I asked him why he bought so much for the guys, he responded, "Well, I just like to see the guys get drunk happy."

The upcoming meeting provided the occasion for some reminiscing on the part of Chivo about the last state conference, which had taken place in Houston. Chivo was in a storytelling mode. About twenty Berets were relaxing at a cantina when several guys—"un bato de Dallas, Toro, Tony y yo," Chivo said—got tangled up in a disturbance because of a Houston Brown Beret named Snake.

[OCT. 2, EVENING]

"We ended up getting maced because Snake was *pedo* [drunk] and causing trouble with others. Snake tried to stop some *racla* [verbal fighting]
between two Chicanos and ended up starting a shuffle among all three.
Meanwhile several *perros* [police] arrived and tried to break up the
fight. They pulled Snake away roughly, and that's when about 20 or so
Berets sort of rushed the *perros*. The cantina owner started to mace the
Berets and the *perros* joined in." All maced, the Berets split.

Chivo said he later came back and shot two or three *plomazos* [blasts]
into the cantina for the macing. He was still upset at Snake, because
his interference in senseless *racla* had endangered the statewide Beret
organization:

[Chivo:] "The *perros* could have wiped out the organization right there.
No one was prepared, just *pedos* y *motiados* [drunk and stoned], rushing
into a fight. Almost all the Berets had *cuetes* [handguns], so the potential
for shit was really high."

Chivo got angry at the thought: "Snake can't control his liquor or *mota*."
I interpreted Chivo's story as veiled advice to the group about how to behave in Dallas.

But the Berets had other reasons to be *al alva* (on alert) while in Dallas.
The city was infamous for its police brutality. The year before (July 24,
1973), there had been a bizarre "Russian roulette killing" of a handcuffed
eleven-year-old, Santos Rodríguez, by Dallas policeman Darryl Cain. According to court testimony, Cain, suspecting that Rodríguez had burglar-
ized a service station, had radioed in: "I've got me an hombre here, and
I'm going to get a confession from him." The policeman then tried to scare
Rodríguez into confessing, but his .357 Magnum revolver unexpectedly
went off, blowing off most of Rodríguez's face.

The Cain murder of Rodríguez expectedly outraged the Mexican American community in Dallas and the state. And the incident intensified Beret organizing throughout Texas. According to the *Echo*, the newspaper of
the Austin Berets, the Cain murder sparked a Brown Beret demonstration
at the Texas State Capitol steps (on November 17, 1973) and galvanized the
various Beret chapters to "begin organizing common goals and communication systems." The first regional conference of Brown Berets had taken

place earlier in the year (February 4, 1974) in San Juan, in the lower Rio
Grande Valley. Brown Beret representatives from Austin, South San Antonio, Houston, El Paso, and Hondo had attended. Also present at the meeting had been representatives from the Denver Crusade for Justice and
the Committee to Free Los Tres in California. The *Echo* article featured a
photo of Toro in his Beret uniform with a handgun in his upraised arm.
The caption read, "San Antonio Brown Beret saying, 'Que no se les olvide
el cuete' [Don't forget your gun]." The major topic was "police oppression"
of the movement. As if to emphasize the point, just two days before the
conference began, the conference organizer, Raúl, was picked up by the
FBI "for reasons unknown." Police surveillance and harassment of Beret
gatherings was to be expected.

When Cain was later found guilty of negligent homicide and sentenced
to five years, a minor riot broke out in downtown Dallas. The West Dallas
guys said they started it "de puro coraje" (out of pure anger). Now these batos had organized themselves as a Brown Beret chapter. The Cain murder,
in short, had set off a number of organizing efforts that now converged at
this statewide meeting of Beret leaders.

GOING TO DALLAS [OCT. 4–5, 4 P.M.–4 A.M.]
As usual everything was somewhat disorganized for our trip to the State
Executive Committee meeting in Dallas. We left finally at 8 P.M. instead
of 5 P.M. as originally planned. The guys are very proud of the make-
shift "camper" affixed onto the pickup from scattered materials. Both
Bennies, Terco, and Primo are sitting in the back of the pickup. Java and
I are in front with Toro, who is driving. Chivo has decided to skip the
meeting.

Meeting in West Dallas, Aztlán

We arrived in West Dallas close to midnight. We were lost, and in the confusion Toro took a slightly improper right turn. Not surprisingly, the gathering of Berets was being monitored by the Dallas police.

We are immediately stopped by the *perros* [dog police]. A Chicano cop
has pulled us over. What a coincidence, I thought, that one of the very
few Chicano cops in the Dallas PD has pulled us over. His gringo part-
ner stands outside the police car in a parade rest position, with his
manaca [baton] in his hand. Some of the guys considered this posturing

with the *manaca* a provocative gesture, as an indication of what the cop thought of us.

The Chicano cop treats us okay; he asks us if we are Berets, a rhetorical question since seven of us are sitting in a pickup with berets on. We say yes, from San Antonio. He asks us if we know where the Beret meeting is being held. No, we respond, could he give us directions? Yes, says the Chicano cop, they're three blocks in the opposite direction. So the cops guided us to the State Executive Committee meeting!

The Brown Beret community center was off Bernal Street in West Dallas in a neighborhood known as Ledbetter. The community had a strange mixture of agricultural and industrial features. It was a semirural enclave of unpaved roads, dilapidated housing, open fields, overgrown thickets, cows, hens, and horses, surrounded by big factory plants with heavy smokestacks and adjacent to a highway that connected the Dallas–Fort Worth metro areas. Ledbetter was dry in terms of liquor. It was a *colonia* where everyone knew everyone, just as in a small town.

We're greeted by about twenty people, mostly Ledbetter Berets, at the Community Center. The Center, which acts as the headquarters for the Ledbetter Berets, used to be an automotive shop. The prominent pieces of furniture are a boxing ring, surrounded by a few chairs, and a pool table. Rent is $50 a month, which they raise with menudo breakfasts every Sunday at the flea market.

A number of informal group discussions and exchanges began. Jaime, one of the leaders from Ledbetter, spoke of the strength of the unity among the raza; others were arguing about various themes about the people's struggle; and one obnoxious bato from Ledbetter kept shouting "¡Viva socialismo!" every so often. In general Toro and Java liked the *perica* [talk] of the Ledbetter guys. Toro got upset with a fat drunk who wanted to touch Java's oak leaf (major insignia); the rule is that no one can touch or wear someone else's beret. The *perica* went on for a couple of hours.

Two Dallas Berets, Perales and Che, came over to tell us to ignore the *mugrero* (filth) of the load socialist. Che was the truck driver who had stopped in San Antonio on his way back from California, the one who had tested the political knowledge of the recruits. Perales I had met before at the No Borders Conference. Dressed in khakis and a shirt with sleeves cut off and unbuttoned to expose a hairy chest and silver chain necklace, with flowing black hair and beard and a beret accented with a star, he looked revolutionary and handsome at the same time. A Ledbetter Beret mockingly called him a publicity-seeker because of his frequent press and radio interviews. It was the first sign of tension among the gathering.

The Dallas Berets seemed to have experienced a fate similar to that of the San Antonio Berets. Like the Westside Berets of San Antonio, the original Northside chapter in Dallas had become inactive, as some of the older veterans had moved on to other things. At one point, the Dallas chapter used to have forty members. Now only three Berets remained from the original chapter. Thus Perales, the Dallas prime minister, had been actively recruiting and claimed credit for the new Ledbetter chapter of West Dallas. Perales described them as "ex-gang members." Che called them inexperienced.

The Ledbetter chapter, only a few months old, was made up of a core group of fifteen to twenty guys, with another twenty who would rise up if the occasion called for it. The chapter included four women Berets. The core group had been part of a *concilio* (community council), but because of dissatisfaction over its inactivity they decided to form their own organization. Then Perales, the Beret prime minister from North Dallas, scheduled a film and talk in West Dallas (in August). After hearing Perales's rap, they talked and argued among themselves and later decided to become Berets because they thought it would draw more support from the community.

The Ledbetter Berets did not like the idea of Perales saying that he was their *jefe*. Jaime Sánchez, one of the Ledbetter leaders, put it plainly: "The Ledbetters do not feel it is fair that they should organize themselves and then accept leadership from some other barrio." Perales, however, said that they wanted to remove him as prime minister and instead have an executive board of six Berets. Now the holdouts from the original chapter and the leaders of the new were trying to figure out a new command structure. The matter would come up for discussion the next day.

We grab blankets and find a place to sleep around the boxing ring. It's about 3 A.M.

Reports from the Statewide Beret Network

[OCT. 5]
The next morning, we went downtown some ten or twelve strong. We happened to be downtown while a parade was in progress. We re-

ceived quite a few stares from the largely Anglo crowd. Even with our mismatched and incomplete khaki uniforms, our berets made us look like part of the parade participants. Later we joked that the crowd was watching us more than it was the parade. A police helicopter followed us around, or at least we interpreted it as that. Some of the batos waved fingers at the helicopter. This act later drew criticism that we shouldn't throw fingers in public while we have our berets on.

The State Executive Committee meeting started at 1 P.M. at the former automotive shop turned headquarters. About thirty or so Berets were present, with about ten non-Berets hanging around outside the center. All those in attendance were men except for seven women Berets from Dallas, Waco, and Austin. Chapters from San Antonio, Houston, McAllen, Ledbetter, North Dallas, Waco, and Austin were represented. Absent was the Hondo chapter, which had become involved in a community protest at the Hondo jail. An irate sheriff had jailed ten of the protesters. Two or three of them were Berets.

Each chapter had two representatives on the executive committee. Others could speak, but only the reps could vote. Because all votes ended up being unanimous, however, no actual head count was ever taken on any item discussed.

José Perales, prime minister of the Dallas chapter, moderated the meeting. Che, minister of security for the Dallas chapter, reminded all about the rule of not smoking or drinking until the meeting was over. Security was posted. The various chapters then began making their reports. These, I would find out, were not just reports of local activities but also opportunities for each chapter to air out grievances or to get a sounding—and to form a consensus—on various issues of interest.

The Ledbetters of West Dallas, after being accepted as a Beret chapter, made the first presentation. Leader Jaime Sánchez provided a quick history. The Ledbetter Berets had formed three months before. The group had been involved in a campaign to rename a local elementary school after Emiliano Zapata. They had gathered nine hundred signatures on a petition as well as the formal endorsement of the recognized organizations of the Mexican American community in Dallas. They had formally presented the idea at the school board meeting but had been turned down. Instead a committee had been appointed to come up with alternative names. Rolo from the Valley suggested that they consider a sit-in at the school if they didn't receive satisfaction.

Previously Perales and Che had described to Toro, Java, and myself how nervous the Ledbetters had been when they presented their petition to the school board. Apparently the Ledbetter spokesperson messed up badly, denied that the Berets were affiliated with the campaign, and then fainted at the end of his presentation. Che was philosophical: "Well, that's the way the guy is going to learn how to speak." But he thought that the Ledbetters screwed up when they shook the hand of the racist school board member who was against the name change: "Now that was stupid."

The question of which chapter—the Ledbetters or North Dallas—represented Dallas on the *mesa directiva* (executive committee) came up and led to a heated discussion. Toro displayed his diplomatic skills and provided an acceptable resolution by saying that each town must resolve its internal problems but that only two reps were allowed per town; how they were selected was up to Beret organizations in that town.

An Impressive Chapter

A report from Austin followed. I had met the leadership from this chapter during my initial contacts with the San Antonio (Westside) Berets when I was still investigating the possibilities of a dissertation. What had struck me then about the Austin leadership was the mix of "gang" youth and college students. In fact, their recognized leader, Polo, embodied both.

As an adolescent, Polo had lived a "double life," as he put it. He had organized the "Purple gang," named after his favorite color, with "batos de mi bloque, batos que había conocido toda mi vida . . . que se daban en la madre con otras gangas" (guys from my block, guys I had known all my life . . . who would come to blows with other gangs). Polo was involved with "cuetazos" (shootings) but never hit anyone. "Mi ganga hacía todo juntos—el cameo, hambeos, boglas, pedos—y siempre hangiaban juntos" (My gang did everything together—work, theft, burglaries, fights—and we always hung out together). Yet because his *abuelita* (grandmother) wanted him to become a priest, she had sent him to Catholic school. At St. Edward's, a college prep high school, he learned how to "chavetiar y en el barrio como pelear" (think and in the barrio how to fight). When they caught him and his buddies stealing, he was expelled from St. Edward's. He got more involved in his gang but dropped out when he got married at eighteen. He also dropped out of high school. He worked for four years at a jewelry manufacturing plant, where he became involved in union organizing. After a heart attack at the age of twenty-six—and three months of reflection in the hospital—he landed a job with Mental Health and Mental

Retardation (MHMR) as an outreach worker. There he acquired speaking and more organizing experience. While at MHMR, he and fellow worker "G.R." began talking about the need for a militant raza organization in East Austin. Together with Zeke and other batos who had attended St. Edward's, they started the Brown Berets in the summer of 1973.

Roberto, a Navy veteran and dropout from the University of Texas, lent some intellectual weight to the Austin Berets. He grew up as an army "brat," lived in various parts of the country, and was quite assimilated. Nonetheless his repeated encounters with racism in high school and in the navy had turned him into an angry, frustrated person. He had participated in the 1969 Del Rio protest, an event that moved him to study and to become more militant. Roberto had an encyclopedic grasp of political literature, and our conversations touched on topics as diverse as Saul Alinsky's tactics, Communist organizing in the 1930s, McCarthyism in the 1950s, and the 1973 coup in Chile. Chavel from Hondo was the only other Beret he communicated with regularly. Roberto acknowledged that he had a bad temper and that this had created conflict between himself and Polo. Roberto had thus decided to relocate to Waco and start a Beret chapter there. He was representing Waco at the meeting.

A third influential member of the Austin chapter was Ana, who had organized a strong contingent of Chicana Berets. She was also the recognized spokeswoman for all the Chicana Berets in the state. Under her leadership, the women had set up a free summer lunch program and had organized hayrides and retreats for the youth. Now they were introducing art and theater to the students in after-school classes and basically building a youth program. Ana was unafraid to speak her mind, whether it involved a scolding of the mayor and the City Council or a questioning of her fellow male Berets. She had created a controversy before the meeting when she discovered that Perales, the meeting organizer, had scored free tickets to the Six Flags amusement park for thirty Berets. "Why not donate the tickets to the youth?" asked Ana in a widely circulated letter to Perales. Although the men criticized her for violating protocol, Ana's pressure moved Perales to get twenty children's tickets to Six Flags.

The Austin Berets, along with other activist contributing writers, published the *Echo*, a community newspaper filled with local news items about politics, social gatherings, and community events, with plenty of critical commentary and Chicano poetry. The *Echo* regularly recorded Beret activities and provided a sustained focus on police harassment and brutality. In July 1974, a few months before the meeting, the *Echo* had pub-

lished a "Brown Beret Manifesto" based on a review of programs and issues "taken up by Brown Berets chapters throughout Aztlán."

The manifesto recognized that "every barrio has its own immediate
needs or stages and it should be no surprise to see each chapter of Brown
Berets active in different programs and issues." That said, some of the key
goals identified were to establish police review boards and community
alert patrols; "lead the community against our present oppressive capitalist system"; and push for an immigration program that protects the rights
of Mexicanos. The next five goals were "revolutionary free schools," free
housing, prison reform, free health clinics, and free mass media for the
community. The manifesto was an elaborate outline of Beret activities
across the region. Clearly the Brown Berets of Austin were the most politically developed chapter of the statewide network.

Zeke, representing the Austin chapter, reported that it had fifteen active members, almost half of whom were women. Like the Ledbetters, the
Austin Berets had a headquarters, the "Centro Chicano," a simple wood
frame house a block from IH 35. The Berets expected to tackle the glue-
and paint-sniffing problem among youths, raise Chicano consciousness
and cultural awareness, and coordinate "community involvement" in matters of concern to the Austin barrios. The main issue they were dealing
with at the time was police brutality. They were lobbying for a civilian
review board. As a lead member of the East Austin Committee for Justice (EACJ), the Berets had pressured Austin's mayor Roy Butler, along
with the city manager and assistant police chief, to come to the Centro
Chicano to discuss the counterproposal of the EACJ. In closing, Zeke invited all the chapters to participate in a protest march against police brutality the following week. (Photographer Alan Pogue would document that
event.)

Other Towns Report

My journal notes on the San Antonio report were brief compared to my
notes on the other chapters, perhaps because I felt most familiar with
the Southside Berets. Toro and Java were articulate in their presentation.
Toro discussed Southside High and the glue-sniffing problem, and Java
discussed the collaboration with TU-CASA and the protest at the Mexican Consulate. Toro and Java then raised issues that had clearly been informed by this collaboration. Toro brought up the question of whether the
American Federation of Labor and Congress of Industrial Organizations
(AFL-CIO) was against *mojados* (illegals). He felt that the Berets should

take a stand and wanted to know what the chapters thought. All comments blasted the gringo unions and favored helping "illegals." One summary comment noted that the border had been created by the gringo. Java then raised the question of organizing Beret chapters in Mexico, but this idea was quickly rejected by Roberto and Rolo, both of whom described Mexico as a fascist state. Rolo mentioned that Mexican undercover agents were working with the FBI in South Texas. It was interesting to see that the TU-CASA rap had influenced the thinking of both Toro and Java.

The three longest reports came from chapters that were largely inactive. The Houston representative initiated a discussion on the new patch for the Berets. The design for the *parche* had been settled at the previous conference in Houston. The Houston rep reminded the gathering of the reason for the new *parche*—to unite all Beret chapters nationally. There would no longer be a difference between the *parche de carnalismo*, the patch with the handshake, and the *parche de la causa*, the patch with the lighting bolt. The California Berets wore berets with the lighting bolt, as did the Midwest Berets and the North Dallas chapter. Most Texas chapters wore berets with the handshake. These differences, reflecting the historical origins of each chapter, had previously caused some tension. The mold for the new patch would cost $450, approximately $50 from each chapter. A unanimous vote endorsed the motion to assume payment.

Perales, whose position as prime minister of the Dallas Berets was in question, reported next, with the now familiar account of how the original Dallas chapter used to have forty members at one time and how he and Che were actively recruiting. Then, as if to signal that he wanted to move the discussion away from the unsettled issue of leadership, Perales asked the members of the gathering what they thought of the Raza Unida Party (RUP). This initiated a fascinating discussion that revealed various tendencies, as well as considerable reflection, among the Beret leadership.

> Rolo from the Valley said that RUP was creating a monster with three heads instead of two. Mique from Austin said that in his town the RUP was running a candidate against a Chicano from the barrio, and the Berets were supporting the Chicano from the barrio. Roberto from Waco and Rendón from Ledbetter called the RUP a reformist effort that would not challenge capitalism.

The criticism was severe, and some seemed to argue that the Berets should take over RUP. At that point, Toro interjected emphatically, saying no, the Berets did not support any political party, that was not their role.

"La Raza Unida nomás trata de meter la pierna en la puerta, pero yo la quiero quebrar con una patada. Es como si tuvieramos un motor chingón. La Raza Unida nomás le va dar un tune-up para que corra mejor, pero no la va cambiar. Tenemos que romperla, deshacerla, y entonces rebuild it from scratch" (The Raza Unida just tries to put its leg in the door, but I want to break it down with a leg kick. It's as if we had a giant motor. The Raza Unida will just give it a tune-up so that it could run better but it wouldn't change it; we have to strip it, take it apart, and then rebuild it from scratch).

Toro had drawn on his background as an automechanic to frame this point. He didn't say much about the rebuilding, what it would look like.

Toro doesn't like to mess with constitutions, descriptions of tasks, etc., doesn't want to be limited by pieces of paper, ministerial description sheets, and so forth, thinks it's bullshit. Toro is basically an anarchist. Other Berets—Clavo from Hondo, Roberto from Waco, Rendón from Dallas, and Rolo from Valley—were clearly conversant about alternative systems. Still the glue that holds the Beret network together is a basic commitment to carnalismo and la causa.

Rolo, the representative from McAllen, made the report for the Valley Berets. Rolo had impressed me as a modest, knowledgeable, and experienced organizer. He was a quiet and attentive listener and was articulate and concise when he spoke. He was of medium height (five foot eight), slim, with brown hair and mustache and a light tan complexion; his wrinkled face made him look older than his thirty years. Rolo said that the chapter had eighty members and that it had been around for two years. There was little activity in the Valley at the moment because the guys were just returning from the north from their seasonal cannery or packing house jobs. Rolo was one of those guys.

Rolo's report then turned into a homily, based on his recent experience in Wisconsin. He had been organizing resistance to a Del Monte company rule that anyone who refused to work overtime would be fired. They had been working seven days a week. The company foreman had told Rolo to pack up his clothes because he was causing a lot of trouble, at which Rolo asked for a switchblade from his companions. The foreman understood enough Spanish to know what was going on and left in a hurry. A couple of days later the company manager approached Rolo and said that he

wanted to be his friend and that they would no longer have to work overtime if they didn't want to. Rolo was driving home a lesson: sometimes
the threat of personal violence is more successful in the short run than legal recourse. The Beret leadership, nodding approval, understood Rolo's
point immediately.

The last report came from a new chapter in Waco. Roberto and Ana,
originally from Austin, had relocated to Waco and had begun organizing
there. The new Waco chapter was accepted. They made no report, but Roberto suggested, as a follow-up to our discussion about the Raza Unida
Party, that we should have a workshop to learn more about the differences
between capitalism and socialism and other systems. The vote was unanimous in favor of education, but not a commitment to a certain system. Roberto mentioned his concern about a "fascist revolution" looming in the
near future and said that we needed contacts in Mexico. Rolo from McAllen noted that *guerrilleros* in Mexico were fighting the capitalist government. A guy from Ledbetter added, "El mismo sistema que tenemos aquí"
(The same system we have here).

Ana, speaking as a Waco representative and as a woman Beret, emphasized in her comments that the notion of carnalismo applied to la familia
and thus to respectful relations between "carnales" (brothers) and "carna-
las" (sisters). All chapters, including the Southside Berets, agreed with her
interpretation. The seven Chicana Berets from Austin, Waco, and Dallas
who were present at the meeting made sure that the idea of carnalismo included women.

In short, the meeting had an upbeat, optimistic tone, in spite of the
internal difficulties besetting some chapters. Three chapters (Houston,
North Dallas, McAllen) were basically inactive, but this was offset by the
formation of two new chapters (Ledbetter, Waco). Meeting in a converted
garage that featured a boxing ring and pool table—the headquarters of the
new Ledbetter chapter—lent an air of progress.

The weekend-long meeting provided an occasion for an exchange of
views, which made the wide spectrum of philosophies rather evident. In
spite of many revolutionary references, no formal ideology unified the various Beret chapters. Although they shared a commitment to carnalismo
and la causa, the statewide leadership exhibited a wide range of political beliefs and knowledge, from instinctual anarchism to utopian socialism. Cultural nationalism kept the diverse strands together. Roberto from
Waco, Rendón from Ledbetter, and the absent Clavo from Hondo were interested in studying communism and alternative systems. But Rolo from

the Valley was down on Marxists, as was Toro. Perales, the prime minister from North Dallas, spoke eloquently about Aztlán, the mythical homeland of the Aztecas. This cultural nationalist sentiment appeared to unify
everyone.

Nonetheless, as the discussion about the Raza Unida Party had made
clear, even here there were limits. Class distinctions restricted the reach
or appeal of cultural nationalism. Although a number of the most articulate leaders—Perales, Clavo, Roberto, Rolo—had some college behind
them, they unanimously agreed that the educated Mexican American was
generally assimilated and would cop out. Thus the feelings toward the
Raza Unida Party, a third political party based on cultural nationalism,
were generally negative.

At the close of the meeting, Toro moved that we name the state executive committee meeting in honor of Che; the anniversary of his death
was coming up. All chapters agreed. Roberto and Rolo then eloquently described the life of a fellow Latino who had died in Bolivia for his revolutionary principles.

The second issue that Toro raised was that we should respect the beret. "Me importa más que la cruz" (It means more to me than the crucifix), Toro emphasized, "porque cuando andaba como Cristiano andaba
plomiando nuestra gente y cuando me hice Beret paré haciendo eso" (because when I was going around as a Christian I was shooting our people
and when I became a Beret I stopped doing that). In oblique reference to
the Ledbetters, Toro referred to the learning mistakes of the San Antonio
chapter. Java, Primo, the two Bennies, and Terco had all complained to
Toro that the Ledbetters didn't know how to wear their berets.

The final item presented by Toro surprised many: we should respect
the women Berets. Toro then gave an eloquent speech on equality for Chicanas in the organization, noting that they also can be soldiers. This was,
of course, inconsistent with his prior position with respect to recruitment
of *soldaderas*. His sudden turnabout, the guys figured out, was related to
his interest in a Beret schoolteacher in attendance. Toro's statement drew
admiration from the Chicana Berets present at the meeting.

The meeting ended at 7 P.M., which also marked the end of the
"Berets only" rule. The guys (Terco, Fat Benny, Java) notice that Toro
has left with the four Beret women who have been attending the
session.

The Ledbetters of West Dallas

Of the various chapters at the statewide meeting, the new Ledbetter chapter of West Dallas was of particular interest to me because of its similar-
ity to the Southside Berets. Like the Southside, the Ledbetter chapter was
a recent formation, and the majority of the batos were ex-gang members;
many were dropouts, but all were interested in promoting la raza. According to one observer, many had been pushed out of other organizations and
some were "muy pelioneros" (too feisty), but most of the young guys had
never been in any organization. The veteran leadership, however, had already been organized as a community council (the Kenasaw House) before they formed the Berets. Moreover, at the opening reception there had
been more than a hint of political ideology when one of the Ledbetters
had kept shouting "¡Viva socialismo!" every ten minutes. Thus the Ledbetter batos seemed to be at different levels in terms of political and organizational skills, experience, and consciousness. This intrigued me. A couple
of months after the statewide meeting, I paid them a visit.

The first person I sought out was the "loud socialist." I wanted to learn
his story. The socialist was named Rendón, thirty years old, intelligent,
sharp, experienced, and confident. At age fourteen, he had gotten together
with two or three guys doing *jales y robos* (jobs and robberies), until they
caught him and sent him to Gatesville Reform School from the age of sixteen to eighteen. There he met Jaime and others from Ledbetter. When he
got out, he worked at a factory and began to learn about unions. He went
from being a member to being a steward and then an organizer. He became a social services bureaucrat but lost the job when he and others took
over a Community Action Project office to press some demands. Now he
had a misdemeanor charge because of the resulting melee and couldn't
find work.

Rendón was turned on to socialism during a recent trip to Puerto Rico.
He was somewhat frustrated because most were turned off by his preaching. Rendón was not thrilled about the Berets. He noted that the majority, including the officers, didn't have any philosophy; they wanted to help
la raza but didn't know how; they didn't have any ideas. When the batos at the Kenasaw House first had discussed becoming Berets, he had
voiced his opposition. Then he left for Puerto Rico for three weeks; when
he returned, they were already organized with officers and everything. He
laughed at the rules about the beret: "That's kid stuff," he said.

[DEC. 15]
Rendón thinks the Ledbetter Berets will collapse within six months
and go back to being a community council. Once the Berets break up,
he will form a group with some batos interested in socialism. Rendón
was a tenuous Beret, to say the least. But ironically he seemed to fit the
"true believer" I had hypothesized about in my initial thinking about
the Berets.

Later at a bar, I got together with the Ledbetter leadership, Jaime and
Bernardo, president and vice president respectively. Also present were
Mando, the minister of information, and Jorge, a young *soldado razo* (plain
soldier). *Rancheras* were playing in the background, and many couples
were dancing.

Jaime, thirty years old, was the recognized *jefe*. His background was
similar to that of Toro and Chivo: former gang member, with ten shootings, two dead, in Gatesville Reform school from age ten through eighteen,
dropped out in sixth grade. Now he worked as a bus driver. His mind was
turned on by *movimiento* literature that a camarada from El Paso passed
on to him. He rapped with others in his *clica*, and in February 1974 he was
elected president of the Kenasaw community advisory board. Then in August they started the Ledbetter Berets. "We didn't know anything about
Beret rules of other chapters; we just got things going." His philosophy
was local activism to make things better—"levantar la gente, hacer por
nosotros, que cuente el barrio, gritar un poco" (lift the people, work for
ourselves, make the barrio matter, protest a bit).

Bernardo, forty years old and second in command, had also been involved in Kenasaw with Jaime and shared the same philosophy about
working for the community. Mando, twenty-one, a college student and the
minister of information for the Ledbetters, looked and talked like a future lawyer. He acknowledged that he was an atypical Beret. He described
himself as a "due process guy" and said that the Ledbetters "were trying to
work within the system to get some needed changes." With regard to the
campaign to change the name of a local elementary school, he had written in a local newsletter that "the children had suggested the idea. As an
identity project, the change of names would make the children feel more
comfortable at their school, and promote feelings of pride and of school
spirit." Now, Mando said, they were being assisted by the Community Relations Office of the U.S. Department of Justice, which was applying some
pressure on the school board and supplying ideas to the Berets. The name

"Emiliano Zapata" was not acceptable to the School Board, so the Berets would now choose the name of a Chicano educator. They were pragmatic about the matter.

In contrast, Jorge, about twenty years old, was a visionary. He said simply: "The thing we're trying to do is get rid of capitalism." He expressed some ideas about a socialist future, how it would look with no credit bureaus, no Seven-Eleven stores, and so on. The Ledbetters were not yet socialistic, he acknowledged, but the guys were for la raza. In explaining how he became a Beret, Jorge mentioned that he had tried the Baptists (until he was sixteen), the Pentecostals (from sixteen to seventeen), and the Jehovah's Witnesses (at eighteen) and since then had been "in nothing" for a while. He said that he had always been interested in politics while in high school. Once he graduated and left the Jehovah's Witnesses, he joined the Berets. Lately Jorge had been hanging out with Rendón. So Jorge had gone through both religious and political conversions! Was he the paradigmatic convert I had been looking for?

Jaime, Bernardo, and Mando were aware of Rendón's socialist rhetoric and were very much opposed to it. Jaime said that Rendón was proselytizing his "mugrero" (filth) to the recruits. With music blaring in the background, Jaime described Jorge as Rendón's dupe, a young confused bato; Jaime was trying to get him to start thinking for himself. Mando simply called Jorge "a tribulation."

[DEC. 16, 7–11 P.M.]
In the bar, the band dedicates two songs to the Berets. Jaime is beaming: "They already know us everywhere in Dallas." Not many organizational memberships are displayed so conspicuously. The guys are proudly wearing their berets and jackets that say "The Ledbetter Berets" on the back. Bernardo, Beret vice president, tells me that if things don't work out, they will re-form as some sort of concerned citizens' group: "si los batos van a seguir dándose en la madre con los berets puestos, mejor ser un concerned citizens' group que no tengan que usar berets, y así se pueden seguir dándose en la madre" [if the guys are going to keep fighting like a mother with the berets on, better to be a concerned citizens' group that doesn't wear berets, and that way they can keep fighting like a mother].

Mando noted that calling themselves the Brown Berets and wearing the beret seemed to add a sense of militancy and determination to the

group: "Our name is one that's disliked, but it's one that stimulates action in the youth. And we plan to stimulate action." He added that some of
the Berets had been Kenasaw Concilio members before, and he could easily see them leaving "the Beret identity" if they saw it getting in the way.
Both Bernardo and Mando had laid their fingers on an important point
about the visibility of the beret.

The Ledbetter chapter, in short, was another case of street veterans
and youth being inspired by the *movimiento* to "hacer por el barrio" (work
for the barrio). Already organized as a community council, they donned
the Beret identity to project an aggressive posture with respect to their demands for the community. Their ideas were diverse. Although a few had a
socialist vision, the leadership and majority of batos were guided by pragmatic cultural nationalism. The campaign to change the local school name
was their priority; if Zapata was not an acceptable choice then the name
of a Chicano educator would be fine. Even joining with the Black Panthers
to protest police brutality, as they would do later, was not an endorsement
of socialist revolution but a sign of frustration with the racist violence of
the Dallas Police.

The main problem facing the Ledbetter Berets was not ideological dis-
sension but lack of basic discipline. If things didn't work out, they might
leave the Berets and reorganize themselves as a "concerned citizens'"
group. The Ledbetters were keeping their options open, it seemed.

Am I Really a Beret?

My visit with the Ledbetters had been made possible by my introduction
earlier at the statewide meeting. At that meeting the representatives from
the various chapters learned that I was writing a book about the Berets.
Toro had made a formal announcement to that effect. He told the gathering to give me ideas, to note what I shouldn't write and what I should mention, and so on.

[OCT. 5, AFTERNOON]
I described my past participation in the Chicano movement and why I
was interested in the Berets. I asked: Why have some batos changed?
Why did the Berets form? These were the main questions I posed
as my interests. I added that I want to spend some time with each chapter, so I can get a good idea of what the Berets are like throughout the
state.

I got a lot of positive feedback and support. Fat Benny said that they were all "curados" (impressed). Perales from Dallas said that it was good that I was Beret because I could write from a Beret perspective. Roberto from Waco said he had pictures for me. Rolo from the Valley asked if I would be using fictitious names; I said I had been planning that all along. Toro, Java, and Fat Benny immediately wanted to know the nicknames I had chosen for them. Jaime Sánchez of Ledbetter was interested in the topic. I told them all that I hoped to spend some time with each chapter to get to know individuals and their activities.

This warm, welcoming reception ironically underscored the ambiguity of my role as observer-participant. I had always been open about writing a book. But this raised the question of whether I was really a Beret. The issue would come up the following day on our return trip to San Antonio.

On the way back in our makeshift camper pickup, we talked about the direction of the chapter and the repeated concern with getting new headquarters that could be used as a community center. The batos had been impressed with the Ledbetter center, which had a pool table and boxing ring. Everyone who spoke (Java, Fat Benny, Toro) agreed that we should rent a place, and Toro concluded that that was our number one priority right now. "When are we going to write proposals?" Toro asked me. "Whenever you want," I answered.

[OCT. 6, 4–8 P.M.]
Then, after fixing a flat, we discussed my book; I received suggestions and inquiries, and I learned the impression Java and Toro had of me. Toro suggested that I include frank conversations "en donde dejamos caer la grena" [where we let our hair down]; he said I wouldn't believe half the stuff he had to tell me about his life. Java surprised me by saying that I just wanted to write the book, that I really wasn't a long-term Beret, at which Toro angrily shouted that he wouldn't have made me a Beret if it was just to write a book.

Java then added that I "had too much education and not enough barrio experience." Defensively, I repeated and clarified my "movement credentials." Java's response to all this, which he repeated every now and then throughout the ride back to San Antonio, was that I should just write my book and let him run the Berets. Did he think that I was competing with him for rank? I interpreted Java's comments as signs of insecurity or jealousy.

Java was generally upset. He got on everyone's case—me and the four guys without jobs (Terco, the two Bennies, Primo)—everyone except Toro. Java was tired of being picked on and laughed at and of the guys not chipping in. He was tired of having to worry about providing for their "mota y vironga" (marijuana and beer) and on this trip for their share of gas and food costs. He was also upset about all the talk about revolution. The batos in turn were tired of hearing Java's complaints. By the time we got to San Antonio, a heavy air of nagging questions had filled the camper.

I couldn't shake off Java's probing question. "Was I really a Beret?" I asked myself. The pragmatic, quid pro quo arrangement between Toro and myself that guaranteed my loyalty and whatever resources I could provide for the organization now offered thin comfort. I might not be a Beret, I told myself, but I was a sympathetic fellow traveler who wanted to know more about the path they had taken. I wanted to write from a Beret perspective.

In short, there was no way that a non-Beret could hang out and write a book about them. Security concerns alone would seriously hamper such observation. The Berets also had an understanding of the necessity of maintaining a positive public image. Thus, when the Ledbetter chapter asked if it was okay to make a statement on the radio, Toro, conscious of the negative image of the Berets, told them to emphasize that we were not a militant organization, we were nonviolent, and we were not trying to overthrow the government. Naturally, I was expected to present a positive image as well.

This expectation had run headlong into my unfiltered observations of the Southside chapter. The lack of discipline, especially in public, was troubling. The cat-calling of women was particularly upsetting. The personal lifestyles of many members were bothersome. After getting to know the representatives from the other chapters, I realized that I was in the rawest chapter in the state. It was a reminder that the Southside chapter was only two months old. Seeing that the other chapters had it together, and that some did think of political education, gave me some encouragement.

An Interim Summary

The batos joined the Berets because of a felt desire to help *la raza*, however vaguely expressed at times by the new recruits. And they joined because Beret membership conferred status and recognition by movement activists. The wearing of the beret was an important public expression of that membership, even as they learned about the group and the movement that it was part of. That learning was shaped through interaction in the broad network of movement organizations and other Beret chapters. The Beret network, in particular, appeared to be key in shaping the perspective and trajectory of the resurgent Southside chapter. The dynamics of the new Ledbetter chapter of West Dallas were similar.

In the Southside and Ledbetter chapters, lower-class Chicano men— most of them dropouts, many of them ex-gang members—were learning about politics and history and taking part in local political events. They had attended meetings, protested before the Mexican Consulate, and petitioned the school board and would march in several protests—all expressions of political action. Becoming a Beret had exposed them to a larger world and larger sphere of action. This was a fascinating political development. The experiences of Rendón and Jorge of Ledbetter offered a fleeting suggestion that my original notion of a political conversion was perhaps not completely far-fetched. But this was a rare occurrence among the Berets I came to know. Among the Southsiders, only Java appeared to be such a candidate. More common, as I discuss in the next chapter, was the mixed bag of politically aware batos who remained fixed to the negative habits of the street. Political awareness and knowledge by themselves were insufficient to change such behavior.

NEGOTIATING *LOCURA*

 THE SOUTHSIDE BERETS returned from the state-wide conference with a renewed sense of mission. Meeting and interacting with the other Beret chapters set off efforts to tighten up. Toro and Java called for more discipline; Toro requested that I give the group political education classes; and Loso and Chivo announced that we had to start working with other Chicano organizations. In a move to soften their image, the Berets also admitted a Chicana into the group. These well-intentioned efforts, however, would come to naught. They would be constrained by a *clica* culture that revolved around drinking and getting high and an underground economy that revolved around peddling marijuana and "found goods." Not surprisingly, the question of what I was recording and writing—and who I really was—became increasingly sensitive and nearly ended my exploration.

Java the Disciplinarian

At the first formal meeting after the Dallas trip (October 16), the new look that Toro and Java were hoping for was evident. Three new members were admitted, including an attractive woman named Concha. She was tall, with brown hair and an olive complexion. Very self-assured, Concha had started hanging out with the batos in early October. She had recently left her husband in Houston and was now staying with her mother, a neighbor of Mosca and Chivo. The residents of these shotgun houses frequently sat outside on their front steps because of the heat, so her introduction into the Beret street gatherings had seemed natural. Java believed that Concha's presence as a Beret would improve the group's public image. I learned later that Concha was a former lover of Toro and considered by the veterans to be a de facto Beret.

George, the second new member, was also part of the new image. He was not the typical bato. George was a journalism student at the local community college and had been referred to the Wesley Center for psychiatric consultation because of repeated verbal confrontations with his professors. There he had met Toro, who told him about the Berets and invited him to the meeting.

The third recruit was the red-headed Rosado, a long-time good friend of Java who had recently relocated from St. Louis. Java had known him since they were kids, from the gang days. Rosado had been hanging around with the group for some time but had never been part of an organization.

At the same meeting, Java announced the confiscation of two berets. One belonged to Catriz, who had been the second in command during the Westside heyday. Somehow Java had come into possession of Catriz's beret. Catriz was supposed to have come to "pelear su causa" (plead his case) but never showed. He was voted out of the Berets, and the carnalismo patch from his beret was given to Primo. Java had also taken away Green Giant's beret, because he had lent it to a ruca. As a result, Green Giant was suspended for six weeks. Java said that these moves signaled more strictness for all Berets, especially regarding attendance at meetings. Java and Toro went over the Beret rules for the new recruits. This also served as a reminder to the "veterans" of two months.

As mentioned earlier, wearing the beret signified courage, service, and solidarity. It was a sign of commitment to "la causa" and, most importantly, a sign of belonging to the group. The beret signified the abstract ideals of the *movimiento*, but these ideals drew their intensity from the concrete, everyday relations between los batos in the chapter. It was the camaraderie of the group that gave meaning to the possession and wearing of the beret. That is how I understood the many expressions of emotional attachment to the beret and the many professed testaments of Berets willing to die for it. Possession of a beret was important symbolic capital.

The scarcity of berets, especially those adorned with the prized patch of carnalismo, had created a "token economy" that Java controlled. As minister of discipline, he attempted to enforce the rules of the chapter by taking away and reassigning berets. The tension over Java's actions had erupted into a leadership crisis immediately upon returning from Dallas.

[OCT. 18, AFTERNOON]

Java comes over to my house to tell me that he has been promoted to colonel and is now second in command; he's still in charge of security and discipline. Apparently Java had some sort of showdown with Toro and Chivo, who were content to let the group continue as it was. But Java wants more discipline, that all the guys should work so they can pay something for the pitch-ins, for funds to go out of town, for rent money for a headquarters, and so on. Java was thinking of quitting if he didn't get his way. Thus he is now a colonel and second in command.

Java repeated that he wanted more discipline. He also said that he was against starting a revolution.

As part of the new beginning, Java had already jotted down names, addresses, and phone numbers in an address book, along with a chart indicating rank and meetings attended and missed. He mentioned that he wanted to have all new Berets pass through a probationary period but that Toro wouldn't let him do this, that Toro wanted to expand and get guys in "nomás asina" (just like that). Java, however, seemed as excited about the Berets as Toro was.

> Java has big plans for the berets. He wants to rent a house that will double as a community center and his residence. He believes that San Antonio should be the national capital of the Berets.

Java was in a talkative mood. He began speaking about why he joined the Berets. Although the Berets were the first organization that he had joined, he explained that he already had a sense of cultural pride. In 1969 he had created a small flare-up at his workplace at Kelly AFB when he placed some "Chicanos United" and "Chicano Power" stickers on his locker.

> His "gringo supervisor" got very upset and demanded that he remove them. The next day all the lockers had those stickers. His camaradas at work were helping him out. The inspector was all upset, but they won that battle.

Now being part of the Berets was helping him at work. Toro had written the commanding officer at Kelly, lauding Java's community efforts. Java had the letter placed in his work file.

Java said that the Berets fixed him; after his get-together with his second wife didn't work out, he was pretty depressed and going around drunk and high on acid "más que la fregada" (more than you can believe). He had heard of the Berets about four years ago; he had seen five guys in uniform accompanied by rucas come into a cantina. The problem with the Berets "es que muchos se meten nomás porque se quieren ver malos y bien chingón" (is that many join only because they want to look mean and manly).

> Java tells me that he joined the berets for many reasons, and that one main reason is that he wants to help lift up his people. He always wanted to help his people, but he had never had the time. Toro had approached him on and off for the past two years about the Berets, but since he had known him from the Circle gang days he thought that this was just another clique. But then he saw Toro with his beret on and thought, "No, this is not like a clique."

One day Java ran into Toro, who invited him to the first meeting of the new Southside chapter. At the TU-CASA No Borders Conference a few days later, Java wore the beret for the first time. He liked belonging to the Berets; it gave him something to do and kept his mind off his second ruca. Moreover, since joining the Berets, he has interested women "all over the place." Java mentioned that Concha in particular seemed to be interested in him.

Java saw his changed appearance as a Beret as an indication that he was now "compuesto" (reformed). He planned to have his new rank blessed by a priest and have Chivo stand as his *padrino* (godfather). Java figured that would make Chivo his compadre. This might also paper over their personal differences, although Java didn't say so. He said that he believed in the blessing and in Jesus Christ. "Jesus was the first revolutionary. Like Villa, Zapata, and Che, Jesus Christ came and showed us how we should live with each other, like brothers." Java then started philosophizing about how all of us—black, white, brown—were brothers and that "the heart and not the head determines what kind of people we are."

Was Java the "political convert" I was seeking—the bato whose developing consciousness signified change in personal behavior? All this time while Java had been talking, I had been recording our conversation mentally. I asked Java if I could tape-record our talk.

[OCT. 18, AFTERNOON]
I want to record our conversation, but Java is reluctant. I'm not sure
why. Java argues that I already know it all, why not write it up? I don't
have to talk to him; I'm a Beret; I've seen what's going on, and so on. As
I am explaining the value of a life history, I drop the tape recorder. As I
pick up the various parts, Java leaves somewhat miffed. This later turns
out to be more than a technical screw-up.

Hangovers and Headaches

While in San Antonio, I was involved in a number of Chicano movement
activities. Mario Compean, chair of the Raza Unida Party, was a friend
and neighbor. Our shared courtyard was the setting for many political
celebrations. One of these gatherings was a party for the Colegio Jacinto
Treviño (an alternative Chicano college affiliated with Antioch College in
Ohio), where I was a volunteer lecturer. Classes took place in a simple
wood-frame house in the Westside, and most of the students were older
batos, a mix of army veterans and ex-cons from the barrios. Several had
been members of the original Westside chapter of the Brown Berets.

[OCT. 18, 5 P.M.–3 A.M.]
Three months into my observations, I invited the Southside Berets to
my house for the Colegio's celebration. This would be the first of many
times that the Southside Berets would come to my house. This particular event would also be the first occasion for a meeting between the new
Southside chapter and the old Westside chapter since the Westside had
disbanded in April. It had not occurred to me that some tension might
accompany this meeting.

Everyone had a good time, and it also made for an interesting meeting between four Westside Berets—Jimbo, Ben, Juan, and Luisa—and
four Southside Berets—Primo, Java, Toro, and Chivo. Chivo said before
the party that we should pay attention to the way the old Berets acted.
Whether this was to set them up for praise or criticism, I was not sure.
I did notice that Ben completely ignored Chivo when passing by. There
were some bitter feelings here.

Previously Toro and Chivo had acknowledged that personal *pedo* (conflict) had driven the Westside and Southside apart. They said that members were screwing around with the women of fellow Berets, that the

Westside batos were tired, and that, yes, the Southside batos were crazier than the batos from the West, "because in the Southside that's the way things are. They throw us out of every cantina we enter." As they intermingled with the Westsiders, Primo and Java were learning about Beret history from another perspective.

At some point, many hours into the party, Primo initiated a discussion with Juan, the founder of the Berets, on why he had quit. Primo said that Toro had explained that Juan wanted to settle down ("se quería cantoniar").

> On hearing this, Juan jumped up from his chair and loudly rejected the explanation. All of a sudden there was tension in the air. Everyone in the room quickly sat up straight, trying to calibrate the situation.

Juan mentioned a meeting with Toro and Loso where he had told them that he was going to resign as prime minister because there was too much conflict and pistol waving among the Berets, because too many guys were "corriendo su cabeza" (going on head trips) and running off at the mouth with rhetoric.

> Java tried to break things up because, as he put it, one shouldn't discuss things when drunk. But Primo was insistent in hearing why Juan quit. So Primo and Juan went to wake up Toro, who had fallen asleep, to confront him, to hear from Toro himself. Toro, half awake, was quiet, but he did say that Juan hadn't quit, that he is still a Beret. Juan, however, remains upset because he wants Toro to tell them why he left, that Toro knows why. Toro never responds to this.

Java, Primo, and Toro told Juan that they had changed; Java stressed that they were going to continue fighting for the people, that Juan had planted some seeds, and that they wanted to see them grow and plant even more.

> Later when the party is breaking up, Java and Primo come and tell me to forget what I saw, that there really is no conflict between the old Berets and the new ones, or between West and South sides, that the batos were drunk and that everything can be resolved. On leaving, Toro asks loudly, to no one in particular and with feigned innocence, "What happened? Why was Juan so *caliente* [upset]?"

Once Toro sobered up, he would have more questions.

A few days later Java showed up, accompanied by Primo, Toro, and Concha. The outburst at the party had triggered some underlying doubts about my work.

[OCT. 21, 7–11 P.M.]
The visit has a definite purpose. Apparently Java had flown off the handle again about my tape recording, saying that my Westside friends were talking bad about the Berets, that I had no permission to record, and why did I want to record since that was a gringo thing, and who thinks of doing these things.

At that point, I realized that Java had exploded in an anxious fit (*tranza*) about being recorded and about the tension at the party. That was why Toro and the others had accompanied him. Toro thought that I might be doing something fishy.

Initially Toro was hostile and wanted to hear the interview of Java that I had taped a few days before. Toro asked how I would feel if he listened to the recording. I said that I had no problem with that and that the interview was about Java's life history. Toro then asked what role the former Westside members would have with this book, because they were no longer Berets: if they wanted to join again and change the rules, fine; but in the meantime they had to follow the rules and orders. I said that the Westside had nothing to do with this, that a tape recorder was a basic tool of all writers, and that Java was confused.

Toro accepted my explanation. He said that he understood the necessity of using a tape recorder to keep notes on all the Berets statewide and mentioned the permission granted by the State Executive Committee. Java acquiesced in this. Later Toro said that the only reason he came was to settle this matter. I believe that Toro was apprehensive because he thought that I was soliciting opinions of him. We both knew that the opinions of the Westsiders would have been negative.

I used the occasion to repeat that I was interested in life histories and the motives for joining Berets, and not in the opinion of others. I emphasized that in recording three rules were in effect: one, I would ask prior permission of the person being interviewed; two, the person had the right to turn off the recorder when he wanted to say something off the record; and three, the person had the right to hear his interview afterward.

The batos hit on me heavily ("me cayeron bien gaucho") before I was cleared and Java put down ("chotiado"). Now I'm firmly in with the group, at least for the time being. I had a certain degree of confidence that such a session could occur frankly and openly. I was upset with Java, who spun a story from bits and pieces and then added his own fear of tape recorders.

The Significance of Not Wearing the Beret

In spite of Toro's initial support of Java, the *soldados* began to react negatively to Java's attempts to tighten up the organization. Increasingly everyone ignored Java ("lo están tirando al loco") because he talked too much and criticized without thinking; he had no tact. Toro said that the guy still needed to mature; the thing to do, Toro and Chivo advised, was just to listen to Java and nod "ah huh" to everything he said. Finally, Chivo and Toro started to come down on Java for always trying to kick someone out for an infraction of these rituals or regulations. Java was seen as too "trigger happy" when it came to discipline, always trying to take away somebody's beret. Chivo in particular still seemed to be smarting over the censure the group had given him.

In response to complaints from the Berets about being trigger happy regarding the confiscation of berets, Java allowed for an exception if the member was drunk or high. Then a Beret was expected to hand over his beret to the minister of discipline (Java) or his assistant (Tino); he would get it back the following day once sober.

[OCT. 23, 7–10 P.M.]
Java mentioned the rule they had made—I couldn't remember when— that a drunk Beret couldn't be disciplined because he was not going to remember what he was doing; just take off his beret or give it to an officer for safekeeping.

This was an interesting amendment that pointed to an important distinction between a guy who was "bueno y sano" (sober and sane) and one was "todo pedo" (out of it). It was also a suggestion of how individuals in the group might navigate between *locura* and *política*. A member could avoid the Beret rules of conduct if not wearing the beret.

This exemption—"if drunk or doped, hand in the beret"—naturally undermined the symbolic import of wearing the beret. The old rules had emphasized the maximum wearing of the beret, and such visibility entailed following the Beret rules of conduct. The exemption made wearing the beret contingent on behavior. This reminded me of the comment of the Ledbetter Beret leadership that "if the batos didn't behave, it would be better to take off the berets and form another organization."

In other words, the Beret uniform mediated behavior. In terms of public or "front stage" behavior, the beret functioned as an important code-switching symbol: wearing the beret demanded proper presentation; not wearing the beret excused an individual from such discipline. Thus personal behavior varied, depending on whether the person was in uniform dress or in street clothes.

This dynamic is similar to the manner in which the military uniform not only highlights the service identity and rank of an individual but also entails certain behaviors—for example, saluting a superior, staying sober, and avoiding hassles with civilians. For the bato loco, wearing a beret signified military-type discipline. Considering that the membership was overwhelmingly recruited from the barrio's "street corner" society, such behavioral code switching seemed to be an important middle ground where batos socialized to everyday street life could acquire a public presentation of self. Wearing the beret not only identified them publicly and thus made them vulnerable to public reaction but simultaneously regulated code switching between "offstage" or private behavior and "front stage" or public behavior.

The guys proved to be expert at code switching.

"Pedo Otra Vez" (Trouble Once Again)

Even when the Berets managed to get a break, they might squander it because of lack of discipline. This was the case with the moderately successful fund-raising event that they organized at Mission County Park in late October. The concession permit was a reward for Beret support of the League of United Latin American Citizens (LULAC) the previous week, the result of their reaching out to other organizations.

Chivo and Java had attended a LULAC meeting at Martin's Ice House to support a pilot project to fight crime and drugs in the community. Chivo, laughing, remembered an old lady who kept saying to "throw them all into the can [bote]." Chivo didn't say anything at first, but after Captain Emil Peters of the San Antonio Police Department had spoken, he got up. Addressing himself mainly to Captain Peters, Chivo said that he was a Brown Beret and that we were working with glue sniffers and drug addicts. He spoke about the conditions in the barrio and said that what we needed was crime prevention, not punishment or more prisons. The audience gave him a standing ovation. Afterward the people present showered Chivo and Java with questions. For such support, Mr. Martin, LULAC bigwig, had secured a concession permit for the Berets.

On an early Sunday afternoon, twelve Berets gathered at a very crowded Mission County Park to sell carne guisada tacos and chalupas at their own food stand. Within a few hours of opening the stand, the food was completely sold out. The Beret concession had grossed a $200 profit. After that the guys started to buy cases of beer. By the time the evening dance started, most of the batos were in various stages of inebriation. I left before midnight and thus missed the fight between two Berets that drew police attention. I reconstructed the scene from several Berets the next day.

FUND-RAISING AND FIGHTING [OCT. 27, 2–11 P.M.]
Tino and López started exchanging words over a woman the two liked. Both were very drunk. Primo and Java tried talking to them when it was clear that the *racla* [talk] was getting out of hand, but they were like lions and wanted blood. Java wanted them to fight elsewhere, in the dark away from the pavilion. But Toro said that if they want to fight, let them kill each other ["que se den en la madre"] right there, just to take off their berets.

And so it happened. After handing in their berets to Toro, the two started fighting and ended up on the ground among the spilled charcoal.

The *perros* [police] with drawn revolvers arrived quickly, but Primo and Mosca stopped them, with Mosca pushing a policeman's gun away, telling him that that the gun was not necessary. Everyone admired Mosca for that action. Primo and Mosca got some mace because they were between the batos fighting and the police. The Berets quickly broke up the fight, separating Tino and López. On the way to the car, in the parking lot, Skinny Benny slashed two tires of a police car in revenge for the drawn gun and mace. The police stopped the guys at the park gate because they suspected that the Berets had slashed the tires, but Toro sweet-talked them out of it, saying that they would help them find the guys who had done it.

The next day, in discussing the fight, the batos tried to minimize the *pedo* by noting that the dance was almost over, not too many people were left, and it was the last function of the year at the park. But they acknowledged that Sheriff Jimmy Flores had noticed that the trouble involved the Berets. Taking off the berets had not rendered them invisible. Chivo was concerned about not being invited to put up another concession next time. Java and Primo felt that Toro as *jefe* should have stopped the *racla* and fighting and that he had to do a better job as prime minister. I was surprised that Toro believed that the organization would be protected if the angry batos simply took off their berets.

The jealous brawl reflected the tension that had developed within the group in the past few weeks.

[OCT. 22–23, 6–10 P.M.]
Primo believes that Java is jealous because Primo is doing good making speeches and he is tired of Java putting him down behind his back. Abe and Terco have exchanged words, and now the two want to fight. Nobody likes Terco, I found out, except perhaps myself, Toro, and Chivo. Giant is also upset with his brother Mosca, says that they always come out fighting. Because of that Java says it would be better if Giant could hustle and start another chapter in Castroville.

To complicate the group dynamics, Chivo and his good friend and ex-Beret Catriz were making things hard for Java. Catriz, whose beret had been reassigned by Java, kept probing Java's commitment to Beret camaraderie, asking if he was really second in command. To such challenges, Chivo and Toro would reply that rank doesn't mean anything, that we were all equal, and that rank was just a formality, thus further undercutting Java's authority.

[OCT. 18]
Java's efforts at imposing discipline were too little and too late to prevent the guys from being "kicked out" of their headquarters. The owner of the house accuses the Berets of being "una bola de bandidos" (a band of thieves) and refuses to collect rent. She wants everyone to leave.

A Different Look

Perhaps because of the tension within the group, the loss of the Beret headquarters, or simply exhaustion, in mid-November, my fourth month with the group, many began relaxing the code about wearing the beret. Given the association between behavior and beret use, this was not a good sign. The leadership, including Java the disciplinarian, set the example.

[NOV. 15, LATE AFTERNOON]
The meeting took place outside Mosca's house. Mosca, a *vecino* of Chivo, lives in one of the run-down $55 a month wood-frame shacks behind the railroad yards. This meeting took place on a wet misty day; it was already dark, and everything was wet since it had rained on and off throughout the day. We looked for a dry spot in the dirt narrow road running by the barracks for a place to hold the meeting. We finally moved under a carport that spanned two look-alike houses and held the meeting there.

Toro was standing against a wall, with his ankle-length army over-coat and sunglasses; Java with his new look was sitting against same wall; Loso and Rosado were on two abandoned chairs next to each other across from Toro; Chivo was hunched in middle of carport dirt space; Abe, López, and myself were over by the concrete porch steps of the house; Terco was sitting on the porch steps. Concha was absent.

None of the officers were wearing berets; only two *soldados* had them on.

Java kiddingly tells Terco to ask Toro where his beret is (laughter). Toro instructs López how to wear his beret, says he is wearing it like a chef. Terco mentions that Green Giant is wearing a star on his beret; the star signifies the rank of prime minister. Everyone is incredulous and smil-ing. "What," says Toro, "little Giant??"

Giant's explanation, it turned out, was that they were always criticizing him for not moving; so now he was moving and had made himself prime minister of the Beret chapter from Castroville. When someone asked, "How many Berets are there in Castroville?" someone answered, "One, Green Giant." Everyone laughed.

We talked about Java's GI-style haircut. It was a radical physical change from his long, flowing hair. Moreover, he was dressed nicely. Everyone was in disbelief that it was Java. Toro said that now Java did not look like a Brown Beret leader, that he looked unfortunately like a Kelly Field worker. Chivo laughed and said that Java was no longer a Brown Beret but a Pink Beret. Java replied defensively that now they would believe him when he said that he earned $13,000 a year and that he worked at Kelly

Field. He added that he was tired of his shaggy hair (*greña*). But the major reason for the haircut, it turned out, was his budding romance with Concha.

[NOV. 6, NOV. 15; LATE AFTERNOONS]
Java announces that he and Concha are thinking of marrying in a Brown Beret wedding and that their house will be the Brown Beret headquarters. We are all surprised. Java is dreaming romance, is head over heels in love. Java wants to get married to a woman who already has the "onda de la raza" [commitment to the people]. He doesn't believe she should always accompany him; there are limits; but they should be able to work together. They're going to live together while Concha gets her divorce. Then in about six–seven months they'll get married.

Toro laughed and shook his head, saying that he would respect the union. Toro added that Java had already scolded him about the way he talked to Concha. There was some tension about which man Concha answered to— Toro or Java. As a result, Java had taken her out of the Berets and made her his own private secretary. Concha now answered only to Java, which entailed calling up all the batos, informing them of meetings, and so on. Thus ended a six-week experiment with a woman Beret.

The gringo landlord comes by on [his] round of rent collection and asks who lived here. Terco, Mosca's brother, says no one, except that I'm his brother. About this time we had moved into Mosca's *cantón*, where Loso continued his *perica* [talk]. Later the landlord came back and said there had been several complaints and that we had better move the meeting. Surprisingly, no one talked back to the gringo, and we all moved over to the house of Concha's mother, where we had the rest of the meeting in the dark driveway while it drizzled.

A Pedagogy for Batos?

Part of the new *onda* (way) about being more strict involved education classes that Toro wanted for the Berets, so that they all could answer when someone asked them questions while they were wearing berets. Toro had become especially aware of this need after the statewide meeting had introduced the guys to some politically sophisticated Berets from the other chapters. Toro asked me if I would be willing to share some of the lessons

I'd been giving at the Colegio Jacinto Treviño. "Of course," I responded. I suggested that we start seeing some Chicano films for starters.

[OCT. 25, 6–11 P.M.; OCT. 27, 2–11 P.M.]
Even though I've been with the group three months now, I have managed to maintain a low profile. Giving classes will put me in a more prominent position, but I have no problems with the request since I consider it my obligation to reciprocate with information and even advice. Moreover, at this point I already know where everyone is "coming from"; I know that there is no contradiction between "being political" and "being underclass." Nonetheless, it would be a supreme irony if I ended up creating the conditions for the transformation that I came to study. But isn't that what I came looking for? A political pedadogy suited for batos locos?

I knew that I was going beyond the proscribed bounds of "field study." One of the prime directives of ethnography was to avoid, if possible, interfering in the "natural settings" under observation. The pitfalls of misguided participant-observation—as taught in graduate school—had been illuminated by the classic example of Leon Festinger's *When Prophecy Fails*. Social psychologist Festinger and associates had been interested in understanding what happens to a cult when its millenarian prophecy of deliverance fails. A critical problem emerged when their appearance as potential followers was interpreted by cult members as righteous confirmation of the prophecy itself. Festinger and associates had interfered with the "natural" evolution of the cult, thus violating a prime directive and rendering their observations suspect.

Now it seemed that I was about to do the same. One key difference, however, was that I had been frank about my intentions and my role; I was not playing undercover ethnographer. Moreover, my up-front presence had not altered group dynamics or behavior, as evidenced by the occasional self-consciousness of the leadership about the unflattering behavior I might be witnessing. Being up front certainly did not circumvent the tensions surrounding my participant-observation, but the ethics of clandestine research was not part of the burden.

Providing education classes to the Berets, however, certainly signified an interference with their political evolution. That did not trouble me, and therein lay another difference from the Festinger study. I wanted to believe in the prophecy. I wanted to believe that political consciousness for these batos meant personal change; and if my intervention might bring this about, I was a willing volunteer. What my participation might mean for my dissertation was a secondary matter. I would worry about that later.

Teaching the Berets, moreover, would simply be an extension of what I was already doing as a volunteer lecturer at the Colegio Jacinto Treviño. I had invited Toro and Java to one of my classes as guests. That may have been the occasion when Toro realized that I was an instructor. Thus when he requested that I provide similar classes to the Berets, I felt no hesitation.

I decided to use films and documentaries as a way of creating discussion. This made sense, since many of the guys couldn't read. The setting for the first session was behind the house of some undocumented immigrants that Chivo knew.

[NOV. 20, EVENING]
I show the film *Yo Soy Chicano* behind the house of some undocumented immigrants. Five or six males live in the house. Chivo once gave them a ride from the border, and they have remained grateful. They lend him money every now and then, when they have some and Chivo needs some. Chivo adds that he has brought "un chingo" [quite a few] from the other side. I asked him if they paid him. He says, "No, I just like to fuck [*chingar*] with the border patrol."

For the first political education session, I had screened *Yo Soy Chicano*, a historical film that began with Aztlán, the legendary homeland of the Aztecs, and continued through Texas independence and the Mexican American War, all the way to the present time of Reies López Tijerina, César Chavez, Corky González, and so forth. It was a classic movement film. Judging from the restlessness of some of the Berets, it also may have been too long.

It was difficult to assess the effect the film had on the group. Only Java was impressed by the history. He picked up on deportations during the Great Depression and asked if this was related to current mass deportations. I said that, yes, basically immigration enforcement was related to economic conditions in the United States. Primo added some comments on this point, and Java appreciated the discussion. Besides Java and Primo, Toro and Rosado showed interest in the film. Chivo, who knew most of this stuff, was just going in and out of the house. The young recruits—the two Bennies, Gabe, Terco, and Mosca—seemed furtive, restless, and just polite. What struck me as the camera panned Corky González's library of Chicano literature was that this meant little to many of the batos. They were functionally illiterate in both Spanish and English. The film was too intellectual.

So for the second session the following week I screened a film about Chicano *pintos* (prison inmates). This would strike closer to home, I thought. The viewing took place outside in the parking lot of the Wesley Center. We used one of the walls as our screen. Cecilio García-Camarillo, the editor of the Chicano literary-political journal *Caracol* and my good friend, assisted me. It was a cold night.

> [NOV. 26, EVENING]
> A good showing of members (about ten batos) on this very cold November night in the parking lot of the Wesley Center. Everyone has berets on tonight with the exception of George, who is a recent recruit. Tonight I am giving the second in a series of political education classes for the batos. Everyone has been drinking and smoking.
>
> Since the Wesley Center is closed, we assemble outside in the parking lot, using one of the walls as our screen. It's very cold. Cecilio and I set up the equipment and begin the film, but only two of the ten guys are paying attention. The others are drinking, smoking, talking, and laughing. The only reactions to the film are the threats the guys make whenever prison guards appear on the makeshift screen.

The verbal insults and playacting prompted by appearance of the guards at least showed some attention, I reasoned.

> Toro and Skinny Benny would reach inside their pants, acting as if they [were] getting their *cuetes* (handguns). The second time Toro did that, Loso bet that his friend (who was visiting) could beat Toro shooting a can at 50 feet. Toro could not resist the challenge and bet five dollars from Java. The betting negotiations became lively, while the film ran in the background. Java was taking care of Toro's handgun. Loso laughed hard because he could not believe Toro was without his handgun. Toro got his *cuete* from Java and started showing it off.

When the film was slowed by a mechanical flaw, I told Cecilio to pack up, and we split. I was pissed and left without saying *adiós*.

Playing with guns

As we're packing the equipment in the car, the guys are still arguing over betting and contest details. As I'm getting in the car, I hear Toro say that it was partly Java's fault because he had given the guys dope, and because we had been drinking quite a bit. Toro knows I am upset. Chivo had been correct: I was going to write that the Berets were "una bola de pistoleros." I leave for Dallas.

Fourth-Month Frustration

I left to visit the other Beret chapters along Interstate Highway 35—Austin, Waco, and Dallas. I needed to get a broader perspective. I needed a break. Yet my frustration was manifest in my note taking. Over four months of hanging out, I had been fairly disciplined about writing my mental record down as soon as possible after every observation. But by the end of November I had become slack. A good part of the reason had to do with my increasing doubts about using this "field experience" as the basis for a dissertation.

[LATE NOVEMBER]

This [sloppiness] is probably due to physical and mental fatigue. Just the sheer hours spent with these guys could account for it. On the other hand, I sense considerable strain in bridging two very distinct social worlds. My working-class background means that I am no stranger to barrio life, but it is no preparation for this organized underclass life. And then the idea of "studying" this group for a Yale dissertation—what contradictions! I sense feelings of arrogance, but also of disillusionment, of having been betrayed by my romantic political expectations. I'll have to deal with this later.

Probably another reason my note taking has become sloppy is that there is less new information coming in. Jesus, why do I sound like an undercover cop?? Ethnography must have that quality to it. I should take a break, switch technique for a while and start interviewing, sound like a welfare intake clerk for a change. Why have I become cynical!?

I was beginning to question the entire project.

7 MY DECEMBER 1974 visit to Austin, Waco, and Dallas reinforced my realization that the Southside chapter I was with was the most "loco" of all the chapters in the state. This may have been due to the seasoned experience of the leadership in the older chapters. The Austin Berets had organized in 1973 and had acquired their headquarters in early 1974. The Waco Beret chapter, although only three months old, was essentially an offshoot of the Austin chapter. The Dallas Ledbetters, though organized in 1974, had been organized previously under different auspices. In comparison, the Southside chapter was still basically one of raw recruits.

Both the Austin and Dallas chapters operated community centers, published newspapers, and were involved in coalition work. An April 1974 issue of the *Echo*, the Austin Beret newspaper, illustrated the chapter's diverse activities. Ana, the leader of the Chicana Berets, had penned an account about an overnight "Kids' Camp Out" at Leander Park for thirty students from Zavala Elementary; fifteen Berets had taken part in the camping trip. An accompanying photo showed a "hay ride" with the kids raising their arms in a "Chicano power" salute. The same issue carried photos of Brown Berets picketing the police and city council as part of a campaign for an independent police review board. The East Austin Committee for Justice (EACJ), of which the Berets were part, was pressing Austin's mayor Roy Butler to respond to its proposal to end police brutality. Since the State Executive Committee meeting a few months before, the Austin Berets, in response to yet another police killing, had organized a protest of 500 at the mayor's house and another of 300 at the police station.

In West Dallas, the Ledbetters continued their push to change the name of their local elementary school. The *Dallas Times Herald* reported: "Thirty Berets and approximately 150 supporters marched seven miles across Dallas to protest last week's refusal by school trustees to rename Gabe P. Allen School in West Dallas for Mexican agrarian reformer Emiliano Zapata." They marched from the G. P. Allen School to the school district's administration building, where they held a peaceful half-hour rally. Shouts of "Chicano power" and "Zapata sí, gringo no" came from the crowd. In both Austin and Dallas, the Berets had clear community support.

The new Waco chapter, consisting of some eight Berets, was about to launch a community newspaper. Roberto, known in Austin as a hot-tempered firebrand, said he would "go easy on Waco" because he recognized that most of the raza was conservative. "I don't want to move too fast with the paper porque no quiero asustar a la gente [because I don't want to scare people]." Roberto understood that the newspaper would require general community support if it was to survive.

Perhaps the relatively small size and compactness of the Mexican American communities in Austin, Waco, and Dallas accounted for the coalition practices and the conscious search for unity of the activist sectors. The original San Antonio Berets had worked with the Mexican American Unity Council, the Mexican American Neighborhood Community Organization, Barrio Betterment, and other organizations in various community projects in 1971–1973. But an increasing estrangement had set in as these organizations secured foundation monies or federal funds. As they moved away from aggressive protest tactics to more conventional politics, they also changed their personnel. They now wanted "educated" people with college degrees on their staff—it was no longer sufficient just to have "barrio experience." The veteran Beret leadership had a clear sense of being sold out by these agencies.

The flip side of this estrangement was the confrontational style of the Berets, which did not endear them to potential allies. Even relations with the Wesley Community Center were sometimes tense. On several occasions, I witnessed the Berets take on a quick adversarial stance when some disagreement with other organizations or individuals arose. The disagreement often turned out to be based on lack of communication or information. The words of Raza Unida Party leader Mario Compean to a Beret leader—"just don't treat us like an enemy"—were to the point.

The reconstituted San Antonio chapter, in contrast to the Austin and West Dallas chapters, was relatively isolated from or had uneasy relations with local movement organizations. The one exception was TU-CASA, the immigrant services center, whose leadership had an explicit Marxist orientation. This relationship would put the chapter on the FBI watch list.

Not being part of a working coalition meant that the Berets had difficulty attracting support or attention for issues they considered important. Inexperience and impatience compounded the difficulty. With the Southside High issue, involving the suspension of several youths for their long hair, the Berets were never able to generate interest from either parents or advocacy organizations. Nor did they ever attract much public attention to the issue. The same could not be said about the next solo action on the part of the Berets.

Preventing an Eviction

It happened suddenly, without much advance warning. Unfortunately, I was out of town visiting other Beret chapters, but Java and the other guys filled me in on the details. The San Antonio newspapers also carried an account of the unfolding saga. Little did I know then that this would be the high point of the Southside Beret resurgence. And I had missed it.

Java and Chivo happened to read that a family was going to be evicted from Cassiano Homes in a few days. So, as Java put it, they went by to talk with the woman, who "sang them a sad story" that really moved them. The next day (Sunday) the Berets held an emergency meeting and decided to prevent the eviction set for the following day. I reconstructed the dramatic event as follows:

> BLOCKING AN EVICTION [DEC. 2, DEC. 11]
> The Berets showed up in strength at 7:30 in the morning and surrounded the Herrera home. Many inactive or former Berets have joined the Southside batos for this action. According to the newspaper account, "Juanita Herrera, her 10 children, and her dishes were to be physically forced out of their home in the Cassiano Homes Monday." They were still hoping that the Housing Authority would change its mind, because "they have no place to go." Bexar County deputies delayed the eviction "when some 20 members of the Brown Berets, a Mexican American all-male service group, stood in vigil outside the home of the Juanita Herrera family."

The San Antonio newspapers quoted Toro's statement that the rights of the Herrera family had been violated. "We intend to help the family and stop

Blocking an
eviction

the Housing Authority from evicting them. They have no place to go." An
assistant manager responded that the Housing Authority "had reached the
end of the rope with that family" and that it was not up to officials to find
a new home for them. Later that day the executive director of the Housing
Authority decided to postpone the eviction for "a couple of days," pending
a full report to his board members.

The Berets appeared to have scored a major victory! The initial news
story about the eviction had elicited positive comment throughout the city.
But then the other side of the story began to leak out. On Thursday the
chair of the San Antonio Housing Authority (SAHA) Board publicly commented on the problems with the children: "These include glue and paint
sniffing, use of marijuana and heroin, public consumption of alcohol by
under-age children, truancy and a general lack of acceptance of the re-

straints of community living." In short, the children were uncontrollable and intimidating. The chair of the board then noted that SAHA had an obligation "to all families residing in public housing to insure that they can live in peace without fear of their neighbors, without being intimidated, harassed or victimized by their neighbors." Apparently the families in the Cassiano Homes, all of them Mexican American, had petitioned the Housing Authority to remove the Herrera family. The complaints had accumulated over the years. The family was considered incorrigible.

All this was portrayed in news articles that followed the story for several days. Conservative columnist Paul Thompson took delight in skewering the Berets for overlooking the welfare of the neighbors who had been urging the Housing Authority to take this action for years. By the end of the week, the Berets looked more funny than threatening. The Berets were furious. Toro "quería cuetear" (wanted to waste) Thompson, and Chivo would go ballistic at the mention of the criticism. Chivo believed that what the Berets did was just. But Java, who was being ribbed by his coworkers at Kelly, was embarrassed by the incident. Nonetheless, the eviction was postponed as a result of the Beret action, and some welfare agencies were pressured to act on behalf of the family. The Bexar County Welfare Department found the Herreras a house with "a leaky roof."

Terrorist, Mafioso, or FBI?

Law enforcement authorities were mindful of the San Antonio Berets and issued occasional confidential reports about them. The San Antonio-based FBI agents had determined on February 1, 1972, that the Brown Berets of San Antonio were a Mexican American civic action group "not affiliated with the West Coast militant group of the same name" but nonetheless maintained some surveillance. It became clear that we were being watched by the police when we traveled to Dallas for the executive committee meeting of the Beret chapters in Texas. As late as 1983, I would discover later, the FBI had conducted a "limited investigation" on the Berets in the state. Regarding possible criminal activities, the 1983 report noted: "Most of the known or suspected members of the Brown Berets have been arrested for violations ranging from failure to obey a lawful order (misdemeanor) to aggravated assault on a police officer (felony). Many members are suspected of being involved in the use and/or sale of narcotics." Basically this meant that I was not privy to information that the FBI didn't already have.

Whether the group itself was infiltrated was an open question. Among the Southside Berets was one mysterious individual I'll call Alberto, who would come by periodically and then disappear for long stretches of time. His occasional presence was notable because of his loud and constant call for armed action. During the Southside High troubles, Alberto, who had just returned from Chicago, recommended that the situation be settled by "offing" the *vendido* (sell-out) principal at Southside. When preparations were being made for the protest before the Mexican Consulate, someone asked if they should take handguns. When I sarcastically commented that that would be a "smart thing" to do, Alberto jumped on me, reminding me of the Beret constitution that I swore to uphold when I joined: "Let it [the protest] go down in the history books." Later at the Austin protest (October 1974), Alberto kept telling Primo that we had come to kill for la raza, to which Primo had said, "Chale [no], the protest is going to be a peaceful one." Primo mentioned in private that he thought that Alberto was crazy; he didn't trust guys that just wanted to kill. There was a question of whether Alberto was a Beret, because someone had lent him a beret for the protest. I had some gnawing doubts about him.

I had met Alberto in the first month of the Beret reactivation when Loso and Toro swung by his house. At that time Alberto was worried about the FBI watching his house and advised us not to stay too long. Both Loso and Toro offered help if he needed to lay low for a while. Afterward Loso told me that Alberto was working with a brother-in-law who was a Mafia "hit man" and that Alberto was doing the same. This explained the certain respect that Toro and Loso accorded him and why he could come and go with the Berets as he pleased. Loso later added that Alberto was "bien loco" (really crazy).

In this barrio underworld, a Mafia connection was plausible. Chale, a Westside Beret, had once described the benefits of a typical bodyguard job to me: $250 per week, a new car, a set of expensive clothes, and all the beer one wanted. The job had only two conditions: no distracting personal conflicts or troubles and the necessity of using a handgun whenever the time came to use it—not using it meant death. Chale talked a friend out of a job offer because the life expectancy of such batos was short. Whether Alberto was a Mafia bodyguard or a government agent, he had a perfect cover for a group like the Berets.

If the Berets themselves did not merit particular FBI scrutiny, the same could not be said about TU-CASA, the Marxist-oriented immigrant services center. TU-CASA activist Rosario, on whom the Berets often leaned

for petty cash, appeared to be a lightning rod of sorts. Owner of a popular Mexican restaurant, Rosario was a self-proclaimed revolutionist and
supporter of guerrilla activity against the Mexican government. He presented himself as a Chicano leader, and the local media accepted the des-
ignation with few reservations. Most Chicano leaders and organizations,
however, had distanced themselves from Rosario because of his public
revolutionary pronouncements. His press conferences and other declara-
tions had spread confusion and undercut the movement. Many wondered
whether his public displays were simply driven by ego or by a plan to embarrass the movement.

The Berets were voicing similar doubts about Rosario, but from a completely different direction. Toro and Chivo wondered about the rumors of
drug use and the immunity he seemed to have from police action. "Had
some deal been struck?" was the implied question. It seemed to be an ill-
disguised secret that Rosario was shipping guns to Mexico; such speculation was fanned by his public statements. The Valley Berets, in fact, suspected that Rosario had taken $30,000 that had been committed to Beret
activities in the Valley and used the money for "hot *cuetes*" (stolen weapons) instead. Upon passing through San Antonio, they decided to pay Rosario a visit; they wanted to apply pressure.

[DEC. 26–27]
The meeting took place at Rosario's restaurant with five batos from
McAllen, Chivo, and myself present. Rosario said that no funds had
come to Texas "period" and, moreover, that the Episcopal church foundation considered several Chicano organizations, including the Berets,
to be subversive. He would try to push their proposals. He was not sure
how it would turn out, but they could count on his support. He urged
the Berets to submit a three-page proposal, and he would push it. So the
guys left with a promise of support, but no money. The guys consider
Rosario to be sly and slippery.

While at the meeting, I realized that the mysterious fund of $30,000 re-
ferred to a failed grant proposal for a delinquency prevention program and
that Rosario sat on the national church foundation board that allocated the
grant funds. Beret suspicions seemed to stem from both misunderstand-
ing and mistrust. All the dealings with Rosario appeared to be shrouded
in ambiguity and wariness, barely disguised by a veneer of Chicano hand-
shakes and *abrazos* (hugs).

Not long after I left the "field," Rosario's name came up in the wake of news that U.S. federal officials and ranking Mexican law enforcement officials were probing the "underworld exchange of high-powered weapons for narcotics in Mexico" (October 1975). The probe had been initiated in part by California congressman Bob Wilson, who claimed that this underworld exchange was "on a dramatic increase" and that some of the weapons were "reaching revolutionary organizations and Communist front groups." Asked to comment to such reports, Drug Enforcement Administration (DEA) special agent Bill Kline of San Antonio said that such speculation was out of his jurisdiction. Kline did agree that the "guns-for-dope" trade was on the rise but described the trade as unorganized and of a mom-and-pop variety: "I'm sure many of the guns are stolen, but they're so valuable in Mexico that . . . some people are just buying the weapons here and then taking them to Mexico."

Barely had the "gun-dope traffic" story broken into print when *El Norte*, a Monterrey newspaper, carried a major story that Rosario was being sought by the FBI "as the founder of a terrorist organization supplying arms to Communist radical groups in Mexico." The story relied on the confession of a suspected gunrunner who had been picked up by Mexican authorities and tortured. The suspect also told authorities that Rosario was organizing terrorists in the Texas Rio Grande Valley. Rosario denied all the allegations and noted that they could "get me killed." He said that the FBI knew where he lived if it wanted to question him. Later a warrant would be issued in Monterrey charging Rosario with sedition and arms trafficking.

Java Quits

Java had warned the Berets about Rosario. He had been "shocked" that Rosario, who had been working with us at TU-CASA, had gone to a meeting of Kelly unionists and proclaimed that he was a Communist.

[DEC. 2]
Java said that he was stunned by the declaration. He didn't understand why one would want to say that, and he began to wonder why we had been working with Rosario. Java repeated something I had heard from him before, that the Berets had to tone down this *perica* (rhetoric) about revolution, because that way we only scare people and ultimately the FBI "nos van a bostear" (will bust us).

Java, in fact, would receive an unexpected visit from the FBI. The reason stemmed from his participation in an anti-inflation protest in downtown San Antonio in mid-November. I missed the protest, but my notes record Toro saying that TU-CASA had asked for Beret participation and that "those who don't have uniforms should wear khaki shirts and pants."

A few days after Beret participation in the downtown protest, two FBI agents visited Java at his work at Kelly Air Force Base to talk to him about his involvement with the Berets. Apparently someone had recognized him and had "squealed" to the FBI, or he had been picked up by routine police surveillance. The local daily noted that the protest had been organized by TU-CASA and that local "Communist Party honcho" John Sanford and members of the Young Socialist League had participated. Enough "radicals" had been present at the protest to draw the attention of local authorities. Although the news story didn't mention the Brown Berets by name, they were very visible in the published newspaper photo.

Java was clearly shaken by the visit and ensuing interrogation. Fortunately union stewards were on hand to assist him in his answers about whether he knew what "militant," "communism," "socialist," and so forth meant. The FBI agents wrote those words down on the newspaper article that they had clipped so that he could learn about that stuff. They also asked questions about the Beret leadership and mentioned Toro and Juan Guajardo in particular. Java replied that the Berets existed only to help the Chicano people, not to overthrow the government. He said that the agents didn't know anything about Chicanos; they asked him why poor African Americans and poor gringos didn't call themselves Chicanos. Fortunately his commanding officer, the same colonel who had received Toro's letter lauding Java's community efforts, supported Java. This resulted in a written apology from the FBI, which Java entered into his file. Java said that Toro's letter saved him and that he was interested in seeing if he could sue the FBI for humiliating him.

[DEC. 11]
Three weeks after the FBI visit, Java, Concha, and her son come by my house. Since announcing their intention to get married, Java has moved in with Concha, and Concha now gently insists that Java call her son "hijo." Java apparently considers himself married and is acting the part of responsible husband and father.

Java had called earlier to say that he wanted to discuss a problem with me, but when he arrived we spent much time bullshitting about events of the last ten days while I had been visiting the other Beret chapters. Java mentioned his embarrassment at the hasty action to prevent the eviction. He had wanted to investigate the case more. When it turned out that the families in the Cassiano Homes, all of them Mexican American, had been urging the Housing Authority to take this action for years, the Berets looked somewhat silly. He had received much criticism, mainly from coworkers at Kelly. Although the Beret action had pressured some welfare agencies to act on behalf of the family, Java felt embarrassed.

> Java then starts talking about the Beret leadership, that Toro and Chivo control everything, that Chivo really is second in command. Java is tired about always being put down by the guys, says there's not much carnalismo within the Berets, that the guys don't move, that everyone depends on him too much, that they bother him at home too much, and that now that he's settling in he doesn't want the guys to visit him so often, that the guys are still into this "onda de gangas" [thing of gangs].

Java was in his usual talkative mood. He said that Toro just wanted to kick ass (*desmadrar*), that Toro had not changed during the fifteen years he had known him, that the Berets would not change until Toro and Chivo left, and that they were just a clique as before. My notes recorded Java's summary judgment:

> "If [Toro] doesn't get into trouble like before it's because the situation has changed, because there are no cliques confronting him like when he was with the Circle gang. But he is still as brave and crazy as before."

Both Java and Concha said that the guys are too violent and that it's the only chapter like this, that has this thing about violence. Java mentioned that he had the Beret letter of commendation removed from his work file.

While Java was out of the room, Concha added that he didn't like the visits by the guys. Java was the jealous type and didn't want anyone hanging around, especially if they had been her lovers before. Java had mentioned something about rumors and that he didn't want to hear more rumors. He wanted to forget about that stuff. The other reasons were important, but that was the "last straw."

> Java is going to continue his struggle, not for la raza but for his familia; he has to work for them. When I remind him that he had once demanded that guys withdraw from the Berets if they wanted to settle

down—for reasons very similar to ones he is now suggesting—he replied that Toro and Chivo made him a fanatic, that this was a military thing and he took it like that. This military thing, Java adds, is for the *gabachos* [Anglos], that our people should stay the way it is, with different colors. He says that he only got in because Toro was after him and that twice he almost got out. Java then hands me his and Concha's berets, his military jacket, Toro's *cuete* plus some ammo, and some Beret records.

I was to hand in the berets, handgun, and assorted materials to Toro. Java saw me as the ideal intermediary, which I took to mean that he saw me as neutral or marginal with respect to the group. I also took it as a sign that he understood my role as an ethnographer.

Java was clearly shaken by the FBI visit and feared that he might be reclassified. He thought that he was going to lose his job. But Toro, when he called to find out what had happened, emphasized the domestic factor. He understood Java's apprehension about batos going over to their *cantón*. He understood that Java "la quiere hacer" (wants to make it) and didn't blame him. Toro said that he didn't want to push Java, but he predicted that Java would be with the guys again when Concha left him. Chivo, however, got very upset that Java had not resigned in person.

[DEC. 29]
Two weeks after his resignation, Java heard that Chivo wanted to kill him, which prompted him to call me to ask why. All I mentioned were the boots—that Chivo had loaned them to Java personally and that Java should return them personally—but aside from that I hadn't heard that Chivo wanted to kill him. Java said he handed in the boots to Chivo and drank two beers with him, and that Chivo had talked okay with him.

Java mentioned that the Junior LULACS were "tercos" (persistent) that he become a member. He told them that he had no time right now but said they are an okay group. They brought toys to Concha's kids and turkey for Christmas, and they were ready to help him with his case against the FBI.

Java's cousin Primo painted a very different scenario for the guys, passing along a rumor from his mother, who had heard it from Java's mother—namely, that Concha had beaten up Java:

"Java was going out to drink beer, and Concha said, 'No, sit down and watch TV,' and pas! Concha struck him a few times and Java sat down to watch TV. 'And don't move from there,' she said, and he didn't." On hearing this, all the batos—Toro, Chivo, Skinny Benny, and Primo—just shook their heads and smiled.

A Raza Unida Infiltrator?

The Berets were never content with my explanation that I was writing a book. I must have some ulterior motive or interest: why write about them? Sometime after I had invited Toro to the class I was teaching at the alternative Jacinto Treviño College, he asked me why I was with the *movimiento*; he didn't understand why, with so much education, I was working with the barrio. The experience had usually been the opposite, he noted. He was trying to understand what made me political. It was an interesting reversal of roles. Likewise, many months into my hanging out, as Skinny Benny was getting down from my car, Primo playfully told him that I was a Communist. I didn't know what had set off that unexpected comment, but I laughed and responded in the same tone that Primo used: "Of course I'm a Communist." The guys were trying to figure out what made me political. They were studying me.

Later I heard that the Dallas Ledbetter Berets referred to me as "José Ángel Gutiérrez" because they thought that I was a Raza Unida activist. The Valley Berets, who heard this while passing through Dallas, brought it up when they arrived in San Antonio. Rolo mentioned the "chisme" (rumor) to Chivo while the three of us were preparing dinner for the batos.

[DEC. 22, DEC. 26–27]
The Dallas Berets told Rolo that "José Ángel Gutiérrez" had just left— they were referring to me—and this led to a delicate discussion of Beret infiltration by La Raza Unida. Apparently Rolo believes it may exist. Rendón had said that the two female Berets in Dallas were really RUP and they had hoped to use the Berets to work for RUP; but when the elections were over, they dropped out of the Berets.

Rolo was trying to understand what a bato like myself was doing in the Berets. I had proven that I was with the *movimiento*, so Rolo was offering infiltration from La Raza Unida as a possible explanation.

Chivo, who has been cooking some potatoes for the guys, says something like "we have to be careful of infiltrators," and after a brief silence
he continues, "but I wouldn't cook una ensalada de papas para un in-
filtrator [potato salad for an infiltrator]." I was silent all this time and
never really responded to these innuendos—in a sense they were non
sequiturs and I was unprepared for them.

It was an awkward situation. But this may have explained Toro's sudden
positive reassessment of Raza Unida in the following days.

WHAT WE DO TO LIVE!

 IN ADDITION TO THE CRAZINESS or *locura* of individuals, another element that created unpredictability in this lower-class world stemmed from the underground economy of drug dealing and peddling of "found" goods. Money-making ventures, especially selling marijuana, were difficult to resist in this world of scarce opportunities. Tension and conflict, in other words, were not simply an expression of unforeseen emotional impulses; they also issued from organized entrepreneurial efforts.

Finding a Trade

The Berets, both recruits and veterans, were familiar with this underground economy. Seven core members of the Beret chapter were unemployed, and five of them were involved in the underground economy. The two Bennies, Mosca, Abe, Tino, Primo, and Chivo were unemployed. Primo had lost his truck job at the soda distributing company because they thought he was stealing—a plausible charge since he had not given up the *tecata* (heroin) that kept him looking for easy money-making schemes. Skinny Benny thought nothing of doing easy "jales" (jobs), as the barely healed scars on his arm, the result of an attempted burglary of a storefront, suggested. Fat Benny had been recruited as a result of his peddling marijuana and pills to the guys. And Chivo, with professed misgivings, had joined a burglary ring. It was a question of survival, he said.

The job with the least risk involved transporting and selling marijuana.

I had been with the group six weeks before I had an inkling of an underground trade among some Berets.

[OCT. 1, OCT. 9, OCT. 13]
Primo and Fat Benny had gone to deep South Texas to pick up some "cosas" [things]. They returned with good stories about the Berets down there; they were treated great, with plenty of beer and *mota*. Primo also learned that Joaquín Murrieta was a Mexican hero. Primo earned a stripe for his trip to the Valley.

In three days Primo made six hundred dollars. The Valley Berets gave Primo a hundred-dollar bill to buy five dollars' worth of gas. They also sent along a tip for the San Antonio Berets. Chivo thought that part of it should go regularly to the San Antonio Berets, and he suggested to Fat Benny that he think seriously about moving to McAllen. Primo now had a temporary job transporting stuff from the Valley to San Antonio.

Primo tells me that the less the Berets know about this business, the better, but it seems most of the guys know already. This is not a Beret-related project but more an individual project necessitated by lack of money. But in view of the obvious connections, at what point is this distinction between Beret group and individual, between official and unofficial, relevant?

While thinking about the vague distinction between criminality and political behavior, I saw an old *Rawhide* TV episode about a "shadowy" deal between Western gun dealers and Indians. A bad white guy (an escaped prisoner) wanted to create a diversion for his own personal interests and arranged to have a hungry dispossessed Indian tribe raid a cattle drive and steal some cattle. I got the sense that when the film was originally produced viewers were not expected to distinguish between the motives of the bad guy and those of the Indians. The show seemed to make no distinction between the criminal intent of the bad white guy and the hunger and dispossession of the Indians.

SHADOWY INDIANS [OCT. 17–18]
Now, after a decade of civil rights protests, one sees clearly that Indians are interested in "stealing cattle" to exact some vengeance or, as the bad guy says in his pitch to them, because their buffalo are no longer around but there are plenty of cattle around. Cattle rustling by hungry, angry

Indians in this old TV Western, once framed as criminal behavior, has become political protest.

I recalled that cattle rustling had once referred to the branding of wild unclaimed cattle and had been a legal activity. Once the frontier had been carved up into ranches, the term and action had become criminalized. A similar criminalization had occurred with cultivating and smoking marijuana. I was searching for analogies that might reframe my observations.

Sometimes when these guys wore their bandanas across their foreheads and began to speak in gestures, I couldn't help but think of them as urban half-bloods. The Southside guys had several passing discussions about an Indian past, much of it wrapped up in pseudo-reconstructions of Aztec culture. But however vague the references, their brown skin pointed eloquently to indigenous roots. I was desperately seeking parallels.

Dealing in marijuana carried no negative connotations for the batos; and given the alternatives, selling marijuana was the least dangerous enterprise. It was not a property crime or a crime of violence. It had long been part of Mexican culture and now was part of the college counterculture. It was relatively easy to rationalize the business transactions of minor players. But the Valley Berets seemed to be a cut above the minors.

Apparently the Valley batos had been engaged in dealing for a while. Rolo, the Beret spokesman for the chapter, had been arrested for two tons of *mota* sometime in 1973 but was later acquitted. Raúl, the prime minister, had been arrested in early 1974 for "contrabando de ilegales" and "tráfico de drogas" (smuggling aliens and drug trafficking) two days before the first Beret statewide conference. Now he was serving time at El Reno in Oklahoma. A few months after Raúl's arrest, a Beret named Sol was arrested in Mexico on charges of gun smuggling. The charges were later dropped, but in the meantime the Valley group had dispersed to various points in the country. The Berets had left town because they thought "que les iba a caier tierra" (they would be implicated). Thus Rolo had spent the summer and fall traveling in Wisconsin and other places. After a five-month exodus, the Valley Berets were just getting back together. This explained why Primo and Fat Benny had found them in such disarray.

In late December I had an opportunity to spend a few days with the Valley Berets. Toro and the guys had come by the house to tell me that the Valley Berets would be passing through town. First, however, they had to explain their strange appearance. Toro was thoroughly covered with mud, and Skinny Benny was drenched with blood. Toro said that they had gone out to the countryside looking for food.

A THREE-LEGGED GOAT [DEC. 19, DEC. 20]

Toro, Primo, and Skinny Benny had been after a pig, so that we could
have a feast when the guys from McAllen hit town. Toro couldn't bring
down the little pig that was as strong as he [was], and it dragged him
around in the mud. He's angry with Primo and Benny because they
didn't jump on the pig and hurried away when the momma pig entered
the pen.

So they went after a three-legged goat instead. Primo described how Toro,
Benny, and himself were all jumping and missing him. But they caught
him, and he became a barbeque *cabrito*. Skinny Benny had taken so much
delight in slicing and slashing up the *cabrito* that he got soaked with goat
blood.

Toro and the guys had come by the house to tell me that two Valley batos, Rolo and Voy, had gone up to El Reno penitentiary to visit Raúl. Apparently ALMA, a Chicano *pinto* organization that Raúl had helped organize, was sponsoring some sort of program at the prison. In any case, they
were on their way back from Oklahoma, and Toro asked if they could
crash at my house. "Of course," I said. They would stay with me for a couple of days.

Marx and *Mota*

I had met one of the Valley leaders previously in Dallas—Rolo, an articulate man knowledgeable about Marx, capitalism, fascism, and the like.
Getting to know him and his fellow Berets would further complicate my
views about behavior and political consciousness.

[DEC. 21–22, DEC. 26–27]

The McAllen Berets arrive at 1 A.M. and we stay up talking until five
in the morning. The guys are on their way back to South Texas, and
they bring with them a lot of news and a surprise—Raúl! What happened at El Reno was that they arrived to see the program that the Chicano *pintos* had organized. They were refused entrance in spite of several entreaties.

The guys were on the guest list, but since Rolo had his beret on, the guards
hassled him and wouldn't admit them. When the guards called the super,
Rolo began explaining what the Berets were and asking why they couldn't
enter. The super got upset and said, "Don't let these guys in."

The batos were pretty angry, having driven some 600 miles to see Raúl. They returned several times to the gate to give the guard trouble. They finally gave up and were in Dallas when they received a call from Raúl that he would be flying down to meet them. Released on an appeals bond, Raúl joined them in Dallas and drove down with the guys. Rolo surmised that the super knew that they would be releasing Raúl the following day.

Chivo and I feigned disbelief at Rolo's account and egged him on to tell us a more dramatic story. Voy chimed in to comply. They were "really sweating it" when they passed through Austin. They ran into a highway patrol roadblock, and they had ten ounces of *mota* with them.

> Voy then describes how in Dallas they were almost arrested for *mota*. They were outside a bar smoking when a cop cruised by slowly. They saw him and decided to go back inside the bar. Before they could go in, the cop had turned around, stopped them, and carded them. Voy ate the joint. Luckily they weren't in their car, because they were carrying a load to sell. "What we do to live!" says Voy.

The next few hours were spent catching up and talking movement politics. The McAllen Berets had all been students at Colegio Jacinto Treviño in the Valley, which they criticized mercilessly. They said that the school had really gone down in terms of community participation and that three individuals controlled the whole show and had sold most of the fifteen trailers they once had. They wanted to know where the money had gone and feared that they would lose the land as well. Voy also complained about "la onda comunista" (the Communist idea), that the faculty couldn't say anything without bringing in Marx. The discussion turned philosophical and centered on Marx and the national question. Marx had not recognized nationalist struggles, so the issue was whether he had any relevance for the Chicano movement.

> Raúl is really down on communism, says that that's all the teachers at the Colegio talk about, and that we're not members of the Communist Party USA but Brown Berets from Aztlán; says that Marx didn't recognize nationalist struggles but only class struggles and that we are fighting for our people. Voy is upset because those *batos del colegio* bring in Marx every which way, even in Mathematics, and he's tired of that. Rolo tones down Voy's criticism by saying that those batos are not really practicing what they preach, that as Communists they should be working with the people, and that those batos are not following Marx.

And so continued on a most sophisticated discussion with the Valley Berets. This would be my intellectual high point with the Berets.

What did Marx have to do with *mota*? Nothing, except that conversations about both were taking place simultaneously among those gathered in my living room, and one could move back and forth between conversations.

For the unemployed and underemployed, survival meant engaging the underground economy. Selling *mota* carried the least risk, but sometimes this was not possible or sufficient. Chivo made this clear. After several hours of talking and drinking with the Valley Berets, he was drunk and talking about "my soldiers" and "my officers."

> [DEC. 21–22]
> Then Chivo starts talking about his burglaries, that it is tough [*cabrón*] working like that but what does one do when one has seven kids to feed? He almost cries when he recalls the time that his boy told him he didn't have shoes to wear, and Chivo didn't have any money to give him. Chivo is getting tired of doing burglaries; he thinks that one of these days they are going to catch him. Toro later tells me that's why he left early, so that Chivo would stay to entertain the guys from McAllen, which he did, and which postponed a *bogla* [burglary], which Toro called "muy pinche [very risky]" and apparently didn't want Chivo to do. Toro says that Chivo is "puñetas" [stupid] for doing burglaries, "but one has to eat."

This juxtaposition of "political" and "criminal" behavior stopped my writing for several days. I didn't know how to deal with this. Built into the ambiguity was the practice of exaggeration, deception, feints, and outright lies. I didn't know how to deal with that either.

> Toro has made back-to-back telephone calls, one involving the assignment of community organizer to a much-neglected part of town, and the other to make contact with a possible buyer.

Chivo as a "Social Bandit"

Perhaps the most complex individual in the group was Chivo, who could both inspire and frustrate. He would have been a worthy candidate for Eric Hobsbawm's roster of charismatic outlaws who have gained popular support or what he called "social bandits." A classic version was a Robin

Hood type who stole from the rich and fought for justice. In the real world, however, such archetypes tended to become muddied.

With Chivo it was difficult to know the difference between truth, exaggeration, and outright fabrication. The scars that crisscrossed his stomach whenever he wore his shirt unbuttoned made it evident that he had experienced a serious brush with death. One evening in late October, after some drinking and smoking, Chivo revealed a bit of his past before the Chicano movement.

CHIVO'S STORY [OCT. 22]
Chivo said that the scars on his stomach were the results of some shots from a guy who owed him $50. The guy shot him in the stomach with two .38 slugs, but he killed the guy with a .22 right between the eyes. Several months later, after he got well, the brothers of the bato he killed jumped him and Toro. They stabbed Toro several times and him only once, but he ended up in worse shape than Toro. The doctors didn't patch him up well, and the result was a stomach infection that almost drove him to commit suicide.

Toro took away his gun, telling him that he would take care of any trouble and would take care of his house. Chivo said that never had he felt so much pain, even when they shot him.

I had heard versions of "Chivo's story" from his brother Toro and from Luisa, a Westside Beret. Luisa told me that the conflict was over something more serious, that Chivo had caught his first wife with the guy. In any case, as a result, Chivo said that when he went into a bar he took out his gun and put it on the counter, asking, "Who here wants to fight with me?"

Then Chivo described his current situation, telling me that "it's a bad time for painters and roofers." He was not working on any houses.

Chivo has been without a job (sin cameo) for some time. Apparently he has joined a burglary ring that his brother-in-law is part of. And he is selling carbines of various calibers. He has sold one and he called me to see if I wanted one. Although his motives are primarily economic, Chivo says "que he mandado chingos pa' [I have sent many to] Mexico for the struggle."

Java, who had also heard "Chivo's story," was skeptical. Java told me that Chivo was "muy embustero" (quite a bullshitter) and that many times he

led on ("periquea") his own soldiers. Java said that if Chivo had done all
the burglaries he talked about, he would be a rich man today.

The Chivo I admired was not the emotional and temperamental drunk
of late nights. In public, wearing his beret, Chivo had aroused many
gatherings with his oratory; he projected courage and charisma. In mid-
December a prime example of his leadership took place quietly and only
came up for discussion when Primo raised it.

[DEC. 18]
Primo criticizes Chivo for his unannounced role in a City Public Service
Board protest: "There we are watching television and then we see Chivo
leading a protest, and he didn't tell us anything about it. What if they
do something to you and we don't know where you are?" Toro supports
Chivo by saying that there are situations when each Beret has to make
spontaneous decisions: "We are all leaders. If a bato doesn't show up,
we'll find out where he is even if we have to look all over town."

Chivo explained that he had no time to call anyone. The protest march
happened "a puro nelson" (on the spur of the moment). He was on his way
downtown, listening to the radio, when he heard about a protest at City
Hall. Since he was so close, he dropped by and found "a big crowd of elderly people angry about their utility bills and they didn't know what else
to do after having protested there." Chivo saw Raza Unida activist Nacho
Pérez, and they agreed "hacemos algo" (let's do something).

They started marching toward the City Public Service Board (CPSB) a
few blocks away, with Chivo leading the way down the street. Chivo ignored the cop who wanted to stop him and just kept walking. They had
no parade permit "o nada" (or anything). Nacho kept the cop busy by arguing with him while Chivo led the crowd onto a busy street, blocking all
traffic. They marched until they reached the City Public Service Board,
about five blocks from City Hall. By that time about six or seven cops
were there, and one was pointing at Chivo. Chivo went inside the CPSB
building, where the people demanded to speak with CPSB officials. Chivo
didn't want to leave because the cops were waiting for him, and he told
some "viejitas" (old women) that "hay vienen los perros a arrestarme" (here
come the dog police to arrest me). The women formed a circle around
Chivo and kept the "perros" away by shouting and swinging their purses
at them. "Se aguitaron los perros" (the cops were surprised) and left Chivo
alone for a while. Then he slipped away from them.

"Pues, asina pasó, a puro nelson" (well, that's the way it happened, spontaneously), Chivo tells us. He didn't leave out the rest of Berets on purpose. He mentions that he was careful not to get arrested because he's on probation at present. Primo ends the discussion on a funny note, saying, "Just don't do it again."

This was the Chivo I admired. Perhaps the essence of the romantic character lay in human complexity, in the mysterious and contradictory behavior of individuals. What if the protest leader by day was a burglar by night? Or if the drug dealer could critique Marx? Was this the political edge: radical critique plus "employment" in the underground economy?

After Five Months

By December, my fifth month of hanging out, it was painfully clear that my idea about a political "conversion experience" had been shot to pieces. My notions about political consciousness and behavior had been simplistic; even the idea of religious conversion, I was beginning to realize, was a questionable one. Despite recurring exhortations about the need for discipline, these batos were not able to escape the gravity of their social world. Yet, as my ethnographic notes make clear, politicization—the acquisition of a political consciousness—did not require a wholesale transformation of personal behavior or withdrawal from an underground economy. There was no necessary contradiction in "locos" becoming and acting "political." As noted previously, the Southside Berets adjusted their loco behavior to that of highly visible political activism through the wearing of the beret. The beret functioned as a "code-switching" symbol that mediated behavior: wearing the beret demanded proper presentation; not wearing the beret excused an individual from such discipline.

[DEC. 29]
After five months of hanging out with these batos, I am ready to leave and return to the university. My observations have become repetitive. There now seems to be little I don't know about these guys. I feel more tired than disappointed. I am not sure how I will write any of this up.

At one of the last meetings I attended the main topics of discussion were the familiar themes of attendance, discipline, and uniforms.

Making a living

ANOTHER RENEWAL [DEC. 29, DEC. 30, JAN. 9, 1975]
I cruise to Wesley, but the meeting is apparently not taking place at
Wesley as I was told so I try Chivo's house and find the guys there.
Chivo's truck "Recio" is parked in front, its bed filled with "hot things"
taken from an abandoned or vacant house. Among these things are a
commode and sink, both conspicuously on top of the pile. I make a joke
that "when Chivo does a burglary, he takes everything," and all the Berets except Chivo laugh. I think I upset Chivo, who says nothing. He is
always solemn about these things. He moves away to talk to someone.

The meeting at Wesley began at 8 P.M. and lasted about an hour. Nine
Berets were present (Primo, Fat Benny, Chivo, Mosca, Toro, Terco, Loso,
George, and myself).

It's a ragtag affair, with the Berets in various degrees of uniform dress.
Skinny Benny is wearing a beret with no cross rifles; Terco and Mosca
have berets on; López has his beret in his pocket; George and Loso have
no berets; and Toro has a *chuco* [gangster] hat on.

Loso, after confessing to his failings, voiced the familiar refrain that "we need discipline" and that dressing up is the least we should expect. Discipline, again, was tied directly to dress.

Loso noted that when the Westside chapter was active, it was no big deal to go to meetings in full dress uniform, "that was the minimum," and when they went to the meetings of other organizations they looked great: they looked disciplined because they were all in full-dress uniforms. At that time "they didn't go into meetings like now, loosely dressed con pedazos de uniforme aquí y allá [with pieces of uniform here and there]." Terco responded, "But carnal, many of us aren't working. Can we buy jackets? Can we buy pants?"

This was not the best moment to inform the group that my time with them was over; but my lectureship, my first teaching appointment, was due to commence within a few weeks.

[DEC. 29]
I resign my commission and explain that I have to go back to start teaching. Chivo, who has turned away and given me his back, asks Toro if I'm quitting. Toro says, "No, he's just handing in his commission." Toro says, "Bueno, David, you can't give orders anymore." I laugh: "When did I ever give orders?" Chivo answers, "And if you gave them, nobody listened to you." We all laugh. Mosca says something like we're losing a lot of batos, and Chivo responds, "That's okay, that's the way it is, there's always a lot of movement con los Berets, old guys leave, new guys come in, and the Berets continue."

I recommended that George, now called "Jorge," take my place. I would train him to handle public relations. Jorge, the college freshman, seemed to be filling the organizing role that Java had. Chivo said that we had to get together before I left to write a proposal for $30,000. We arranged a get-together for the following day.

Seeing beyond the Mask

The next day, an urgent matter arose that made me reassess my image of Toro. I had pegged Toro as a macho with an authoritarian style forged in his gang days. Basically I had seen him as a prototypical *jefe* with fairly rigid views. Then came a surprising indication of tolerance, if not acceptance, of difference. This question arose as I was getting ready to train Jorge as my replacement as public relations officer.

ON *JOTOS* [DEC. 30]

I went for Jorge, now secretary of the Berets, to start his training, but he wasn't ready. I went to the Wesley Center, but no one was there. I then drove to Chivo's house and found Chivo, Toro, and Mosca. Mosca is glad that Jorge didn't make it because he has a secret to share—"Es joto Jorge" [Jorge is gay].

Mosca said that we shouldn't train Jorge because he was a "homosexual":

[O]ne night Jorge was drunk and while Mosca was sleeping on the sofa and Jorge on the floor, Jorge goes over to him and begins to massage his penis. I ask Mosca what he did while Jorge was stroking him. Mosca responds exasperatedly, "Well nothing, what could I do!" I consider this a strange answer.

The problem was what to do with Jorge. Toro, Chivo, Mosca, and I discussed the matter. Mosca said something like "the guy can blow it and embarrass the Berets; we can't have *jotos* in the Berets." Toro then surprised me and said that gays can be in the movement. I was momentarily taken aback. This was the Toro who had called draft-dodgers "culeros" (turntails) and was opposed to admitting women into the Berets. Toro drew on his experience and said that Mena, the manager of the Wesley Center, was ex-clergy and a *joto* but that he was for the people. Toro explained that Mena had never approached him, and although he had said some "weird things, and he looked like a *joto*, he was still a good guy." Toro seemed to be relying on appearances for his assessment of Mena, but I didn't question him. Instead I said, "Well, I don't want to train someone if you're going to kick him out of the Berets tomorrow." Toro decided to keep tabs on Jorge for a while; if it happened again Toro would have a talk with him. I suspected that Mosca was just trying to undermine Jorge's rise in the Beret chapter.

Later, as I accompanied Toro to get some brake pads for the Beret truck, he told me that Mosca didn't stop Jorge because he probably liked it. I pointed out that this also made Mosca a "homosexual," at which Toro became incredulous. His eyes widened. Toro had the old Mexican belief

that only the "female" of the pairing was homosexual. "Are you sure?" he
asked me.

As we're driving, we're conscious that Recio doesn't have any reverse
and hardly any brakes; Jorge messed up the transmission night before
last. As we drive through the freeway maze, Toro tells me that he has
ten brothers and sisters, and they are so different that one of them—a
lifer in the army—told Toro and Chivo if the Berets start some conflict
against the United States he himself would come to kill them. He and
Chivo were the "black sheep" of the family.

Now that I had announced my imminent departure, Toro, Chivo, and
others seemed to be offering me final commentaries on their lives. Toro
was talking as if being interviewed.

By sixteen Toro had learned all about guns, calibers, etc.; he saw his
first killing when he was 13 when the Dot gang killed a guy from the
Circle with a shotgun. When he graduated in 1964 from Harlendale, he
received his diploma with a handgun strapped to his waist. He has no
record, either as a juvenile or an adult, because the cops always messed
up on some technicalities.

Toro said that there are three rules among gang members: don't screw
around ("no chinges") with the woman of a companion; don't screw around
with a companion; and if they are going to screw you, screw them first.
    In spite of his machista exterior, Toro was open to modifying his ste-
reotypes based on his personal relationships and information, advice, and
experience. Basically he was open to learning and overcoming earlier prej-
udices. He felt confident about his ability to size people up.

Toro likes to drink and smoke *mota* with a guy, because he wants to
know the guy and what he thinks; he wants to know "more than the
mask the guy has on."

I too was seeing beyond the mask.
    Somewhere around Southside Woolco we ended up at a bar to have a
few beers. Toro wanted my feedback on several things. He was interested
in Colegio Jacinto Treviño and asked for my advice; we talked about how

slick Rosario was and how los batos didn't get anything from him. Toro asked me how the Berets rate in comparison with other organizations, saying that he had never had someone tell him how Berets compare and wanted an objective ("a la graba") assessment. I told him that the Berets were a unique organization in the batos they recruited and in style, and that was good, but that much more discipline and training was needed. I repeated this several times in different ways.

We finished our beers and headed back to Chivo's *cantón*. While we were driving, Toro started talking about his wives and relations with women. "Why am I such a jerk?" he asked rhetorically.

> By [the] time we get back to Chivo's house, Toro is talking about a shoot-out at El Chicano Lounge with drug-pushers. Clara, his woman at the time, was feeding him bullets; he is still proud of Clara for that. The shootout lasted several minutes, and at the end no one was hurt—"just two holes in the refrigerator and lots of bottles busted."
>
> Toro is still talking and laughing about that time as we get down from the truck. Chivo and Mosca overhear Toro, and Chivo says, "Don't tell him; he'll write it down in his book! That's why I am very careful with what I say to this guy." Toro looks at me and asks, "That's why you want to know?"

I got out of this quickly by saying, "I didn't ask you anything; you're telling me the story." Toro said "oh" and then terminated the story by saying that nobody was hurt. The book was never very far from Toro's or Chivo's consciousness. They never said things to me that they didn't want me to take note of.

> We all continue drinking beer. We're sitting outside a row of old shotgun-style houses next to a railroad yard where the trainmen are assembling a freight train. It is already dark. Chivo, dressed in greasy blue denims, is trying to start a fight with his woman so he can spend the night out. He begins to sing *rancheras*—sad ballads about betrayal and bittersweet love. His friend Manuel joins in, but his high-pitched voice makes us laugh. Every now and then a *ranchera* is punctuated by a *grito* or a boxcar slamming into another.

One of the guys listening was a "mojado" by the name of Juan. Apparently Juan had been romancing the daughter of the gringo landlord of the shotgun houses, the old man who kept telling us to move our meetings elsewhere. Toro and I gave Juan a ride to the landlord's home, where Juan hoped to see the daughter. "Depende," Juan said, if the husband's truck was there; if not, he could go in. Toro told me later, after leaving him off, that Juan had been "screwing her" for some time.

A Special Invitation

Apparently Chivo thought that I was missing some important experience, that there was more to observe. He understood my role as a writer. Or at least that was how I interpreted his unexpected visit and invitation.

A week before my departure, Chivo and his friend Mique, an erstwhile Beret, dropped by to sell me a tape player that they had just found. We discussed Skinny Benny's shooting up of his mother's *cantón* while his mother, brother Marty, Marty's family, and Primo were all inside. Skinny Benny shot two bullets into the house and almost hit someone inside. He was trying to shoot himself; but when Mique grabbed his wrist, Benny had to let go of the gun. Primo moved Benny's hand. Benny was upset because of some girlfriend. Chivo said that they would not return the gun to Benny and that they would probably kick him out of the Berets. Later I found out that Benny had been suspended until he saw a psychiatrist, apparently at Toro's suggestion.

After many minutes of such casual conversation, Chivo brought up the primary reason for the visit.

[JAN. 2]
Chivo then invites me to join them in a *jale* (job, trick). I say "no" but I feel my face flush. It's a strange sensation; I feel honored by the invitation. This was an invitation to cross the line that these batos had long ago crossed, to a social world where notions of ownership were suspended, where private property was seen as part of a "commons." This was the "best spin" I could put on burglary.

A worse interpretation was that we lived in a "mondo cane" (dog's world) and that we should take what we can. Either way, these ideas were what made the batos locos dangerous and what made the politicized element among them doubly dangerous. If an ideology could be affixed to these practices, could the bato loco become a radical agent of change? Wasn't this question at the core of my exploration?

But I had no idea, no expectation, of discovering a distinct social world, a culture sustained by a subeconomy of occasional labor, petty theft, the drug trade, gift exchanges, and bartering. Now I was being invited to cross the boundary and visit this world. This could have been a possible climax to my entire journey. I would have had a rare glimpse at the practice of burglary that set off this underworld from the conventional world. But there were no ideas or politics involved in Chivo's proposal.

Chivo was not troubled by such questions. He did not claim any political intent. His was a target of opportunity. This for him was a basic economic matter governed by calculations of risk.

I thanked Chivo for the invitation but turned it down. Chivo understood and nodded.

I figured that Chivo was trying to introduce me to all the spheres of his life before I left. Or perhaps he was trying to make me understand, after my jokes about the commode on his truck, that even an easy burglary required some courage. His invitation forced me to acknowledge something I had sensed before—that I was not sufficiently loco. I was not so radical after all. I realized in that instance that I had a deeply ingrained respect for private property. I should have recognized this earlier, given my reactions to Primo's and Skinny Benny's habit of finding lost bikes.

Chivo tells Mique that I'm a heavy (*pesado*) in my own way, that I had told them at the beginning that I wasn't a *pistolero* ("un bato de tiros"), but nonetheless I worked for the people and that they have much respect for me.

I was somewhat surprised but pleased by Chivo's sudden appraisal of me. I felt honored by his comments. Before they left, Chivo "borrowed" my prized serape.

La Despedida at Food City

I drove down South Cross Boulevard, a major thoroughfare of the Southside, looking for the batos for one last *despedida* (farewell).

[JAN. 9, 1975]

At the Food City grocery story, I unexpectedly see "Recio," Chivo's truck. Chivo, whom I haven't seen for days, is sitting in the truck cab. I sneak up from behind and jump on the truck bed and raise hell to surprise Chivo. Chivo is surprised and ready to shoot me, he tells me; we hug. Mosca, outfitted with sunglasses and beret, comes out from the store, and a small reunion and discussion takes place outside the store. Then Toro, Primo, and Skinny Benny happen to be driving by and see us. They are all wearing their berets, including Skinny Benny, which I take to mean that his suspension is over. Five Berets and I are now gathered in the store's parking lot, hugging, saying goodbye, and exchanging last minute words. It's an unusual scene at Food City. I feel like I'm on speed. Everything seems to be happening in double-time.

I reminded Toro about the possibilities of working with Raza Unida and the commitment of Barrio Betterment to push the glue-sniffing proposal that I had written for the Berets. Toro expressed his disappointment with Mena of the Wesley Center; Mena was supposed to set up a Beret presentation before Barrio Betterment but apparently screwed up and forgot to tell them the right time. Chivo wanted to know if we were going to burn down his house. Toro said, "No, but we'll go talk to him and maybe rough him up." Chivo remarked that we never should have given up the old tactics, and Toro said something like "Yeah, we might have to return to them." In a passing comment, Chivo mentioned that they caught a guy with a shipment because he was speeding. A stupid arrest, we all agreed.

The guys want to know when I'm leaving and I tell them whenever I get a ride, probably next week. Chivo wants me to take "Recio" so that I could stay longer, and he seems serious. I decline, saying that after all we only have two trucks. The last thing Toro tells me—"Si algo te pasa, nomás nos das un pitazo [if something happens to you, just give us a call] and we'll find a way to get up there."

Toro then started talking about the new year and said that Berets were really going to start moving, with training and discipline as priorities and that they were going to get a center. Toro said, somewhat dramatically, that in this new year, "If I fall asleep, awaken me; if I betray you, kill me." While Toro spoke, I could not resist imagining a surrealistic scene of a group of batos confronting my Yale dissertation committee, in the shadow of some ivy-covered tower.

A Spring Break Visit

During my spring break from teaching, I went to see the guys, who were meeting at the Wesley. Toro and Jorge were there early. From Toro I learned that Primo had done "algo gacho" (a terrible thing), taking off with Margie, Skinny Benny's sister-in-law. Toro said: "Imáginate, after Skinny Benny let him stay in the house; after all the help the family gave him." Almost all the Berets were upset by Primo's "movida" (action). The turmoil that an affair can create within a group—the reason why Toro had opposed admitting women to the Berets, the supposed cause of the breakup between the Westside and the Southside Berets—now worked its havoc among the Southsiders. Primo and Margie were in Dallas, and Skinny Benny, husband Marty, and their brothers were looking for them. Skinny Benny was the "crazy" Beret who had been suspended for his impulsive gunplay. The gravity of the situation—"they're still looking for them"—had been plainly expressed.

> [MARCH 23, APRIL 1]
> Jorge picks up the train of thought and begins gossiping about several things: Java and Chivo ran into each other at Mission County Park, and Chivo gave him a shove and Java left practically crying; Terco has returned from Ohio, where he left his woman; Mosca was out [of the Berets] for a while, getting over his woman leaving him, but his absence was more directly related to a fight he had with Manuel at a bar when both were drunk; and of course, Primo had left town.

Jorge said that there was too much resentment among the Berets. "Well, at least they haven't killed each other," I said. Jorge laughed and replied, "But they're close to it." Jorge added that the Berets had no direction at the moment: "We're just going down. I hope we hit rock bottom soon so we can't go any further down. Nothing's really happened since you've left." Jorge was fed up with the inactivity and internal conflict and was thinking of quitting soon. He had become involved in Harlendale school elections and was chairperson of a voter registration drive there. Was Jorge the bato I had been looking for?

Jorge represented the intellectual voice that was missing from the group. He was writing for *Caracol*, the literary-political journal, and had gotten two or three pieces published already. One of his stories described how Mrs. Herrera and her ten children finally had been evicted from the Cassiano Homes public housing. The police, with "sarcastic laughs and twitches of the eyes," had thrown Mrs. Herrera's furniture into the street, but the Bexar County Welfare Department had found her a house with a leaky roof. The piece ended with a plea to join the Brown Berets in fixing the roof. "Nothing has come of the project," Jorge noted. He had suggested to the guys that they help the evicted family fix up the house, get donated lumber, and work on a project together. "That would have brought the guys together as a group; but the guys don't want to work."

[APRIL 1, 8–9 P.M.]
Eight people are present for the meeting at Wesley's parking lot. For some it's the first meeting in a while. Only three are wearing berets; and Toro has a chuco hat on. Chivo drives in with Olga but leaves without getting off the car, a reminder that personal conflicts continue to make their influences felt.

As expected, attendance, discipline, and uniforms were the main topics of discussion. Loso and Jorge said that they knew several guys who were ready to join, "But why recruit them? We're not doing anything." Both Loso and Toro expressed the need to get back in touch with organizations. Toro remarked that TU-CASA had changed leadership—it had gotten rid of Rosario. This was not good news. Through Rosario, TU-CASA had been the main political ally and financial supporter of the Berets. The meeting ended on an inconclusive note, with Toro saying that he would get back with everyone for another meeting.

Before I left San Antonio, I saw Primo and Margie, whose affair had thrown the Beret group into disarray. They were visiting San Antonio, were obviously in love, and were talking about having a baby. They were being treated well in Dallas and were staying with two women Berets.

[APRIL 2, AFTERNOON]
Primo tells me that the Berets are on the move in Dallas. They're having meetings with the City Council, and a mere soldier (*soldado raso*) did great telling them off. [He says] that both groups are together and have about two meetings per week and that everyone hates Perales, who thinks he's the *jefe* of the combined Dallas chapters.

Primo said that the Berets were planning to march with the Black Panthers to protest the killing of an old man who was eating a 10-cent coffee cake without paying for it. In Primo's words, "We're marching with the Black Panthers because maybe this could happen to us as well." A few days after Primo's comment, police mishandling of a party disturbance in West Dallas generated support from the Mexican American community for the march.

The FBI and a tactical force from the Dallas Police Department were keeping a close eye on the Berets and the planned march in Dallas. The FBI report, which I would secure later, noted that Brown Beret leader Perales had "announced to the local media that if there is any violence connected with the march, it will be initiated by the PD, and they will accept no excuses from the city council in defense of the PD in the event of violence." The FBI assessment determined that the Berets would be joined by members of the Black Panther Party and the Bois D'Arc Patriots. The teletype identified the Black Panthers as a "Black extremist organization" that "has advocated the use of guns and guerrilla tactics to bring about the overthrow of the U.S. Government." The Bois D'Arc Patriots was "a small local organization" that "rejects traditional racism, which pits color against color, and was formed to protect the interest of working-class whites in an economic society controlled by money interests" (Dallas teletype, April 23, 1975). The march participants were a striking interracial networking of progressive organizations in the area.

The protest march took place on April 26 and drew 152 participants. One of the participants was Primo: Brown Beret, occasional heroin user, bicycle thief, and absconder with a married woman. I note this not to highlight the faults of individual Berets but to underscore the often forgotten point that there is no purity within social movements. A microscopic ethnography of a movement organization—or of any complex collective— can easily uncover the flaws of people. At the human level, movements are built by individuals whose ideology and behavior are less than consistent and sometimes contradictory. One finds populists who are racist, Marxists who are classist, people of color who are homophobic, and so forth. A campaign for the emancipation of X may be carried out by individuals with a distaste for Y or a weakness for Z. It is not a surprise that contradictions between political goals and personal behavior abound in the history of social movements. Add "sinful" or unethical behavior to the mix, and the complexity increases exponentially.

In short, my field experience had eaten away at the sociological notion of ideal types. Complicated people did not fit neatly into boxes. In retrospect, this seems commonsensical. Yet such ethnographic nuances were absent in the dominant sociological discussion of lower-class people. The ideal typifications of Lewis Yablonsky, Edward Banfield, and so forth recognized little variation and no constructive agency among this population; lower-class men were basically parasitic, apathetic, hostile, and dangerous. This work did not admit the possibility of flawed humanity, a notion that acknowledged problems but allowed for breaks, ruptures, contestations, and even transformation.

FROM THE ISLAND KINGDOMS

 AFTER SEVEN MONTHS of hanging out, coupled with intensive interviews, I felt I had developed an accurate snapshot of the complex and uneven political development of the Brown Berets throughout Texas. In the case of the Southside Berets, one might wonder whether a much longer stay would have yielded more nuanced observations and conclusions or at least have given the chapter more time to find its footing. The question was moot. This reconstituted chapter of raw recruits was in decline in 1975, as was the general Chicano movement.

The inactivity and listless direction of the Southside Berets reflected the general condition of many movement organizations in the mid-seventies. The movement network was breaking down. The farmworker campaign in Texas had split into two factions. The TU-CASA national network had splintered. Serious divisions had surfaced within the Raza Unida Party, the electoral arm of the Chicano movement. In 1976 the party would suffer a fatal setback when its two-time gubernatorial candidate, Ramsey Muñiz, was arrested for transporting marijuana. This did not bode well for my dissertation, which was already burdened with ethical questions, methodological "two steps," and theoretical doubts.

A good part of the problem should already be apparent from my journal notes. Even after conceding the flaws and disguising their identities, I still found it difficult to write about individuals who had befriended me. And I had been naïve to think that I could critique political organizations in motion. I faced the common dilemma of ethnographers—how to critique or describe those who have welcomed you into personal and communal space. I was reminded of Clifford Geertz's point that a certain "moral tension" or "ethical ambiguity" is an inevitable mark of ethnography.

Greatly compounding the writing difficulty was the matter of evident police and FBI interest in the Brown Berets. They were as interested as I was in knowing more about the political orientation and background of these batos locos. Although my perspective and intentions were radically different from theirs, nonetheless this overlap in interest created many awkward moments for me. Even though I had been "cleared" to write about the Berets because of my movement connections, my presence continually raised questions about what I was doing, what I was writing and for whom. To say that I was writing a dissertation did not allay any suspicions. In fact, I myself began to wonder for whom I was writing. One of the most despised "tags" in barrio youth culture is the *relaje*, the stoolie or snitch who gives insider information to authorities or more generally to outsiders. In what sense is the ethnographer not a *relaje*?

Although these were critical ethical and political questions, I faced the equally daunting problem of not having an appropriate descriptive frame for the batos locos. I saw myself as an interpreter lacking the vocabulary to translate the reality I had experienced. I faced a conceptual impasse. I knew what I wanted to say: despite the abject circumstances of their lives, and despite the imperfections of their thinking and behavior, these crazy guys had nonetheless risen above parochial boundaries and begun to fashion a political philosophy. "Damaged" as they might appear to outsiders, they retained the capacity to identify injustices and to organize accordingly. Indeed, in light of the sociological literature about the underclass, their attempt to reach for a broader understanding, and to act upon that understanding, was impressive. Basically I had witnessed a group of lower-class men trying to right the wrongs of the world as they knew it. Yet when they stepped out into the public arena, their actions were lauded as courageous and idealistic or damned as threatening and foolish. My story line about the Southside Berets pointed to the difficulties of transcending the limits of a lower-class barrio world. I needed a metaphor that could carry such an argument.

This chapter describes my search, conducted in spurts over many years, for this metaphor. Ironically, the spatial boundaries of the places where I studied and wrote—in New Haven, the Grove Street divider between Yale and the African American ghetto; in Santa Fe, the adobe walls of the faux hacienda of School of American Research; at Stanford, the lofty

The Island Kingdoms

perch of the Center for Advanced Studies in the Behavioral Sciences in the Palo Alto foothills—all seemed to remind me that no other subject seemed so laden with ethical and political minefields as an ethnography on the underclass. Although these were places of reflection at some remove from everyday society, the matter of race-ethnic difference kept intruding itself at every turn, making me a self-conscious translator and interpreter. That self-consciousness may perhaps best explain why I turned to literature to find a bridging metaphor for my narrative explanation.

In retrospect, it is easy to follow the path that led me to Cervantes's classic tale of Don Quixote. The frame was initially inspired by my experience with the Berets: they were bold, visionary soldiers venturing into strange territory; and I, as their secretary observer, felt like Sancho Panza. Over time, as the project evolved and other figures and organizations became prominent actors, the reference to Quixote expanded beyond the Berets to encompass the entire Chicano movement and even its antagonists.

As a disclaimer, I should note that I am not a Cervantes scholar, and what I knew of Don Quixote and the tension between "dreaming" and "reality" I had learned in high school and college. As a graduate student, I thought of Quixote as a literary version of the tension between agency and structure, one of the fundamental oppositions in social science. The dialectical play between agency and structure was a basic principle of social change: structure (reality) shaped agency (social action), agency shaped structure, and so on. The figure of Quixote introduced the elements of perception, aspirations, and imagination into this dialectic, as a critical component of agency. Thinking of Quixote made me approach the opposition between agency and structure from the perspective of the agent or actor. But the idea of invoking a literary metaphor for a sociology dissertation never entered my mind in graduate school. Even later, when I returned to the ethnography during my privileged sabbaticals, I was not convinced of its appropriateness.

What settled the question was my second encounter, metaphorically speaking, with Professor Lowenthal, some twenty years after our hallway bump. With Quixote in mind, I was able to answer his earlier inquiry about the Berets with an explanation that I believe he would have appreciated.

Not Writing a Dissertation: New Haven, 1975–1976

I had been with the Berets a couple of months before it dawned on me that I might have serious problems in writing about this ethnographic experience. The political problems had become clear: how could I critique a movement organization that was concerned about its public image? I had observed much confidential or private misbehavior, so ethical questions also arose. Once I returned from the "field" and attempted to explain what I had witnessed, the difficulties became unavoidable. How was I going to portray these "crazy guys"? How could I deal with the negative side of men who had befriended me and convey the complexity of what I had witnessed to a committee of Yale University professors?

In large part, the problem I faced stemmed from the fact that I was straddling very different worlds. I could not avoid the stark contrast in

status between my "research subjects" and the promised academic certif-
icate, and this awareness raised fundamental questions about what I was
doing. Of course, I had been conscious of class and race difference from
the moment I stepped on campus. In the early seventies, Yale was an elite
university situated next to a restive black ghetto in an economically depressed city. The Grove Street divide between campus and the African
American community was a constant reminder of stark difference. The
contrast was all the more accentuated because Yale was still as much a
finishing school for undergraduate white men as it was a great intellectual
center. Undergraduate women had only been admitted two years earlier
(in 1968), around the time the campus dress code had been relaxed. Even
at the graduate-school level, "proper manners" were subject to scrutiny
and evaluation. This represented a challenge for a naïve twenty-something
from the Westside of San Antonio. The academic part I was able to manage. But in the area of social graces, sherry tastings, polite intellectual
banter, and the like I did not fare too well. Tweed coat, bow tie, and pipe
tobacco were alien to me and would remain so. A cultural chasm separated this academic world from the social worlds I knew in Texas. Now
that I had to begin writing on lower-class Chicano males, I could no longer ignore the gulf.

This conflicted sense was accentuated by the ethnographic gaze I had
consciously turned on for seven months. I began to see that being at Yale
graduate school was just as much an ethnographic experience as hanging
out with the batos locos of San Antonio. I was in a strange position. Being
familiar with the sociological literature, I was aware of the adverse reactions that my descriptions could stir up, in spite of my empathy with the
group. Moreover, given the sparse literature on Mexican Americans at the
time, my portrayal ran the real risk of becoming generalized to all Mexican American males. Although I was an interpreter and defender of the
Berets and its world, I was a curious defender, ambivalent but also hopeful that my analysis might somehow help advance some of the political
goals of the Chicano movement.

Complicating matters were my mounting doubts about sociological perspective and methods. The country had experienced one of the most tu-
multuous decades in its history, marked by antiwar protests, civil rights
movements, ghetto riots, and a conservative white backlash. But sociology
seemed to lack the tools and vision to address such significant events. The
discipline remained committed to the idea of a "social physics," that is, to
being a science of hypothesis testing and measurement of human behav-

ior, with the aim of rendering such behavior as predictable as the dance of atoms. My dissertation prospectus, in fact, had listed eight such hypotheses. Sometime during my field experience, I had concluded that the notion of a social physics was absurd.

In sum, having rejected both the theory and method expected in a sociology dissertation, my prospects for molding the Beret material into acceptable form looked very bleak. The dissertation about the Berets would not be the romantic portrayal that the guys wanted; nor would it be the academic treatise of hypothesis testing expected by my dissertation committee. I finally ceased writing when it became apparent that I would have to address the reigning framework of deviance and social pathology. My dissertation would have had a defensive tone from the start; it would never have risen above the din about "macho culture."

My predicament was made worse by that fact that I was reaching these conclusions while holding down an *acting* assistant professorship at the University of California at Berkeley, with the expectation of a finished dissertation in the short term. The UC Berkeley time clock was ticking away toward a dissertation completion deadline. Professor Lowenthal had warned me to finish if I wanted to stay. Setting aside the Beret ethnography and starting a different project meant that I would not finish in time.

I decided to set the Beret material aside. From a career standpoint, it looked like a foolish decision, for it signaled the beginning of an odyssey through several universities. Yet intellectually and politically the decision was the correct one. A basic history of Anglo-Mexican relations had to precede any examination of such a specialized group as the Brown Berets. Such a topic became my dissertation, which in time evolved into *Anglos and Mexicans in the Making of Texas.*

A Literary Turn: Santa Fe, 1987–1988

Many years passed before I returned to the ethnography. I had serious doubts about the material I had gathered, but I had not given up. My first sustained effort to resuscitate the project came when I was privileged to receive a residential fellowship at the School of American Research (SAR) in Santa Fe, New Mexico. What better place to write ethnography than at an anthropological institute in Santa Fe?

The School of American Research was the former hacienda of eccentric sisters Elizabeth and Martha Root White, daughters of *Chicago Tribune* publisher Horace White and benefactors of the arts and anthropology. Their eight-acre estate, named "El Delirio" after a bar in Madrid, Spain, was an inspirational place for five residential scholars to do their stuff, a writer's dream.

Outside the adobe walls of SAR was a society with a complex history of ethnic relations. Santa Fe was the first permanent Spanish settlement (founded 1598) in what is now the United States, and its residents prided themselves on this history. The adobe structures, old missions, multistory Pueblo dwellings, and kivas exuded history. The quaintness of Santa Fe had been carefully preserved, a policy influenced in large part by the artists, writers, anthropologists, and wealthy easterners who had settled in New Mexico. By the 1980s Santa Fe was a world-renowned contemporary arts and anthropological center. Preservation of ethnic architecture and tradition was the unquestioned philosophy, and ethnic tourism and arts were the driving force of the local economy. The annual Indian and Hispanic Market fairs drew thousands of visitors from across the country and the world. New Mexico advertised itself as the "land of enchantment" and as a place of "tri-ethnic harmony."

Underneath such romantic spin, some signs of tri-ethnic tension or dissonance would occasionally surface. I recall the muted but bitter tone of the Hispano gardeners at SAR as they pointed to the nearby hills and named the old families who had once lived there. Over time many native Hispano residents had been displaced by wealthy but *simpático* Anglos who appreciated the ethnic culture and lifestyle. Preservation and celebration of tradition had ironically been accompanied by displacement of the original families. Likewise, the monument to the Franciscan martyrs and the annual Santa Fe fiestas, which commemorated the Pueblo uprising of 1680 and the "reconquest" twelve years later (in 1692) by Don Diego de Vargas, suggested an earlier displacement and colonization.

Nearly three hundred years after Don Diego's entrada into Santa Fe, I witnessed its annual reenactment. Into the plaza rode a mounted conquistador, adorned with armor and steel helmet, though softened with a colorful plume, solemnly leading a dutiful procession of friars, "native chiefs," and various "native princesses." I was stunned. I had never seen a conquistador or a reenactment of Spanish conquest before. Unlike the local residents who were accustomed to such imagery, for an outsider like myself the procession brought to mind the harsh reality of colonization.

Somehow my reaction to these celebrations of tradition and authenticity led me to think of the Cervantes tale, which I had read as a seventeenth-century parody of warrior culture. Don Quixote struck me as the anticonquistador, whose erratic actions were both heroic and foolish and thus shrouded in ambiguity. As a description of my complex feelings about the entrada and about the colonial history that Santa Fe represented, the image of Quixote seemed to fit. And the image also seemed to capture the complex feelings I had about the batos as barrio soldiers. But it took another discovery—no less surprising than witnessing the commemoration of a conquistador entrada—to link Quixote with the batos locos.

LINGUISTIC AND METAPHORICAL CONNECTIONS

The elaboration of a Spanish legacy influenced much art, music, and literature in New Mexico and also became an intellectual current among some scholars who studied the Spanish-speaking culture of the Southwest. Yet I was surprised to find an extensive discussion in the relevant social science literature that harkened to seventeenth-century Spain. A circle of linguists and anthropologists was engaged in an intriguing discussion about whether the Caló (argot) of contemporary pachucos or batos locos of the Southwest was related, as Adolfo Ortega put it, to the Gypsy Caló of "the Spanish Golden Age."

According to this reasoning, constant persecution had caused many Gypsies to migrate to the Spanish colonies of the New World, thus implanting Caló in Mexico. Once it came in contact with the United States border (most dated this to the 1920s) it began to mix with English, and a new variety, "Pachuco," was born. Anthropologist George Barker had traced the origins of *pachuquismo* to the *grifos* (marijuana smokers) and peddlers from El Paso, who were influenced by the Caló of the Mexican underworld. When marijuana was made illegal in the 1930s, the need for a secret form of communication was reinforced. This underground language, unintelligible to speakers of standard Spanish or English, became part of the gang and prison culture and spread in the 1940s and 1950s to working-class urban youth. During the Chicano movement of the late 1960s, Caló experienced a resurgence. Indeed, "Chicano" was originally a pachuco word, often used derogatorily to refer to a low-class individual.

Whether Caló was a reflection of youth alienation from both Mexican and Anglo American cultures or a creative fusion of both remains a matter of debate. But the suggestion of a legacy dating back several centuries struck me as somewhat fanciful. Perhaps it seemed far-fetched only because historical accounts of lower-class social life are rare or not given much attention. Could a genealogy of this sublanguage point to a history

La Entrada del Conquistador

for the Spanish-speaking fraction of the world's lower classes? Could it suggest an underworld culture of *longue durée* passed down from one generation to the next?

These attempts to trace linguistic inheritance seemed concerned mainly with form and not content. But it was not necessary, as linguist Rogelio Reyes noted, to establish a tight lexical or historical connection between the Caló of the bato loco and the Caló of the *gitano* (Gypsy). Both argots shared the same infamy of being seen as "a secret language peculiar to a group of thieves, tramps or vagabonds." Both varieties were spoken by marginal communities, which was perhaps sufficient sociological ground upon which to draw suggestive parallels. This is where matters rested back in the late eighties.

Is it a coincidence, then, that I began to play with the notion of Don

Quixote as an interpretive metaphor while living in Santa Fe? I began to experiment. I outlined the argument in my journal:

[DECEMBER 1987]
Why couldn't the Berets be seen as a collective Quixote? If they used distinct language; dressed up in a uniform (berets, sunglasses, army jacket); emphasized their threatening appearance; emphasized their role as defenders of the community yet alienated almost everyone including their potential allies; believed they were the vanguard of the movement; were awkward in dealing with any situation other than through the politics of confrontation and intimidation; yet were continually in search of injustices in order to right them—then the allusion seemed promising. The confrontation between illusion and reality made Quixote an ideal allegorical metaphor for my interpretation of the social world of the "crazy guys."

Of course, if the Berets were Quixote, then I was Sancho Panza. Framed in this way, my role as participant-observer was cast in a different and revealing light. Sancho Panza, we may recall, was the peasant squire who accompanied Don Quixote (though with misgivings) because of the promise of a governorship of an island kingdom. After a while, the naïve Panza realizes that the promise is a hollow one but in the meantime has become attached to the old man who wishes to be remembered as a knight in shining armor, though the armor consists of rusted tin and cardboard.

Panza's experience resonated with mine as a participant-observer trying to understand the reasoning, tactics, and behavior of the batos locos. My notes explained the parallels:

In Cervantes's tale, Panza represented the world of reality, the counterpoint to Quixote's madness. Panza gets confused when observing that others act as if Quixote's fantasies were in fact real. How many times did I, as the Panza of political realism, shake my head at Beret analyses of situations, and yet bite my tongue because they and others in their world saw their assessment as correct?

The hypervigilance of Berets regarding security at meetings, for example, often seemed to be disproportionate to the nature of the meeting. Posting security at times seemed to be more of a dramatic performance meant to impress young members and observers than a necessary measure.

I had written about one instance when Austin's mayor Roy Butler, along with the city manager and the assistant police chief, had accepted an invitation from the Berets to discuss the police brutality issue at their Centro Chicano.

[MAY 7, 1974]
The meeting took place outside beneath an enormous oak tree, with the mayor, city manager, and assistant police chief sitting behind a card table draped with a Mexican flag. The setting had all the historical symbolism of a treaty meeting. Three armed Beret guards were posted on the rooftop of the Centro as lookouts for possible police interference. While the meeting progressed, they chatted via walkie-talkies with security on the ground. Given the nature of the meeting, the security measures appeared excessive. Yet over the course of the afternoon meeting, several police cars passed by the scene just to let everyone know of their presence. The rank and file police, upset that the mayor and chief were meeting with the Berets, had played their dramatic part perfectly.

The reaction of authorities and movement organizations to Beret activities often confirmed or reinforced the Beret interpretation of events.

QUIXOTE AS A CROSSOVER SUCCESS

Being at an anthropological institute undoubtedly influenced my thinking as well. Fortunately for my interests, during this time the discipline of anthropology was undergoing serious introspection and confessing to its literary conventions. This postmodernist critique essentially argued that all ethnography was "fiction" in the sense that it was a "literary construction." Social scientists, the argument went, employed a number of rhetorical devices in order to compose an authoritative text—establishing authority through "I was there" statements, jargonistic embellishment, the claim to represent the native point of view, and so forth. I was not concerned with advancing this postmodernist critique, but the critique did open up the possibilities of deliberately using literary images if they served the purpose of explanation. What better way of circumventing the books of sociology than by invoking a literary metaphor to carry the argument? Referencing the classic tale of Don Quixote and Sancho Panza was a way to avoid, if not challenge, the dominant sociological narrative of deviance.

Here was a literary metaphor that could humanize the lower classes and emphasize their multidimensional character as they negotiated a life of poverty.

When I presented my ideas about the Quixote metaphor to my SAR colleagues—"admittedly an experiment," I said—this literary turn received encouragement. I had expected that my invocation of literature as a frame for my ethnographic observations would be the main point of discussion, but my fellow anthropologists saw nothing unconventional about this. Instead the discussion revolved around why I had chosen "a Hispanic metaphor."

I was surprised by the question. Of course, I replied, the tale of Don Quixote de la Mancha had a long and revered place in Hispanic culture and letters—but no longer was Quixote limited to Hispanics. I wanted to say that it was like the city of Santa Fe, but I held back. Quixote, I said, was a universal tale and certainly American. Quixote had crossed the linguistic divide and had been adopted by English speakers. Although the genealogy of Quixote was clearly Hispanic, its acceptance and appreciation by non-Hispanics had made Quixote a "crossover" success. In fact, I noted, it may have been the first Hispanic crossover in American popular culture.

Later I did the research to back up my assertions. By the 1960s Don Quixote had become part of America's literary and cultural canon. The Broadway musical *Man of La Mancha* drew rave reviews in 1965 and won a Tony award for Robert Goulet in 1968. The musical's signature song, "The Impossible Dream," which emphasized the notion of striving and fighting in spite of impossible odds, had become Quixote's song. The Americanization of Quixote was completed when Elvis Presley included "The Impossible Dream" in his regular Vegas performances in the early 1970s (recorded live in January 1971). Hollywood finally stamped its imprimatur with a screen version, featuring European acting stars Peter O'Toole and Sophia Loren, in 1972. The popularization of Cervantes's tale, however edited and interpreted, had nonetheless introduced the figure of the heroic fool or idealistic adventurer to the English-reading audiences of the country.

In sum, my sabbatical at a faux hacienda in Santa Fe, where Spanish influence was celebrated and enshrined in museums and pageantry, inspired my experimenting with the idea of Quixote as a thematic underpinning for my interpretation of the Berets. Then I shelved the project. With too much work to be done on the ethnography, I put it aside. I would not return to it until my next postdoctoral leave six years later.

Finding Meaning in Protest and Literature: Stanford, 1993–1994

Nestled in an idyllic California setting in the foothills above Stanford University, the Center for Advanced Study in the Behavioral Sciences (CASBS) is a bucolic retreat for scholars. In 1993–1994 this was the privileged setting for thirty resident scholars, an interdisciplinary lot that included philosophers, psychologists, political scientists, sociologists, historians, even linguists and musicologists. Other than the fact that we were all working on manuscripts and other writing projects, the group had no overall theme. Shared lunches, rotating seminar presentations, and volleyball matches were the glue that held us together. One objective of my fellowship year was to revive my long-delayed Beret project.

This tranquil setting stood in contrast to what was happening below on the Stanford campus and in the surrounding communities. Proposition 187, an anti-immigration referendum on the state ballot, had made immigration a contentious public matter. I recall driving down El Camino Real and witnessing the Mountain View Citizens' Council hectoring the Mexican day laborers gathered on a street corner. The "citizens" carried signs that said "Don't Make This a Third World City" and "Go Back to Mexico." I was reminded of the White Citizens' Councils in the South of the sixties and seventies.

The resident fellows were expected to give a presentation on their work during their time on the hill. I debated whether to present my Beret material for my CASBS lecture. Again I felt that few could understand the world of batos locos and was even more unsure about the Quixote metaphor. This was not an audience of anthropologists. I expected skepticism, and I myself was not completely convinced about taking a literary turn. Rather than complicating social reality, was I distorting it by linking it with possibly facile and overworked literary imagery? Ben Olguín, at that time a graduate student of comparative literature, thought so. Olguín was finishing a dissertation on Chicano prison art and literature, so in a sense we were writing about the same social stratum. We faced similar questions about representation and interpretation and had many conversations about these questions.

I had explained that I wanted to get away completely from the images of pathology that dominated sociological discourse. What interested me was the ambiguity, the interplay between dreams and reality, that the Quixote figure represented. Olguín was sympathetic but nonetheless did not like this particular literary turn. "It's too European," he said. "Why are you catering to the *gabachos* [whites]?" Later (October 1994) Olguín called and left a long message on my recording machine:

> Hey bato, this is Ben. It's about 10:45 P.M. on Wednesday. I was calling because I remembered I had read a book called *A Taste of Power: A Black Woman's Story* by Elaine Brown, who was Panther chief after Newton. I just snapped that basically it is, in a sense, what you may be trying to do, or it may give you ideas about how to approach the Berets, from within, again as a participant-observer, in a mode that's different from Elaine Brown's, but still very much within it.

Olguín said that without mentioning any literary traditions Brown had framed her story as "a romantic idea, a romantic movement, with romantically inspired individuals, who are still very much into the *locura*, who are very much tragic heroes as well."

> So again without invoking some problematic legacy, such as *el quixote*, which is about Spaniards, or about the tragic hero, which is also a problematic genre or character in literature, she still draws upon it and presents a really good candid vision, a female perspective, even dealing with the attacks on women, on the use of sex to subordinate women. All that crazy contradictory shit is still dealt with in a positive way. So anyway, check it out. I'll talk to you later, man. Bye.

Olguín argued that "truth" is often impure and adulterated and we should be prepared to deal with that reality.

I had no problem with the notion of complex and contradictory human behavior in everyday life and especially in social movements. The problem I faced was how to communicate this complex and contradictory truth about lower-class men to others—and especially to *gabachos*. Yes, I told Olguín, I wanted to use this European character to speak about the pachuco, so that nonpachucos could understand. I was conscious that I was trying to communicate across class-ethnic lines. The crossover metaphor of Quixote seemed to offer a bridge that could link our various social worlds.

Yet when my time came to present before the CASBS fellows, I switched topics. I teamed up with fellow resident scholar Patricia Williams, who had also been somewhat reluctant to discuss her work. Both of us worked in that sensitive intellectual space known as "race relations," and we expected that a frank discussion might generate some discomfort. Williams spoke on contemporary media constructions of African Americans, and I lectured on the future of Anglo-Mexican relations in the United States, based on what was happening then in California with Proposition 187. The response was cool and defensive.

The climax came when a behavioral psychologist began talking about how lizards, with a cortex and nervous system similar to that of humans, segregated themselves by color. Was the comment a facetious one? "Have we have not progressed beyond the lizard stage?" I asked rhetorically. This was the only time that tension, so evident in the surrounding cities, had wafted through this foothill retreat. The experience later moved me to compose a bit of sarcastic poetry:

LIZARDS, LAGARTIJAS [SUMMER 1994]
Images, memories of recent past,
happy hour conversation strikes chords,
raises questions: why is animal imagery used to discuss
race & gender: monkeys, gorillas, cows, bulls, dogs, felines,
stallions, mares, bucks, deer,
rabbits, mice—the reverse of anthro
po morphizing?
I remember too that
color preference pervades the lizard world
and since we have a similar
nervous system & genetic disposition,
well, you get the drift.
But of the animal images I can think of,
the one I like best: cockroaches.
Especially the flying kind.
Some speak of us as mosquitos
pestering the mighty lion to nagging misery
or the flea, tiny & seemingly powerless but nonetheless
the plague of the land.
I prefer the cockroach. But I could get used to the lizard.
I like lizards. Desert creatures, fast like speedy Gonzalez or the wily
    coyote. I like coyotes too.

A HUNGER STRIKE AT STANFORD?

Unlike the experience of my retreat in the Palo Alto hills, the tension on the Stanford campus below was palpable. Much like the drama of the conquistador entrada in Santa Fe years earlier, another drama would make me clarify my thinking about quixotic activism.

The "farm" was not immune to the immigration controversy being waged visibly along the Camino Real. On campus, differences over this question had morphed into questions about affirmative action, ethnic studies centers, the "American Cultures" breadth requirement, and the like. A vocal conservative student group openly supported the anti-immigrant Proposition 187, accused the Chicano organization MECHA (El Movimiento Estudiantil Chicano de Aztlán) of being racist, and generally maintained an aggressive antiethnic campaign on campus.

The tension was kindled into a smoldering flame on April Fool's Day when the deanship of Cecilia Burciaga, an outspoken critic of the Stanford president Gerhard Casper and provost Condoleezza Rice, was eliminated as the result of a "budget reduction." Burciaga's termination, after twenty years of service, also meant that she and her husband, artist-writer José Antonio Burciaga, could no longer serve as residence hall masters of the theme house Casa Zapata. Through this house the Burciagas had been the primary organizers of Chicano student events on campus for nearly two decades. José Antonio Burciaga's artistic imprint was part of Casa Zapata, most notably with the iconic mural *Last Chicano Supper* that adorned the dining room. Basically the Burciagas were symbols of the Chicano presence at Stanford.

The dismissal met with immediate protests from a cross section of faculty, staff, and students. No one believed or accepted the budget rationale. Meetings of the Chicano faculty, students, and Provost Rice "did little to resolve the crisis of confidence," reported the campus newspapers. The Chicano Graduate Student Association called Burciaga's layoff "an act of disrespect to her and the entire Stanford community."

Against this tense background, a blowup took place in Memorial Auditorium over the showing of a ten-minute United Farm Workers *No Grapes* documentary (about pesticide spraying) before a regularly scheduled Sunday feature film. Some impatient students shouted "Fast forward!" and "Yea, pesticides!" and "Beaners, go home!" The Chicana sponsors of the documentary were shocked by the jeering. This incident triggered the unexpected decision by MECHA to wage a hunger strike; it was, according to a spokesperson, "the last resort after a string of insults and attacks against them."

On Wednesday (May 4), a few days after the jeering incident, four Chicana students began a hunger strike on the campus Quad, vowing to not eat until the university agreed to their demands: the establishment of a community center in East Palo Alto, a university boycott of grapes, the establishment of Chicano Studies, and the rehiring of Cecilia Burciaga in some capacity. About fifty protesters, many dressed in black shirts and red armbands, picketed in the Quad for much of the day. They pitched two tents and hung signs reading "Stanford stands 4 ignorance," and "¡No uvas! Boycott grapes."

President Casper and Provost Rice met with the hunger strikers and supporters at the Quad for nearly an hour and had a "testy" exchange. Casper and Rice stated that the demands had caught them by surprise. Rice said: "You may dislike what I've done . . . but the fact is, I'm provost, and if you don't work with me, we aren't going to get anything done." President Casper said the students were "holding a gun to my head" and that "if you believe that will solve problems at Stanford and make us work together as a community, you are mistaken." He claimed that the strikers put him in a bad position by demanding immediate answers to questions that would take a long time to settle.

On the second day of the hunger strike, May 5, more than 250 students rallied in the inner Quad to show support. News of a hunger strike at staid Stanford had galvanized various student groups, parents, alumni, and public opinion and cast an unwelcome spotlight on campus affairs. As the standoff entered a third day, pressure mounted on both the student activists and the administration to reach a settlement. MECHA negotiators met with faculty intermediaries, while Casper and Rice met to discuss wording in a proposed agreement. Civil engineering professor Jim Leckie, one of the intermediaries, said that the administration "and particularly Rice" took a hard-line stance: "Condi is one tough nut. You would have thought she was negotiating with the Russians and not with students. She clearly received her management training in the Pentagon."

The three-day hunger strike ended late Friday (May 6) after university administrators agreed to consider adding a Chicano Studies program and to form committees to address the demands regarding the grape boycott and an East Palo Alto youth center. Although the protesters were not successful in getting Cecilia Burciaga rehired, they did force Provost

¡Huelga!

Rice to publicly recognize her contributions to Stanford and the distress caused by her layoff. For the students, this had been a matter of showing respect.

The following morning (Saturday), both sides held a joint press conference to announce the agreement, but the public session did not go smoothly. As the *Stanford Daily* described the scene:

> While a dreary rain fell, University President Gerhard Casper and Provost Condoleezza Rice squirmed uncomfortably in their seats as the crowd of onlookers chanted "Uvas, no! Chicano Studies, sí!" with increasing fervor. Then, in a scene that recalled a similar meeting between Israel and the Palestine Liberation Organization . . . Casper

refused to sign the written agreement. For a moment, an ugly confrontation seemed imminent.

Casper at first refused to sign the agreement, saying that "trust had to
be the basis [for the agreement] rather than signatures," but he relented
and decided to sign. Provost Rice, who had "been opposed to any sort of
symbolic signing," went along with the president's decision and signed the
agreement as well.

On such tentative grounds did the angry protests and hunger strike end.
A hard-fought negotiation yielded no clear winner. This inconclusive ending prompted much campus discussion about whether the hunger strike
had been a "gimmick," a "gun to the head," or an "alternative tactic to the
armed man" for producing change. I thought I had witnessed a prime example of quixotic political behavior. The hunger strike moved me to coin
a term—"quixotic agency"—to refer to dramatic political action motivated
by a righteous belief in a cause or vision and taken with little concern for
tactical success. The strike also made me expand the idea of "Quixote's soldiers" beyond batos locos to refer to movement activists generally. Quixotic
agency seemed to be an integral part of large-scale social movements.

The Stanford protest seemed like a late aftershock of the Chicano movement: all the student demands—a grape boycott, Chicano Studies, community outreach, and hiring of faculty and staff—seemed to have been
taken from a twenty-year-old script. Certainly the intensity of emotion
and disruption of everyday routine for four days was reminiscent of the
heady days of the late sixties and early seventies. But whether an aftershock or a harbinger of something new, the hunger strike made me realize—or reminded me—that quixotic behavior was not limited to any particular segment of the community.

A SECOND ENCOUNTER WITH PROFESSOR LOWENTHAL

What finally sealed my choice of Quixote was my chance discovery that
Leo Lowenthal, the distinguished scholar who had stopped me in the hallway so many years before when the Beret material had been a working
dissertation, had also been a Fellow at CASBS in 1955. He had used that
year to complete his classic work on literature and society, *Literature and
the Image of Man*. The book was shelved along with others in the CASBS
library. Discovering Lowenthal's book was an unexpected coincidence.

Even more unexpected was finding that one of Lowenthal's key chapters was devoted to the work of Cervantes!

Lowenthal had died long before, and my memory of him only evoked a sense of smug authority. In fact, after many "hallway encounters" at different universities over the years, Lowenthal in my mind had dissolved into a general sentiment of the race-class divide I kept experiencing; he had become a metaphor of sorts. But on reading his chapter on Cervantes, I was stunned to find a description and interpretation that I could use to communicate my ideas about the Berets.

According to Lowenthal, the Cervantes critique of the status quo was "cloaked in images of artistic irony." His work described "the society of the poor as the only place where genuine human feelings still exist, because there people remain uncorrupted by interests in worldly goods." Cervantes even allowed himself the extended joke, in the tale of *Rinconete and Cortadillo*, "of picturing a society of robbers and thieves as exemplars of true human solidarity." All the marginal creatures—the beggars, the crooks, the Gypsies, the insane—had been forcibly cast out from society; but while they were accused "they themselves in turn are accusers. Their very existence denounces a world they never made and which wants no part of them."

Lowenthal had grasped the irony of the social world of the bato loco. He described what the batos of the Southside would call "carnalismo":

> Paradoxically enough, the robber, whom we would expect to place a high valuation on possession, displays only indifference to worldly goods. Money as such has no meaning for him; the principles which govern his life are honor among thieves and responsibility to his fellows. The highest moral law he recognizes is that of solidarity. The society of the robbers calls itself a "brotherhood"; the society of the gypsies obeys the "law of friendship."

Moreover, these "grotesque Utopian prototypes" not only served to indict the social order:

> they also positively demonstrate the idea of man. They all serve to show the possibilities of Utopia, where everyone has the freedom to be his own deviant case—with the result that the very phenomenon of deviation disappears.

Meeting Professor Lowenthal again

Inside the book image:

LITERATURE
AND THE IMAGE OF MAN
Sociological Studies of the European
Drama and Novel, 1600–1900

By Leo Lowenthal

The Beacon Press   Beacon Hill   Boston

Lowenthal understood, then! Any goatherd could become a Don Quixote and pursue justice: "Man, any man, contains a creative potential, although his condition, his social role, may not allow him to realize it." Through his reading of Cervantes, Lowenthal had expressed the essence of my interpretation of the world of these batos locos.

The appeal of employing Quixote as a bridging metaphor was now rather apparent. As a universal story about the disjunction between idealism and reality, it provided a platform for communication across several worlds of experience set off by race, language, class, and gender. Invoking Quixote seemed to be a fitting way of conveying my message about the Berets and the Chicano movement to my colleagues and to a general reading audience. The metaphor was sufficiently complex and imbued with mixed and debatable meanings. A reference to Quixote raised the question of whether the Berets were heroic or foolish, a much more interesting and intelligent discussion than one about whether they were pathological or irrational. The metaphor also seemed to be an apt description of much movement activism and related aftershocks, such as the Stanford hunger strike.

So, after many years and after some experimentation inspired by local environments, I finally settled on Quixote as the master metaphor for my interpretation of the Chicano movement. Such resolution did not result in a rush to complete the manuscript. I had other competing projects that demanded attention. But now I felt I had a workable and interesting conceptual framework for my movement project.

Quixote, an Unoriginal Metaphor

To say that the Quixote frame was "too European," then, was not an effective critique, because the crossover appeal rested on such affinity. A more telling critique of the frame might have been that it was somewhat trite, at least judging from Chicano movement documents. The image of Quixote had been used during the Chicano movement in both positive and negative ways, to represent courage and idealism, on the one hand, and foolishness and materialism, on the other. As George Mariscal has noted, the newspaper of the United Farm Workers, *El Malcriado*, had adopted Don Quixote as its official logo to invoke both idealism and militancy.

A few years after my stay at CASBS, a literary work appeared that reminded me that my use of Quixote to describe the Chicano movement was not very original. Professor Genaro González published a novel about the Mexican American Youth Organization (MAYO) and the Chicano radicals of the late sixties, which he titled *The Quixote Cult* (1998). The author was a movement activist and the novel a thinly veiled autobiography.

Through the eyes of the protagonist (De la O), we experience or learn of the Del Rio protest march, the "Kill the Gringos" press conference in San Antonio, a statewide conference at a seminary where the statue of the Virgin Mary was painted bronze, and the demise of MAYO as it transformed itself into a political party—all key events in the Chicano movement. De la O runs into gunrunners, dope runners, heroin addicts, and undercover agents: "Just last month we discovered that a guy provoking us to jump on cars at the Del Rio rally was ATF: Alcohol, Tobacco, and Firearms." But the batos on drugs turn out to be just as threatening as the overzealous undercover cops, as De la O realizes:

> We're not that different from black militants who treat pimps and pushers like they're a guerrilla vanguard. But the closer you get to these guys

the less they look like revolutionaries. Sometimes people have a hard time telling the difference between heroes and assholes.

In a similar vein, a cynical De la O pokes fun at movement iconography: "Che Guevera . . . is our ultimate Rorschach. We see in him whatever we want to. Roque draws his eyes somewhat slanted; he could pass for Zapata's cousin. He also tans him up like a lifelong migrant."

González clearly intended his novel to be a critique of the movement. As he explained to William Childers, using Quixote as the antihero allowed him to "take the leaders of the movement off their pedestals, viewing events from a more human perspective and including the negative side of their activities." The "Quixote cult" is not heroic but idiotic, ridiculous, and out of touch.

Yet because the author called his work fiction, we must treat it as such. González collapsed characters and events and perhaps created situations as transitions or explanations. In a work of fiction, truth and imagination may interweave inextricably and unapologetically. González never claimed to be writing history. The novel was fiction, apparently because the experience of the movement was still too fresh, too young, to be critiqued directly. I understood why it was fiction. I also understood the cynicism.

The intrigue and appeal of literature often comes from the unexplained or barely explained, from the omissions, implications, and ambiguities in the narrative. This is one major difference between literature and the social sciences. Just as social science must ground its argument in ascertainable facts, it must be clear about its argument. The historical or social science narrative does not have the luxury of being intentionally opaque.

As strange and alien as my description of the social world of the bato loco may appear, it has not been made up or invented. This journal hews closely to the interviews and field notes that recorded my observations, thoughts, and feelings at the time. My narrative contains no composite characters. I had no need to invent human complexity and ambiguity. What I have redacted are the countless hours of just hanging out, talking, drinking, smoking: the mundane minutes and hours that make for solidarity and friendship.

The Southside Berets were an unusual band of rebels: soldiers with no cars, jobs, phones, money, or discipline but armed with plenty of spirit, commitment, and dreams. To call them "quixotic" would be misleading if it obscured the difficult and serious side of living in a poor barrio. Living a lower-class life was not what made them quixotic. It was their attempt to move beyond the circumscribed limits of their underclass environment that made them quixotic. I thought of Quixote because these guys sometimes fought illusory enemies, because ambiguity was so much a part of their world, and because the militancy they symbolized became irrelevant with the decline of movement activities. As irrelevant political actors, the Southside chapter dissolved in the late seventies, its members returning for the most part to the invisible social world of lower-class life.

AND THE POLITICAL EDGE?

10   I RETURN, FINALLY, to the questions that moved me to undertake this ethnography in the first place. After my long, fitful search for an appropriate metaphor, the material has aged and thus become harmless. The passage of time has taken care of the ethical and political dilemmas that paralyzed me in the mid-seventies. In retrospect, letting the material become dated may have been the only resolution I had.

In this concluding chapter I provide a summary of some key observations and conclusions. I want to be clear about what I learned from my exploration. I explain the rise and fall of the Southside Berets, while noting the different levels of political development among the statewide Beret network. Cultural nationalism was the unifying oppositional ideology of the network and the beginning point of political consciousness for many recruits. One might argue that the appeal of cultural nationalism may have been the illusive key that I had been searching for. I include some observations made in 1983 by the FBI and by myself—unconnected accounts from very different perspectives, naturally—that may help clarify, but not settle, this question.

A Long-Delayed Assessment

What motivated these young barrio men to create and maintain a militant political organization? As noted, I found that there was no mysterious or unique key to the politicization of the Berets. The mystery had been created by a social science literature that said that the underclass, males in particular, was supposed to be apathetic, violent, impulsive, and apolitical. Yet in the late sixties and early seventies Brown Beret chapters composed of young men and women, often gang youth, spontaneously emerged throughout the urban Southwest and Midwest as part of a broad-based Chicano movement. They were part of a youth movement "from below" that was based on an awakening cultural nationalism and ethnic pride.

Given the segregated context in which Mexican American youth lived, it was understandable that opposition to that segregation could be mobilized through ethnic nationalistic appeals. A desire to do something for "la raza" was the beginning point of political consciousness for many Beret recruits. Beyond that desire, some were drawn by the uniform and status it conferred; others were attracted by the camaraderie of the group; and still others joined only because a relative or close friend had invited them. In fact, most of the recruits were drawn from kin and friendship networks. Regardless of their individual reasons for joining, the recruits shared a basic understanding, even if vaguely expressed, that the Berets were for the people. This was the kernel for further political development, as evidenced by the sophisticated veteran leadership of the Austin and Valley chapters.

The Brown Berets with their paramilitary organization and fashion were an organic expression of the street youths, the noncollege youths, who became "turned on" to the Chicano movement. Like the college activists, these street youths learned about politics through discussion, sharing information, participating in political events, and so on. Unlike the college activists, most had been gang members or were familiar with the gang culture of the barrio. Now these batos locos were preaching carnalismo, la raza unida, and la causa to barrio youth and working to calm barrio warfare. Ethnic-racial identity as Chicanos and Chicanas became more important than neighborhood identities.

For their organization and mission, the Berets borrowed from the armed forces to create paramilitary units whose purpose as *soldados de la raza* was to address the problems of their neighborhoods and advance the Chicano movement. The focus on community protection and police brutality was a natural step. The important point was that the barrio youths had organized themselves. They created rules, rituals, and a token-economy of promotions and began to join other organizations in protest activity. These

¿Pos? Well?

young barrio men and women left their private barrio worlds and ventured onto a public arena.

THE METEORIC RISE AND FALL OF THE SOUTHSIDE

One might easily argue that the reconstituted San Antonio Berets never really escaped the gravity of their lower-class environment. Formed in August 1974 from the remnants of the original Westside chapter, this second-generation chapter was clearly fraying by the following spring (April 1975). Nonetheless, in that time I was able to observe how raw recruits learned to become Berets, that is, to become visible, public actors.

From my observations of the San Antonio chapter, I discerned two steps that were learned simultaneously. The first was mastering the rituals expected of members—the special handshake, maximal wearing of the beret, and spreading the word about carnalismo. The second step was learning that the Berets were an organization as opposed to a clique or social club. This signified learning and following rules of conduct and interacting with the network of movement organizations, or what I have called the "organizational field." This network included such politically diverse organizations as LULAC and TU-CASA. Interaction with the statewide network of Beret chapters, in particular, was key in shaping the knowledge and perspective of this emergent Beret chapter. A third step might have been the pedagogical one of developing political literacy and voice, as evidenced by the older chapters. The recruits of San Antonio never reached that point.

Basically these lower-class men adapted their street lifestyle and habits to accommodate their emergence into the public arena of politics. In public the group expected conventional behavior and disciplined members through reclaiming berets and at times through suspension or expulsion. In private the group acted as a support group by containing individual acts of *locura* and by providing moral and economic assistance. Many members negotiated *locura* and *política* through behavioral code switching: they were on good behavior when wearing the beret but free to become "loco" when not. Wearing or not wearing the beret mediated their conduct.

The local activist network had been significant in reinforcing commitment to the movement, educating and providing information, giving material support, and—of special import for the Berets—providing opportunities for group and individual performances. In a seven-month period the

Southside Berets had been part of an immigration conference and a protest before the Mexican Consulate and had participated in at least three marches. These events, with one exception, were the result of a collaboration with TU-CASA, an immigrant rights organization with national and international connections. Once TU-CASA began experiencing serious internal problems, the Berets lost an important ally that had provided political space and opportunities for Beret performances and education.

This collapse of the organizational field had two effects on the Berets. On the one hand, the increasing isolation of the Berets led to erratic and hasty actions on their part. One memorable occasion, for example, was their action to prevent the eviction of a family of twelve from a public housing project. This generated considerable front-page publicity, which quickly turned negative once it became clear that the Mexican American residents of the housing project had petitioned that the family be evicted because of drug dealing, troublemaking, and so on. Nonetheless, their dramatic blockade of the eviction ensured that the family received the social service attention it needed.

On the other hand, with fewer public appearances, the Berets increasingly had less need for discipline, leading to considerable violation of the rules. With no material support, the default economic activity for some was a return to drug dealing and petty theft. They saw no contradictions between "being political" and "being loco." As might be expected, in a situation where they could code switch (and with a decreasing call for their services), a great deal of ambiguity could attend any political action: was it taken because of perspective and commitment or because of some non-political personal reason? This ambiguity was a structural element of this barrio world.

ON THE DIVERSITY OF THE BROWN BERETS

One of the strengths of ethnography is its focus on a group or community in the "real world," that is, in an unrehearsed or unstaged environment. This is usually also one of its limits, because the ethnographer may have no comparative cases on which to anchor generalizations. How is it possible to know if the dynamics of the group or community under observation are like those of other groups or communities that appear similar? How generalizable are the ethnographer's observations? This is the problem of the "single case" study. Thus the ethnographer must seek comparative opportunities and learn to take advantage of those that may unexpectedly come along.

Fortunately, along with the recruits of the reconstituted San Antonio Berets, I was introduced to the statewide network, which gave me the opportunity to study the contrasts in political development among various Beret chapters. My observations and interviews with the leaders of these chapters introduced me to the diversity of the Berets throughout the state while confirming my assessment of the chapter I was hanging out with.

If the San Antonio chapter was the rawest in the state, the other chapters, with their headquarters and newspapers, illustrated the developmental possibilities. In the mid-seventies the Austin chapter, with its bungalow headquarters and *Echo* newspaper, set the pace for Chicano activism in East Austin and was a leader in the coalition to stop police brutality. The Waco chapter, although a small group and relatively new, was publishing *El Coraje*. The original (North) Dallas chapter had dwindled down to a few members but still published *La Onda Chicana*. The Valley Berets, having been dispersed by police actions, were locked in a battle for control of an alternative Chicano college, Colegio Jacinto Treviño, where they were students. Another student from the college led the Hondo Beret chapter, which published the community newspaper *Los Barrios*. The new West Dallas/Ledbetter chapter had no newspaper, but it operated a community center complete with boxing ring. The San Antonio chapter had lost its garage headquarters, as noted, and my attempts at political education had failed.

In terms of political philosophy, the Beret network had no coherent ideology beyond cultural nationalism, a frame that pitted Chicano against *gabacho*. The idea of Aztlán, a liberated homeland for Chicanos or Mexican Americans, was a goal shared by all. Yet some chapter leaders wanted to study Marx, while other leaders expressed a reflexive distaste for communism. Seeming contradictions existed even within a chapter. Within the Southside Berets, I heard an odd mixture of revolutionary slogans and devotion to Che Guevara and denunciations of communism and Vietnam War draft resisters. As one bato put it at a meeting, "Communism is another gabacho system." Yet at the same time the Southside chapter was working with TU-CASA, a Marxist-Leninist organization. Any ideological contradictions were papered over by an assertion of heroic masculinity and cultural nationalism.

Heroic masculinity, however, did not make for smooth relations with women. The experience of the Southside Berets had made that patently evident. Machismo was a general problem in all the chapters, even in those that had admitted women. Many years later, Ana, the leader of the Chicana Berets, would recall that she had many good memories from her time

	Organization	
	+	−
+ Ideological Development	Austin Berets (a, b)	Dallas (Northside) Berets (b) Waco Berets (b) Valley Berets (c) Hondo Berets (b)
−	Ledbetter (West Dallas) Berets (a)	San Antonio (Southside) Berets

a: headquarters; b: newspaper; c: college students.

Diversity of the Brown Beret network in Texas, circa 1975

with the Austin Berets but that "sexism hurt." Although the women did much of the work, "the guys took credit." At local protests, there was no problem with being inclusive. The women would be given time to speak. "But at the big events, the women were pushed to the side. With thousands marching, egos got into play." If the family was to be the model for the Chicano movement, then "it couldn't be just men speaking." It wasn't a matter of credit, Ana added: "We didn't care who got credit, but the Berets were not just a militant male group." The gender issues were never resolved.

A simple typology illustrates the diversity of the Brown Beret chapters in Texas in the mid-seventies. One axis indicates the degree of organization, basically a division between chapters that had a physical headquarters and those that did not. The other axis points to ideological development, with a plus mark for those chapters that engaged in regular political discussion and a minus for those that had no structured sessions. Perhaps not surprisingly, the more developed chapters (with the exception of the Valley chapter) also published community newspapers. The resulting typology, based on the material facts of having a headquarters and publishing a newspaper, corresponds well with my observations of the various chapters.

What should be emphasized is the potential for change within each chapter. Some individuals in both the Ledbetter and San Antonio chapters, for instance, were calling for political education classes and more discipline. The collaboration with TU-CASA—pointing again to the importance of the organizational network—might also have led to more political development had TU-CASA not changed leadership in 1975 and folded shortly thereafter.

Although I left the field in 1975, I maintained a watch on the Berets for many years after. While the Southside chapter dwindled to a handful of active members by the late seventies, newspaper coverage suggests vigorous Beret activity in Austin and Dallas. These chapters continued to be involved in anti–police brutality campaigns. In addition, the Austin chapter waged a bitter but successful community campaign to stop the annual boat races on Town Lake. The two Dallas chapters kept raising community issues at city council and school board meetings and in 1979 led nearly two thousand angry marchers through the streets of Dallas in protest against a Ku Klux Klan march. By this time, according to an interview with Dallas Beret leader Perales, they had "put aside the rifles and revolutionary rhetoric" that had characterized the Berets of the sixties. They still had as their objective "the liberation of Aztlán" (the Southwest), but now they would wage "a nonviolent struggle" against oppression by advising groups on the proper way to conduct legal and peaceful demonstrations and assisting individuals with police brutality and harassment complaints. The Berets had toned down their militancy. Gone were the days when Toro could raise his *cuete* at a conference and remind those gathered "que no se les olvide" (don't forget the guns).

Brown Berets or Brown Shirts?

As pointed out earlier, the segregated environment of Texas made Chicano cultural nationalism a natural mobilizing point for political consciousness and agency. But, as George Mariscal notes in his excellent analysis of the Chicano movement, nationalism based on such platforms could produce separatist, chauvinist impulses or could lead in a broad internationalist direction. Mariscal, who recalled witnessing a fascist youth march in Madrid, understands the extreme sentiments that nationalism can arouse as well as the various forms it can take. If there are different kinds of nationalism, as Mariscal states, what kind were the Berets practicing?

This question dovetails with a lingering fear in the scholarly literature that the "authoritarian" nature of the lower class predisposes it to fascist or cult movements or to any charismatic leader who promises salvation, regardless of political ideology. Although I have likened the Berets to quixotic soldiers, for some observers the Berets conjured up images of fascist paramilitary groups such as the Brown Shirts of Germany and the Black Shirts of Italy. The revolutionary nationalist rhetoric, along with the paramilitary dress and posture, ensured that the Beret chapters would be seen as a militant and threatening organization. The FBI reported that the Berets "appear to be a pro-Castro group" because their uniforms were "an exact duplicate of the military uniforms of Castro's Army." The similarities to the Brown Shirts and Black Shirts or to "Castro's Army" are superficial at best, limited perhaps to matters of military dress, for the political contexts and movements to which the groups were attached are simply not comparable. Yet the charge of authoritarianism or fascism merits a response.

An incident I witnessed in 1983 forced me to confront this question. The Beret project, although on hold, was still on my mind. I had an unexpected "comparative opportunity" to observe batos locos who entered the political arena in the service of personal interests, shorn of any apparent ideology or political philosophy. I was reminded of the political "thuggism" feared by many. It was this incident that made me appreciate the importance of Chicano nationalism—with its mantra of "la causa, carnalismo, la raza unida, la familia," and so forth—in terms of creating a collective orientation.

In 1982–1983 I was doing political consulting work for associates of the Southwest Voter Registration Education Project. In the spring of 1983 I was called to assist in the reelection of city councilwoman Alicia Chacón in El Paso. Chacón, former school board trustee and longtime public servant, had been forced into an unexpected runoff by the flamboyant private investigator Jay J. Armes. In this overwhelmingly Mexican American district, I witnessed the authoritarian behavior of batos locos that many scholars associate with cult movements. This election contest provided a sobering check on any tendency to romanticize batos locos.

Armes, whose surprising support had forced Chacón into a runoff, was already a legend in El Paso and throughout the world of private investigators. His hands were hooks, the result of a childhood accident with dynamite. Billed as the "world's most famous private investigator," Armes provided security services for governments, royalty, and entertainers. His international fame had come from rescuing Marlon Brando's son Christian when ex-wife Anna Kashfi took him to Mexico in 1972. Armes had played the role of the "rooftop sniper" in an episode of *Hawaii Five-O*. And in 1976 his fame was guaranteed when Ideal Toys made a Jay J. Armes bionic action figure, which included interchangeable gadget hands and a "super hook." In the South Valley area of El Paso, Armes was known for his flashy lifestyle and eccentricities. He lived with a pet tiger and cheetah in his walled compound, drove a late seventies Shark Corvette, and sported exotic weapons. He was an ultra-conservative Republican, but this was a moot issue in a nonpartisan election.

The Armes strategy was to rely on his fame and band of faithful followers. Philosophical or policy differences were not at the center of the election. He had no need to flex his ideology. Instead the small company of batos who saw themselves as his loyal soldiers flexed muscle. I was a poll watcher at one critical polling place when I saw them arrive.

> They arrived in a small bus. About ten–twelve batos, sporting sunglasses and headbands, got off. Then they lined up on both sides of the sidewalks leading to the polling place and began wolfing at women and taunting the men. After many minutes of such campaigning, one bato laid down on one sidewalk so that voters were forced to walk around him. I was stunned by what I was seeing. There were no police around.

The scene was surreal and become even more so. Lack of discipline doomed these intimidation tactics. An apparently drunk low-rider, cruising in support of the batos campaigning on the sidewalk, had circled the block several times.

> Then he crashed his car in front of the polling place. In a 20-mph zone, with obvious traffic around, he had rear ended another car. When he opened the car door, several beer cans spilled out. Now the police came, and their appearance put a damper on the tactics of the bato campaigners.

Alicia Chacón won this critical polling precinct and prevailed in the runoff. Later she heard that Armes had become furious at the behavior of the batos.

These campaigners with the sunglasses and headbands forced me to clarify the political nature of the Southside Berets, the least developed of the Beret network. The Armes supporters and these Berets were drawn from the same sociological material; at times they exhibited the same kind of antisocial aggressive behavior and could be embarrassed by the same lack of discipline. Whether the Southside Berets were a gang under a different name had been a topic of discussion within the local Chicano movement network. But what set them apart was their conscious attempt, as noted earlier, to create a disciplined organization in service of la raza. Armes soldiers were not committed to any notion of a collective raza.

If the San Antonio Berets were the least politically developed when compared to other Beret chapters in the state, their rudimentary organization and ideology was still of consequence. Commitment to "la causa" oriented the Berets toward public rather than private or individual goals. Moreover, because they saw themselves as bound to follow the basic tenets of carnalismo and la raza unida, cultural nationalism also signified a change from gang-based behavior and thought. Although at times little more than a reflexive sentiment of resistance, cultural nationalism oriented them toward collective goals rather than personalistic ones.

On Cultural Nationalism from Below

Brown Berets or Brown Shirts? At about the same time when "Armes's army" was intimidating Mexican American voters, the Brown Berets were participating in and sometimes leading counterdemonstrations against the Ku Klux Klan throughout the state. In 1983 the Klan had scheduled marches in several Texas cities. The Berets were working with black activists and Anglo progressives to counter the KKK presence. Documentation of this activism comes not just from community newspapers but also from FBI records that provide a good overview of Beret activities of this time. The FBI, as I found out much later, was also thinking of the Berets in 1983. Of course, it was asking different questions from a very different perspective.

George Mariscal has pointed out that Chicano nationalism was not a homogeneous or simple ideology but ranged from a narrow separatist tendency to one with broad, internationalist influences. If the Texas Berets are judged by the allies they kept, then clearly these chapters tended toward the internationalist side.

From February 16 to May 16, 1983, the FBI initiated a ninety-day "limited domestic security investigation" because of Brown Beret communication and involvement with the John Brown Anti-Klan Committee (JBAKC) of Chicago, which was already under a "full domestic security investigation." The JBAKC had alerted Beret chapters throughout Texas about planned Ku Klux Klan activities in their respective cities. On February 19, 1983, three days after the initiation of the FBI security investigation, eight hundred protesters led by JBAKC, the Berets, and a Black Citizens Task Force, along with pro-Palestine and pro–Central American groups, counterprotested the Klan march in Austin. The Klan parade had an estimated fifty-five to sixty KKK members and a spectator audience of approximately two thousand. "There were 8 to 10 arrests, mostly for crossing barricades." Several members of the Berets were arrested, including Beret leader Polo, who was injured during his arrest (San Antonio teletype to director, February 16, 1983).

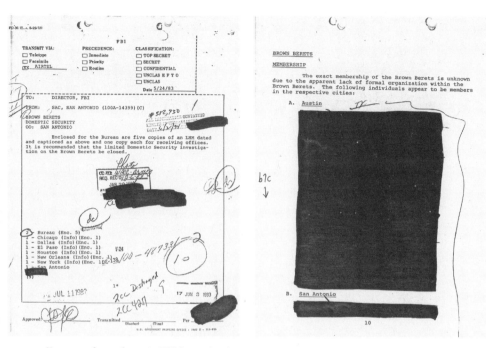

Excerpts from the 1983 FBI investigation

The Berets were also present at the other Klan rallies held that year in Houston (April 1983), San Antonio (May 1983), and Dallas (July 1983). According to the report:

At least one member from San Antonio was observed in Austin on February 19, 1983. At least two members from Austin were observed in Houston on April 2, 1983, and several members from Austin were observed in San Antonio on May 1, 1983.

The FBI observer could recognize individual Berets from different towns and knew the members from Austin and San Antonio by name. These names were blacked out in the report; but judging from the size of the blacked-out areas Austin appeared to have between nine and eleven members, whereas San Antonio had only two or three known members in 1983.

According to the 1983 investigation, although the "initial goal" of the Brown Berets had been "total nationalism of Mexican Americans in the United States and the establishment of a separate territory," their philosophy and current goals were unclear:

There is no indication that they produce any written literature regarding their goals, philosophy, or purpose. They support local causes which give them a public forum, most often these dealing with the alleged violation of the rights of Mexican Americans or police brutality.

A suggestion of the decline of Beret activity and energy comes from the report's conclusion that "the Brown Berets appear to be small localized groups lacking defined goals or purpose and lacking strong, coordinated leadership." The report recommended closing the investigation, "subject to being re-opened at a later date if additional information is developed." The Berets were no longer considered a terrorist threat.

The KKK campaign and associated anti-KKK protests of 1983 reminded me that it is necessary to distinguish between cultural nationalism "from above" and "from below" to indicate the structural location of the mobilized groups. Chicano nationalism was cultural nationalism from below in the sense that it represented a challenge to "Anglo supremacy" and basically called for the redress of inequities, whereas the nationalism of the KKK, a cultural nationalism from above, called for the maintenance and reinforcement of white supremacy.

The element of class, in other words, must be introduced to sort through the various kinds of nationalism that inform social movements. The relevance may be this: a social movement from below pressing for equality and justice is subject to various recognition claims from its constituent elements regarding other inequalities—claims based on gender, ethnic-racial, subclass, and religious differences, for example—whereas a movement from above pressing for order, morality, or a return to foundational values is less subject to such recognition claims and, in fact, might tend to suppress claims based on difference. Since my history and ethnography have explored only one side of this argument, I can only offer this as a working hypothesis.

In the case of the Chicano movement, the internal logic of its ideology and the political realities facing a movement from below influenced it to take a more open direction. As I have discussed elsewhere, this movement for ethnic-racial equality awakened other desires for equality, as Chicana feminists began to challenge machismo and patriarchy. Like the question of identity, the demands for respect and equity, couched in the ideas of la raza unida, carnalismo, and la familia, were amenable to reinterpretation. Even the *machista* Southside Berets were under constant pressure from other Beret chapters to admit women into their ranks. In the case of the Austin and Dallas chapters, cultural nationalism had been only one step in political development. It made possible additional steps, some of which led to coalition-building with other racial-ethnic groups from below, as documented by the "limited domestic security investigation" of the FBI in 1983.

The anti-KKK protests may have been the last hurrah for the Berets in Texas. Although individual Berets continued to appear at protests, by the mid-eighties most organized Beret activity had ceased. What happened to the batos? A few veterans told me frankly that many dropped out when "drugs and guns" started getting big with some batos. As I have noted, in this lower-class barrio world, individual members could drift back and forth between underground economic activity and political activity without any sense of contradiction. I have emphasized the importance of the local activist network in encouraging the "political" side of this divide. With the shrinking of this activist network and the decline of protest tactics, the Berets became increasingly irrelevant as a standing group, and many batos simply went back to the anonymity of their barrio world.

MANY YEARS LATER

11   I NATURALLY WANTED TO KNOW what happened to the Berets, as a group and as individuals. I returned to this book project in earnest in 2007 and began reconnecting with several ex-Beret leaders. My interviews with them confirmed various features of my assessment thirty years earlier, including my evaluation of the Austin Berets as the most politically developed and the Southside as the least. The life trajectories followed by some ex-Berets did not surprise me. Reality provides the limits as well the inspiration for romantic frames.

Austin Beret leader Polo became an influential, if controversial, political voice for the East Side. One feature magazine story from the 1980s described him as a "revolutionary in a pin-striped suit" and "a champion of the barrio who knows how to get under the skin of the Anglo establishment." Polo's distractors call him "a publicity-hungry agitator, an extortionist, a terrorist." Polo rose to become an aide to county commissioner Marcos De León, who himself had been a Beret.

Equally influential was Ana, the leader of the Chicana Berets, who has built an environmentalist organization called People Organized in Defense of Earth and Her Resources (PODER). PODER had its political baptism when it launched a campaign to force a gasoline storage facility to relocate from its East Austin site. Since then PODER has grown into a powerful neighborhood organization. It represents an interesting "second generation" movement organization that has merged concerns for racial justice with environmentalism.

Other accounts point to success stories. Zeke, the manager of Centro Chicano, became a professor of education and a dean at a southern California university. Roberto continues to work in social services in Waco while publishing a community newspaper on the side. Perales, the charismatic, Che look-alike Beret leader, has become an evangelical minister in Dallas.

In San Antonio I was able to draw much finer distinctions and balance the success stories with stories of losses. Among the original Westside Berets, I found a housing agency inspector, a high school teacher, a successful artist, a settlement house worker, and so forth. But I could personally count seven Berets who "got lost" on drugs for a while. One Chicana Beret overdosed.

Among those who were lost for a few years was José Morales, former field marshal and spokesman for the Westside Berets. When I saw him in 2008, he was a street minister, preaching the gospel to other batos. He was sixty-five and had been clean for thirty years. "From hooked to hope" was the way Morales put it. He had kicked his heroin habit while in the Berets; but after leaving the group he got back into the habit, along with two other ex-Berets. "Me torcieron, pasé tiempo en el corre [They arrested me, I spent time in corrections], and then I was back out in the streets doing heavy shit." José almost killed a bato and almost got killed. "At that point I found Christ. He was my salvation." He got a job as a nurse with the Veterans Administration and became a minister. His religious conviction has been his salvation from drugs and crime.

The epiphany and religious conversion of Morales brought to mind my original thesis about a political conversion experience. For a few of the thirty Berets I had interviewed in 1974–1975, the near-death experience— an unexpected heart attack, being wounded in Vietnam, or having a gun pointed at his head—had been the existential crisis that led to personal and political transformation. But for others, such near-death moments had created no such crisis. Again, a more common path to political consciousness and literacy was the less dramatic "drift," to use David Matza's term, of individuals following kin and friendship networks.

Morales's experience introduces a realism that steps in to check, if not undermine, romanticism. Heroin addiction is not romantic. Trafficking in drugs is not romantic. Spending years in the penitentiary is not romantic.

Once the Berets ceased functioning, that was the trajectory followed not just by Morales but also by Toro, the Southside leader.

The Deep Fall and Rebound of the Southside

With regard to the Southside Berets, the main subject of these journal notes, the future of the group looked uncertain the last time I saw them in 1975. The 1983 FBI report suggested that two or three San Antonio Berets were still active then. A visit with Toro thirty years after my field experience filled in the gaps and confirmed some of my worst fears about the group.

> [MARCH 31, 2008]
> I am in San Antonio specifically to find out what happened to the Southside chapter. The South San area remains depressed. One sees working class neighborhoods of single family homes, many adorned with burglar bars, with the occasional strip mall of "mom & pop" businesses and evangelical storefronts. Catholic churches and schools are still a dominant presence. Razor wire around driveways and parking lots is not an unusual feature. Elaborate graffiti, restaurant signs, and billboard exhortations from Jesus compete for attention.

I met Toro, the old *jefe* of the Southside Berets, at Dos Carmelitas on Southcross Boulevard, a neighborhood restaurant not far from where the batos used to congregate.

Toro, of course, had aged, but the most significant and visible difference from the last time I saw him was the scar tissue that covered his right eye socket. The right side of his face was paralyzed. It was the first thing he clarified. He lost the eye, he told me, in a shootout over drugs.

> Toro takes my hand, takes my finger and presses it against the socket of his right eye. I feel a hard knot. "This is where the bullet hit. The bone made the bullet go down. It came out through the back of my neck instead of the back of my head."

Toro related the story of what happened in a matter-of-fact tone. In the mid-eighties Toro and his brother Chivo were no longer active Berets. They began selling soft and hard drugs but never got hooked themselves. By 1990 they had a thriving business. Soon they became embroiled in a struggle for control of the drug trade. "We had three stores going all day and all night. This guy wanted to take over the territory." Some shootouts occurred, and the last one nearly cost Toro his life.

> The guy called him while he was at the hospital—"Cabrón, you're still alive. I'm coming over to finish the job." "Vente, vente, puto" [Come on, come on, whore], Toro replied, but the guy never showed.

Toro's voice took on a sharp edge as he expressed some bitterness at what happened next. On leaving the hospital, Toro looked for his assailant but heard that the bato had left the state. After a year of waiting, he heard that the guy had been sighted in town and started making plans to exact his revenge. Then he read about the guy's murder in the newspaper! Toro said that he was so upset that someone else had killed the guy that he contemplated going after his murderer. "Can you imagine that!?" he asked rhetorically, amused that he once felt that way.

Toro was busted shortly afterward, in 1992, in a drug raid. He was sentenced to ten years. Those were "a tough ten years" that he wanted to forget. He did not want to talk about them. Shortly after his release in 2001, his brother Chivo died from a heart attack, caused by the long-term complications of a motorcycle accident that had left him in a wheelchair. Chivo's health was never the same after the accident. Toro noted, with a crooked grin on his face, that Chivo was never busted for anything, even though he was the "baddest" of them all. We both nodded and smiled in agreement.

I asked Toro about the other Berets. We recalled that Java, Concha, and Primo had left the group just as I was ending my time with the batos. Java's brother Abe and Abe's friend López had followed next. Jorge disappeared. The three brothers—Terco, Mosca, and Giant—went their separate ways. "Loso se cantonió y quién sabe que pasó con los dos Bennies" (Loso settled down and who knows what happened with the two Bennies), added Toro. All of them left one by one until the only active Berets in the late seventies were Toro, his brother Chivo, and Tino. They would go to the protests, but they were becoming more involved with the drug underworld. Tino was never able to kick his heroin habit, and "it cost him his life," Toro said. I mistakenly thought Toro was referring to an overdose.

Toro had sent Tino to Pearsall to organize a Beret chapter, but he ended up ripping them off for money. The Pearsall guys came to San Antonio to even things up with Tino, but Toro and Chivo defended him. "Ahí perdimos un chapter en Pearsall" (there we lost a chapter in Pearsall), said Toro. Then the same thing happened later with some batos from Houston. Tino ripped them off (a gold watch and other effects) to support his heroin habit.

> They [the Houston guys] called Toro and told him that they were going to make Tino pay for being a *ratero* [thief]. Toro alerted Tino to watch out, that they were after him. Toro offered his *cuete*, but Tino said he was armed and fine. Six months later, however, the Houston guys offed Tino while he was sitting on his front porch. Toro later found out that Tino had pawned his *cuete*. "Fíjate [Imagine]," Toro tells me, shaking his head, "he pawned his handgun for his chiva [heroin]."

It was a tragic end for Tino, Luisa told me later. Tino had been the intellectual "nerd" of the Berets. He was a Vietnam veteran and had been a great field worker for a local mental health agency, "but he sunk deeper and deeper into his drug habit."

I had criticized sociology because of its tendency to freeze or reduce lower-class males into "ideal types" of pathology. I had turned to literature to humanize them and to emphasize their potentiality. Now, however, as in the Cervantes tale, reality upset the dream, and the promise did not come forth. Was I still hoping for some sort of political epiphany? I had to stop thinking in religious terms. The idea that someone could drift back and forth between addiction or criminality and movement politics had to sink in. I had to remind myself that this was not contradictory.

As if to confirm this very point, Toro began to tell me about the new Brown Beret chapter he had recently organized. I was still digesting the stories about Tino's drug-related death and about Toro's stint in prison when Toro told me that the San Antonio Berets had started up again. This was unexpected news. The hand of agency must be irrepressible, I thought. It must be.

A New Generation of Berets

Now in his sixties, Toro is an advisor to the newly formed Brown Berets. Six years after his release from prison, he started the Berets again, because "we are still treated like a second-class people." He had both local and general concerns. He recalled going to a neighborhood meeting where the president of the neighborhood organization threatened to have the police expel an elderly woman who was sharply challenging the district's

A Beret family,
César Chávez
Day, 2008

councilman. The woman had lived all her life in the barrio, Toro said, and this incident upset him. Then he read about the Minutemen announcing that they would begin patrolling the border in search of illegal immigrants. He felt that it was time to regroup.

Together with a few family friends who had "similar views and passion," Toro organized a new chapter of twenty members. The new Brown Berets are very different from the group that I hung out with thirty years ago. These Berets are an aggregation of extended families, with wives and children as members, rather than a pseudo-gang of males. Three generations belong to the new Berets, with the oldest being sixty-seven and the youngest eleven. With wives as partners, the gender question appears to have been resolved; and with the family as the core unit of the organization, the image of hoodlumism seems to have dissipated. They are explicitly clear that, unlike the Berets of the seventies, they no longer carry weapons. In fact, the motto of this resurrected chapter is "Our only and foremost weapon is knowledge."

The Berets still wear berets with the red patches of carnalismo, with an image of two brown hands clasped in front of the United Farm Workers eagle. The language of their first press release (2008), with phrases about "giving voice to the oppressed," retains the militant tone of before. Toro said the group's goals remain the same: "to serve the people in every way possible, to observe the conditions in our barrios and organize for appropriate action."

While these Berets are concerned with a number of community problems, their main issue revolves around immigrant rights and immigra-

A Brown Beret at
the Alamo, César
Chávez Day,
2008

tion reform. The presence of Minutemen, an armed private citizens' group described as "over-enthusiastic racists," has been a mobilizing factor. In their press release, the new San Antonio Berets declared that "we need to stand up against the people that want to close the borders and send back thousands of families who have made this their home. . . . We stand tall against the minute men and the other organizations that intend to stop the flow of immigration."

The press release also made it clear that the Berets looked forward "to working with the Black Panthers and other chapters of the Brown Berets towards one common goal: equality in every facet of the word." In ad-

dition to these organizations, the San Antonio chapter has begun working with labor unions such as the Southwest Workers Union and civic organizations such as LULAC. In 2007 they attended the LULAC National
Convention held in Chicago and were given a standing ovation. They
have participated in the Christmas protests at the Hutto immigration de-
tention center, where undocumented families are housed. And they have
"faced off" against the Minutemen when they have shown up in San Antonio. They vow to be vigilant in protecting the community from these
threats. As San Antonio journalist Elaine Ayala announced in her news
blog (June 29, 2007), "The Berets are back"; but this family-oriented chapter clearly reflects a new organizing model.

The announcement by the Minutemen that they would begin monitoring the border also aroused the old Berets of the Valley. The Valley newspapers quoted Rolo, identified as prime minister of the South Texas Berets, warning the Minutemen to "think twice before you come here." Rolo,
now in his sixties, said that he led more than one thousand Berets in the
state and that they would oppose the Minutemen "with physical force if
necessary."

The exaggeration about membership was characteristic of the Berets,
but the determination to defend the Mexican American community was
certainly real. Rolo noted that he had fought for the people for forty years
and had been shot twice. Thus members no longer wore berets, Rolo explained: "If we use the brown beret, we will be a target." He added that he
planned to fight for the people as long as he was alive.

The Beret veterans still surfaced to rally the troops as the situation
dictated. The examples of the Valley and San Antonio were not isolated
ones. Throughout the Southwest, new youth groups with no relation to the
original Berets of the 1970s have arisen, seemingly spontaneously, to protect the community. In Watsonville, California, for example, some youths
studied the history and "linked up with the founders and OGs [old guys]
of the past and re-birthed the Berets after the tragic killing of a young La-
tina" in 2006. They remain "in the forefront of helping elevate the mind
state of troubled youth." They are also "knee deep" in the immigration
debate.

In 2009 in nearby Salinas, where gang violence has claimed several
lives, a nineteen-year-old Salinas native is hoping to start a chapter of the
Brown Berets "to make a change for the better in the community in a nonviolent way." William Medrano grew tired of hearing about all the shoot-

ings. He felt that it was time to make a change and thought the Brown Berets were the answer. It reached a point, Medrano said, where the shootings "became common."

> I lost this and that buddy. I don't think it's okay, [that] we can't do anything about it, but we can. That's what I'm here for. That's why we want the community to come out and do something about it. We want to do the right thing.

Medrano was inspired by the active chapter in Watsonville, which has been successful in doing community service projects. Their latest project included fixing up and donating bikes to kids. With a rise in violence, Medrano sees this group as a way for young people to become a positive force in the community.

The recent and surprising reappearance of Berets in San Antonio and elsewhere in the Southwest, some thirty years after the original chapters, affirms the hope and symbolism of the Brown Berets. The youths recruited into these new groups may have only a vague awareness of Beret history. But the fundamental idea of Brown Berets as an alternative to gangs, as a legitimate organization that can act as a community patrol, has taken hold in the imagination of barrio youth. Such an alternative identity constitutes a significant legacy. For the youth, it provides a pathway for their irrepressible agency.

A Last Word about Quixote

I returned to this book project in earnest in 2007 when I began to work with the papers of Texas congressman Henry B. González, a prominent adversary of the Chicano movement. These papers provided the impetus, not to mention ample material, for finally composing my interpretation of that frenetic period, titled *Quixote's Soldiers: A Local History of the Chicano Movement* (University of Texas Press, 2010). That history, in turn, set the context for these journal notes. Among the congressional papers, I discovered a satirical caricature of Congressman González as a "Don Quixote de dinero [of money]," futilely chasing a pesky Chicano movement bird. The cartoon, apparently part of a political leaflet circulating in the Mexican Westside in 1969, lampooned González not only as a "sellout" to wealthy interests but also as a fool for posturing as the heroic savior from a few brash college students. This was an ironic discovery. After I had settled on

Quixote as my metaphor for the Berets and for movement activists gener-ally, I was not expecting to find Quixote used to ridicule the main oppo-nent of the Chicano movement.

So Quixote was clearly nonpartisan, and the allusion could be used as either critique or praise. But regardless of its use and by whom, Quixote's essential meaning remained: it pointed to the disjunction between vision and reality. Thus the actions of Congressman González, the Brown Berets, or the Stanford hunger strikers could be described as "quixotic." What made behavior or agency quixotic was its visionary impulse in the face of reality. In this sense, many quixotic elements—figurative and thematic—surface in my local history and ethnography of the Chicano movement.

Our society is a complex reality made up of distinct social worlds. These worlds may overlap and interlock, but distinct strata or layers are visible. How is it possible to communicate across these strata without stripping away the complexity of the social worlds involved? As Professor Lowenthal put it, "Human communication depends upon language which is oriented toward commonly shared experience and insight."

We search, then, for metaphors that might provide a bridge across the divide of experiences. Without such metaphors, we might as well not talk—or write.

BIBLIOGRAPHIC NOTES

THESE NOTES SERVE TO INTRODUCE the body of evidence and referential material that guided or influenced my account of the Berets. I close with an anecdote about the role of bridging metaphors.

My journal consisted of some two hundred single-spaced typed pages of field notes from mid-August 1974 through mid-April 1975, with a two-month break from mid-January to mid-March. I interviewed all thirteen Southside Berets and fifteen of the disbanded Westside Berets, as well as the leadership of the Chicago Berets, the North Dallas and West Dallas (Ledbetter) Berets, and the Waco, Austin, and Valley Berets. These interviews took place in 1974–1975. A second round of interviews with a few former leaders took place between 2006 and 2008. These materials have been donated to the Benson Latin American Collection of the University of Texas at Austin.

In addition to the field notes and interviews, the Beret newspapers— *Echo* (Austin), *Los Barrios* (Hondo), *La Onda Chicana* (Dallas), *Coraje* (Waco), and *Mi Sangre* (Chicago)—were important sources of information. Also invaluable were the Chicano movement newspapers *Caracol*, *Chicano Times*, and *El Degüello*, all from San Antonio.

The diverse activities of the Berets in the state can be suggested by the following newspaper items. For the Hondo Berets, see "Hondo Sheriff Jails 12 Chicanos for Protesting Arrest," *Chicano Times* (San Antonio), October 11–18, 1974. The eviction action of the San Antonio Berets was covered in "Eviction of 12 Delayed," *San Antonio News*, December 2, 1974; and in "10 Children, Mom Face Being Evicted," *San Antonio Express*, December 3, 1974. The protest marches of the Dallas Berets were reported in "Brown Berets March," *Dallas Times Herald*, October 27, 1974; and in Javier Rodríguez, "Brown Berets March On," *Nuestro Magazine* (June/July 1980). The intense community organizing against police brutality and the Town Lake boat races in Austin during the 1970s surfaces in Jim Shahin's profile piece "Hoodlum or Robin Hood? Just Who Is Paul Hernandez?" in *Third Coast: The Magazine of Contemporary Austin* (June 1983).

The neighborhood of Columbia Heights, where most Southside Berets lived, has been described by social worker Ernesto Gómez in "The Barrio Professor: An Emerging Concept in Social Work Education," in *The Chicano Faculty Development Program* (New York: Council on Social Work Education, 1972); and by sociologist Buford Farris in "A Comparison of Anglo and Mexican-American Stratification Systems in San Antonio, Texas, and Their Effects on Mobility and Inter-group Relations" (Ph.D. dissertation, University of Texas at Austin, 1972). For a description and interpretation of the larger setting in which the Chicano movement and Berets developed, see my book *Quixote's Soldiers: A Local History of the Chicano Movement* (Austin: University of Texas Press, 2010).

Regarding gun running and police surveillance, see "Swaps across Border: Gun-Dope Traffic Up," *San Antonio Light*, October 8, 1975; "Chicano Leader 'No Gunrunner'—Mexican Paper Blasted," *San Antonio Light*, October 12, 1975; and Dick Reavis, "At War in the Mexican Jungle," *Mother Jones* (May 1978). The FBI report titled "Brown Berets—Domestic Security Limited Investigation, February 16, 1983–May 16, 1983" was part of thirty-three pages that I received after my Freedom of Information request from the U.S. Department of Justice, Federal Bureau of Investigation, Processed Documents on Brown Berets (Texas), unclassified June 2, 1994.

The Stanford "troubles" began on April 1, 1994, when the university administration announced a six percent budget reduction that eliminated the position of long-time dean of students Cecilia Burciaga. The weekly *Campus Report* and the *San Jose Mercury News* carried accounts of the troubles from mid- or late April to mid-May 1994. The *Stanford Daily* carried major stories from May 5 through May 10, with a final story on May 23.

For the resurgence of the Brown Berets in Texas and California, see "Brown Berets Threaten Minutemen to Think Twice before Patrolling," *Monitor* (Edinburg, Texas), July 28, 2005; and Elaine Ayala's blog entries "Brown Berets Are Back," June 29, 2007, and "Find S. A. Brown Berets Online," September 28, 2008, posted on www.MySanAntonio.com. Also see Davey D., "Fighting the Power—Meet the Brown Berets," May 1,

2006, posted at www.myspace.com/seg831/blog/116140623; and "Salinas Teen Fighting Violence One Beret at a Time," Central Coast News, Fox 35, March 24, 2009, posted at www.kcba.com/Global/story.asp?s=10059566 &config=H264.

The most relevant secondary sources on the Chicano movement for this work were George Mariscal, *Brown-Eyed Children of the Sun: Lessons from the Chicano Movement, 1965–1975* (Albuquerque: University of New Mexico Press, 2005); and the autobiographical novel by Genaro González, *The Quixote Cult* (Houston: Arte Público Press, 1998). See the interview with González in William Childers, "Chicanoizing Don Quixote," *Aztlán* 27:2 (Fall 2002): 87–117. Important referential works were Ian Haney López, *Racism on Trial: The Chicano Fight for Justice* (Cambridge, Mass.: Belknap Press, 2003); and Diane Espinoza, "Revolutionary Sisters: Women's Solidarity and Collective Identification among Chicana Brown Berets in East Los Angeles, 1967–1970," *Aztlán* 26:1 (Spring 2001): 17–58.

The social scientific view of the lower classes as unworthy and pathological has a legacy that stretches back to the birth of sociology as a discipline. As a graduate student in the seventies, I found that tradition well represented by Walter B. Miller, "Lower Class Culture as a Generating Milieu of Gang Delinquency," *Journal of Social Issues* 14:3 (Fall 1958): 5–19; Lewis Yablonsky, *The Violent Gang* (New York: Macmillan, 1966); and Edward C. Banfield, *The Unheavenly City: The Nature and Future of Our Urban Crisis* (Boston: Little, Brown, 1970). The "left," in spite of its sympathy, has not been much more charitable. For a view of the lower classes as politically inept or limited, thumb through Eric J. Hobsbawm, *Primitive Rebels: Studies in Archaic Forms of Social Movements in the 19th and 20th Centuries* (New York: Norton, 1959); George Rudé, *The Crowd in History: A Study of Popular Disturbances in France and England, 1730–1848* (New York: Wiley, 1964); and Antonio Gramsci, *Selections from Political Writings, 1910–1920* (New York: International Publishers, 1977). For "revolutionary hope," see Frantz Fanon, *The Wretched of the Earth* (New York: Grove Press, 1963).

The application of these views of the lower classes to Mexicans and Mexican Americans dates back to early twentieth century American sociology and anthropology. Sociologist Emory S. Bogardus was a pioneer in studies of Mexican immigrants and gang youth. See, for example, his "Gangs of Mexican American Youths," *Sociology and Social Research* 28 (September–November 1943). Work with Mexican and Puerto Rican families by anthropologist Oscar Lewis popularized the notion of a "culture of poverty." See, in particular, his *Five Families: Mexican Case Studies in the*

Culture of Poverty (New York: Basic Books, 1959). For a classic portrayal of machismo, see Lola Romanucci-Ross, *Conflict, Violence and Morality in a Mexican Village* (Palo Alto, Calif.: National Press Books, 1973). Such studies have lent support to widely held stereotypes that have occasionally surfaced in public.

A notable example was the controversy over the meaning of Mexican machismo that erupted in the San Antonio news media in October 1974. The controversy began with the story by Mike Hess ("Machismo: Manhood's Proof No Joking Matter," *San Antonio News*, October 9, 1974) and ended three weeks later with the editorial response of the *San Antonio News* ("The Evils of 'Machismo,'" October 28, 1974). Between those dates, radio stations KUKA (October 11) and KCOR (October 16), and KTSA talk show host Logan Stewart (October 15), all aired critical commentaries. In that same month U.S. attorney general William Saxbe warned about a million illegal aliens who had "burrowed deep" within our society, a reminder that anti-immigration views and policy were (and continue to be) inextricably associated with negative views of Mexicans as potential American citizens ("Saxbe Calls Illegal Aliens a U.S. Crisis," *Los Angeles Times*, October 31, 1974).

The social problems associated with Mexican Americans can be seen most clearly in the gang and "pachuco" literature, which along with the immigration question is perhaps the most developed theme in American social science and history regarding Mexican Americans. Even sympathetic scholars have to acknowledge the conflict and dysfunction associated with pachucos and gangs. For a historical view, see Octavio Paz, *The Labyrinth of Solitude* (New York: Grove Press, 1985); Luis Alvarez, *The Power of the Zoot: Youth Culture and Resistance during World War II* (Berkeley: University of California Press, 2008); and Eduardo Obregón Pagán, *Murder at the Sleepy Lagoon: Zoot Suits, Race, and Riot in Wartime L.A.* (Chapel Hill: University of North Carolina Press, 2003).

The classic texts on pachuco linguistics are George Barker, *Pachuco: An American-Spanish Argot and Its Social Functions in Tucson, Arizona* (Tucson: University of Arizona Press, 1970); and Beatrice Griffith, *American Me* (Boston: Houghton Mifflin Company, 1948). Very different views on the matter have been offered by Lurline Colthorp, *The Tongue of the Tirilones: A Linguistic Study of a Criminal Argot* (University: University of Alabama Press, 1968); and Adolfo Ortega, *Caló Tapestry* (Berkeley: Editorial Justa Publications, 1977). For a critical review of this discussion, see Rogelio Reyes, "The Social and Linguistic Foundations of Chicano Caló," in *Research*

Issues and Problems in United States Spanish, edited by Jacob Ornstein-Galicia, George K. Green, and Dennis Bixler-Márquez (Brownsville, Tex.: Pan American University, 1988).

In addition to historians and linguists, sociologists and anthropologists are naturally well represented in the Chicano gang literature. I have already mentioned Emory Bogardus. Joan Moore and James Diego Vigil have also been pioneers in this area. For their candid analyses, see Joan Moore, *Homeboys: Gangs, Drugs, and Prison in the Barrios of Los Angeles* (Philadelphia: Temple University Press, 1978); and James Diego Vigil, *Barrio Gangs: Street Life and Identity in Southern California* (Austin: University of Texas Press, 1988). Also see Ruth Horowitz, *Honor and the American Dream: Culture and Identity in a Chicano Community* (New Brunswick, N.J.: Rutgers University Press, 1983); Martín Sánchez-Jankowski, *Islands in the Street: Gangs and American Urban Society* (Berkeley: University of California Press, 1991); and Felix M. Padilla, *The Gang as an American Enterprise* (New Brunswick, N.J.: Rutgers University Press, 1992). None of these texts, however, are concerned with social movements or political consciousness.

For research that addresses the question of political consciousness and gangs, one must look at the literature on African American youth during the black civil rights movement. See, for example, David Dawley, *A Nation of Lords: The Autobiography of the Vice Lords* (Prospect Heights, Ill.: Waveland Press, 1973); John R. Fry, *Fire and Blackstone* (Philadelphia: J. P. Lippincott Company, 1969); Reginald Major, *A Panther Is a Black Cat* (New York: William Morrow and Company, 1971); and Elaine Brown, *A Taste of Power: A Black Woman's Story* (New York: Pantheon, 1992). This was the social movement literature I found most relevant for my research. In addition, an early influence on my thinking was the work of Luther P. Gerlach and Virginia H. Hine, *People, Power, Change: Movements of Social Transformation* (Indianapolis: Bobbs-Merrill, 1970), which compared the Pentecostal and Black Power movements.

The issue of "field methods" and related ethical and political questions naturally command considerable attention in sociology and anthropology. It is a vast literature, and my acknowledgments here are quite incomplete. Of the referential books important in the early stages of this project, I recall four: Leon Festinger, Henry W. Riecken, and Stanley Schacher, *When Prophecy Fails* (Minneapolis: University of Minnesota Press, 1956); William J. Filstead, *Qualitative Methodology: Firsthand Involvement with the Social World* (Chicago: Markham, 1970); David Matza, *Delinquency and Drift* (New York: Wiley, 1964); and Dell Hymes, ed., *Reinventing An-*

thropology (New York: Pantheon Books, 1969). My ambition to link the local everyday world with larger structures and forces was first inspired by C. Wright Mills, *The Sociological Imagination* (New York: Oxford University Press, 1959).

After my field experience, I found solace among the anthropologists troubled by the ethical and political dilemmas of ethnography. See, for example, Clifford Geertz, *Local Knowledge: Further Essays on Interpretive Anthropology* (New York: Basic Books, 1983); and Vincent Crapanzano, "On the Writing of Ethnography," *Dialectical Anthropology* 2:1 (1977): 69–73. The introspective or reflexive tendency within anthropology within a short time led to a position that portrayed ethnographies as a type of literary text. Elaborated discussion can be found in James Clifford and George E. Marcus, eds., *Writing Culture: The Poetics and Politics of Ethnography* (Berkeley: University of California Press, 1986); and George E. Marcus and Michael M. J. Fischer, *Anthropology as Cultural Critique* (Chicago: University of Chicago Press, 1986). A recent contribution is Walter Mignolo's *Local Histories/Global Designs: Coloniality, Subaltern Knowledge, and Border Thinking* (Princeton, N.J.: Princeton University Press, 2000).

For a sociological take on these questions, see Richard Harvey Brown, *A Poetic for Sociology* (Chicago: University of Chicago Press, 1989). Social movement theorist Mayer N. Zald has likewise urged sociologists to see "the humanities as a source of hypotheses and theoretical frames" in "Sociology as a Discipline: Quasi-Science and Quasi-Humanities," *American Sociologist* 22:3–4 (Fall/Winter 1991): 165–187.

Historians, of course, have been profoundly impacted by the postmodernism of the seventies and eighties. To cite just one example, for a critique of this tendency, see Bryan D. Palmer, *Descent into Discourse: The Reification of Language and the Writing of Social History* (Philadelphia: Temple University Press, 1990). On the other hand, literary scholars have been delighted to demonstrate that the social sciences use literary conventions, and some even argue that the historical and social sciences may be considered a certain type of fiction. Of direct relevance to my history and ethnography was the work of Louis Mendoza, *Historia: The Literary Making of Chicana and Chicano History* (College Station: Texas A&M University Press, 2001).

As should be obvious, rather than denying such claims, I would argue that exploiting the richness of literary metaphors may help us gain a better understanding of the complexity of human agency. This point was driven home by my ironic discovery of Leo Lowenthal's interpretation of Cervantes's work in *Literature and the Image of Man: Sociological Studies of the European Drama and Novel, 1600–1900* (Boston: Beacon Press, 1957). So I turned to Quixote as a "bridging metaphor" that could humanize the lower classes: they have political ideas and imagination, they are fearless and can be courageous, but they are poor and have to hustle to survive, and they lack information and have little organizational capacity. Here, as noted, lies the importance of a movement's organizational field, which provides both stimulus and information for political action among the lower classes.

Although my turn toward literature helped me circumvent the sociology of deviance and delinquency, this only enmeshed me in Cervantes studies, where every passage—even every syllable—of *Don Quixote de la Mancha* has been analyzed and interpreted. Cervantes literary societies around the world stand ready to do battle, to defend or promote certain views that have crystallized around the figures of Quixote and Panza. Here I stand with the opinion of Miguel de Unamuno, who noted: "If Cervantes were to be resurrected and returned to the world, he would have no right whatsoever to complain of this Quixote, of which his own is no more than a hypostasis and point of departure" (*Selected Works*, vol. 3 [Princeton, N.J.: Princeton University Press, 1967], 445–462).

Today's Quixote, as I argued while experimenting with my literary turn, was no longer Spanish or European. I wish I had possessed Mary Malcolm Gaylord's essay *"Don Quixote* and the National Citizenship of Masterpieces" in my arsenal at the time. Addressing the question "To whom does a masterpiece belong?" Gaylord writes that Don Quixote has long been "naturalized" into the research and teaching agendas of professors of English and literary theory. In the United States, the work is "probably taught at least as often in English as in Spanish." She also argues that Don Quixote is not just "an Old World book": Cervantes was aware and critical of the practices of Spain's empire, "putting the very words of conquistadores and chroniclers in his characters' mouths." The Gaylord essay appeared in Marjorie Garber, Rebecca L. Walkowitz, and Paul B. Franklin, eds., *Field Work: Sites in Literary and Cultural Studies* (New York: Routledge, 1996).

Naturally, after four centuries of an active "shelf life," it is remarkable that Quixote retains contemporary significance and can still inspire debate. In this work, my aim was only to explain why I turned to the classic tale of Don Quixote as a bridging metaphor. I have no interest in advancing a particular interpretation of Quixote beyond my pragmatic application of it to my field experience.

On Bridging Metaphors

I close with an anecdote that at first may appear whimsical but which, on further reflection, may suggest the critical role of bridging metaphors in society. For if a seventeenth-century novel seems too distant or removed from the present to be a satisfactory frame for an argument about communication across distinct social worlds, then we might consider a futuristic tale about "the island of Tanagra." Again, reference to an imagined story may help convey the thrust of my argument.

The writers of *Star Trek* have often turned to the social sciences in their search for material. This was evident in one of the most fascinating adventures of the *Next Generation* series, "Darmok and Jilad at Tanagra," where linguistic understanding became a literal as well as figurative struggle.

In this episode, the Starship *Enterprise*, under the command of Captain Jean-Luc Picard, is carrying out the difficult assignment of establishing relations with the Tamarians, a mysterious alien race. The Tamarians are described as peaceful but incomprehensible, because previous Federation attempts to communicate have failed. It is not a translation problem but a conceptual one, for the Tamarians speak English in strange disjointed phrases such as "Darmok and Jilad at Tanagra" or "Shaka, when the walls fell." The Tamarian language, we learn as the episode unfolds, consists of metaphors drawn from their culture.

Needless to say, the crew aboard the *Enterprise* cannot understand the Tamarian greeting. When the Tamarians unexpectedly beam Captain Picard to a nearby planet to join Dathon, the Tamarian commander, the officers of the *Enterprise* interpret this as a hostile move. They are further prevented from taking any remedial action by the shields of the Tamarian ship. On the planet, Picard and Dathon are forced to learn to communicate as they defend themselves against a strange beast. Picard slowly begins to understand that they are reenacting the story of "Darmok and Jilad at Tanagra," the tale of two strangers who met on an island and became friends as they fought "the beast of Tanagra" together. Picard starts to comprehend that the Tamarians use metaphors, drawn from history and folklore, to establish analogies and express concepts. "Sokath,

his eyes uncovered!" Dathon exclaims when Picard comes to this realization. Dathon is fatally wounded in the battle with the beast, but he is able
to teach Picard enough Tamarian vocabulary before the *Enterprise* beams
him back through the Tamarian shields. Picard then defuses the armed
stalemate with the Tamarian ship by communicating with the metaphors
he learned from Dathon.

Devoted fans of *Star Trek: The Next Generation* have created websites
where they discuss and debate the specific meaning of Tamarian phrases.
"The river Temarc in winter," for example, a phrase uttered by Dathon at
the beginning of the episode, has been taken as a reference to the silence
of a frozen river, thus meaning "be quiet, chill out." But some have argued
that a great river can be crossed only during a certain season, thus meaning
"we'd better try to communicate now." It's difficult to know, as web-blogger
Tim Lynch has noted, because "brief translations strip the Tamarian language of a world of richness." See, for example, the websites of Raphael
Carter, "Discursive Dictionary" (www.myspace.com/darmokisdathon/blog
/281711913), Tim Lynch, "Review of Darmok" (www.macs.hw.ac.uk/~hwloidl
/TL/tng5/darmok.html), and Dr. Mality, "Darmok" (www.jacksonhu.tcu
.edu.tw/myweb2/wo2.htm).

Of particular interest: a Google search for Raphael Carter's "Discursive Dictionary" of the Tamarian language also yields Lurine Colthorp,
author of *Tongue of the Tirilones*, as a first page hit. Links to discursive
dictionaries for Tamarians and tirilones or pachucos share the same web
page space. The point, again, is that our complex society is made up of distinct social worlds. Some are so distant from one another that one might
as well be speaking of alien worlds and languages. The pachuco or bato
loco, speaking in a distinct Caló argot, dealing with everyday *locura*, sur-
viving in a zero-sum environment of poverty, lived and continues to live
in such a distinct world.

The river Temarc in winter!